UNLIMITED REAL ESTATE PROFIT

Create Wealth and Build a Financial Fortress Through Today's Real Estate Investing

MARC STEPHAN GARRISON, M.B.A., & PAULA TRIPP-GARRISON

Adams Media
Avon, Massachusetts

Published by
Adams Media, an F+W Publications Company
57 Littlefield Street, Avon, MA 02322. U.S.A.
www.adamsmedia.com

ISBN: 1-58062-948-2

Printed in the United States of America.

J I H G F E D C B

Library of Congress Cataloging-in-Publication Data
Garrison, Marc.
Unlimited real estate profit / Marc Stephan Garrison & Paula
Tripp-Garrison.
p.   cm.
ISBN 1-58062-948-2
1. Real estate investment—United States. 2. Real estate
management—United States. I. Tripp-Garrison, Paula. II. Title.
HD255.G364 2003
332.63'24—dc21
2003011089

Cover photo © Goodshoot / Superstock.

This book is available at quantity discounts for bulk purchases.
For information, call 1-800-872-5627.

Contents

■ To my wife, coauthor, and editor, Paula Tripp-Garrison, you are my best friend and greatest blessing. Thank you for colorizing a black-and-white life . . . I see you in each of our combined ten children. You always see the forest in spite of the trees. Your grace will see us through.

—*Marc Stephan Garrison*

■ To my husband, dear friend, and partner in life. You taught me to dream and I love you. To my sons, Jasen, Ryan, Marc, and Luke—I physically gave you life . . . each of you have taught me the true essence of life!

—*Paula Tripp-Garrison*

Foreword

TIME FLIES WHEN YOU'RE HAVING FUN. Sixteen years ago, in my bestselling book *Buying Right: Getting Started in Real Estate Investment,* I wrote that I thought if interest rates ever went below 7 percent, this country would be in deep financial trouble. At that time, in 1987, interest rates had just come down from the middle teens. As I write this foreword, interest rates are in the low single digits, and our wonderful country is doing just fine, thank you. Our world continues to change. Today, I can talk on my cellular telephone and at the same time write a letter on that same telephone, which can be printed at my law office and delivered by e-mail to my clients, without my having to even be in the office. Today, I can obtain a new loan on a piece of real estate without ever having to meet with a loan officer; more importantly, I can close on that new loan in less than a week's time.

As my son used to say, "Things are a-changing." He is correct. Today we have new types of mortgage (deeds of trust) loans. Today, it is easy to obtain a real estate loan from a local lender for 97 percent of the purchase price. Today, you can obtain your credit report on the Internet and have a much better understanding of whether you are going to get approved for a loan and—just as important—of what you need to do in order to clean up your credit if necessary. Today, important pieces of investment information are available, within a minute's time, just for the asking. The old investment tools are good initial building blocks, but if you rely on them, you are going to be left behind tasting the dust of those investors who have and are using the up-to-date tools.

In *Unlimited Real Estate Profit,* Marc Garrison and Paula Tripp-Garrison are going to teach you the New Tools for Real Estate Investing. Follow closely, and you shall succeed. They will tutor you on the new paradigm, the "Fifth Migration," which I believe will be the most important new investment technique of the twenty-first century. They will push you to have educated persistence and help you make plans for your future financial success.

Marc and Paula correctly emphasize that you need to know the market potential of the area you are about to invest in, as well as the supply-and-demand factors of that area. They point out that purchasing real estate properties in the absorption stage of the investment cycle is the only viable approach in today's explosive real estate market. They stress that you can live where you want to live, but you should invest only where it makes common sense. These and other important lessons are taught herein.

We all owe Paula and Marc a big THANK YOU for this wonderful book and the information and techniques it espouses. Correctly use this information and techniques, and you can only become successful as a result thereof.

—Stephen A. Wayner, Esq.

A Letter to the Reader

Dear friend,

In 1977, I began what would become a never-ending search for the sound, enduring principles of creating wealth and building a financial fortress. What I have come to realize, though, is that the answer is not found in magical tricks of financial wizardry. Instead, it is a mental mindset that pushes you when all else fails. The book that you hold is my eighteenth. My writing career started in 1984, when I wrote my first real estate investing book for Simon & Schuster. I found out what it felt like to become a bestselling author—but that fame is rather hollow in comparison to the satisfaction of getting to know the men and women all across the United States and Canada whom I have helped to become self-made millionaires through their real estate investments.

Ever since 1986, I have personally selected fifteen investors a month (people just like yourself) to spend most of a week with my wife, Paula, and me in our very best real estate investing target markets. Paula and I have now personally taught just over 2,500 people—again, just like yourself—our tools for creating wealth and building a financial fortress. For that group of both new and experienced investors, I have been able to take their back yard investing to the next level. And during that entire almost seventeen years of experience, we have now taught, mentored, pushed, and loved just over 700 of our students to become documented self-made real estate millionaires. Nobody in the United States or Canada invests like we do. The economic research that we provide is available nowhere else. The hands-on training that we do is found nowhere else. With this new book, *Unlimited Real Estate Profit,* we are for the first time ever publicly teaching our strategies, tools, and tactics for becoming a self-made real estate millionaire in the next three years. But first, let me share something with you that can help you to get to know Paula, our children, me, and the collective vision that we have been extending to our students since 1986—and now into the book that you are holding in your hands.

In 1980 I achieved the dream of a lot of people. I became a documented self-made millionaire. Funny, but this new status had never been my goal. I just wanted freedom. I wanted enough money to buy myself the time that I needed to do the things that I really wanted to do in life. Time for my children. Time to go to school. Time to relax. Time to enjoy life. And time to fulfill a few of my dreams. Somewhere along the way, I came up with this crazy idea. I made it a goal to get to really know as many other self-made millionaires as I could and to try and extract from them their secrets for creating wealth, for finding freedom, achieving balance, and for living life to its fullest. I didn't want to interview self-made millionaires who were living lives of self-destruction. Heaven knows there have been all too many examples of that—John Belushi, Elvis, and Marilyn Monroe, just to name a few. Instead, I wanted to find self-made millionaires who were happy, fun-loving men and women who were enjoying life, working hard, and making a difference in this world. This search would continue through the 1980s into the 1990s, and if I know myself, it will continue for the rest of my life. Since my start, I have sat down to lunch or talked on the phone with literally hundreds upon hundreds of self-made millionaires. I have pumped these individuals and listened to their life stories. I have kept notes and boiled these interviews down into twenty-nine secrets that embody the collective wisdom of all the self-made millionaires whom I have met, personally taught and helped create, or have gotten to know.

Recently, I wrote these secrets down for the very first time. My motivation was to prepare them and to package them as a Christmas gift for our ten children, their future spouses, and their future children.

Slowly, my wife and I began to share these ideas with the students we have trained on our "BuyingTour." Our students, in turn, have shared these twenty-nine secrets with their friends. And now, before we jump into this book, we are going to share them with you as a way for you to understand where we are coming from—our hearts—and the reason why, as a family, we feel so honored to have been able since 1986 to personally teach over 2,500 people how to become totally financially independent. Think how it would feel to have been the personal mentor, teacher, and coach to over 700 documented self-made real estate millionaires. What a responsibility. What a blessing . . .

I present these secrets with as little commentary here as possible. Paula and I will talk about them more in a book that will quite aptly be titled *The 29 Secrets of a Self-Made Millionaire.* If you keep in touch with us via our Web site, *www.narei.com,* we will tell you the minute when that new book is going to hit your local bookstores. But for today, just realize that you can become all of these things in harmony with our real estate investing tools—tools that are made stronger in every single way by your guided use of the Internet. The bottom line is that if you are willing to devote one to two hours a day, five days a week (with weekends off for good behavior), in the next few years you will be able to become one of our newest documented self-made millionaires in what we call our InnerCircle. Spend some time with these twenty-nine secrets. Write them on your hand. Send them to your friends. Memorize them. Copy them, and put that copy on your desk at work or on your bathroom mirror. The power of these secrets lies in their simple clarity. And by the way—each of these twenty-nine secrets comes from people who all became documented self-made millionaires through real estate investing. Not only that—I almost forgot—but these twenty-nine secrets all were given to me by members of our InnerCircle. Who do you think learns more? The teacher or the student?

The Twenty-Nine Secrets of Self-Made Millionaires
by Marc Stephan Garrison and Paula Tripp-Garrison

1. They are married to the right person.
2. They are loyal.
3. They view money as a tool to buy time so they can afford to work at something that they enjoy and that's worthy of their time and talent.
4. They give people more than they expect and do it cheerfully.
5. They work to become the most positive and enthusiastic person you know.
6. They are honest.
7. They have a grateful heart.
8. They have persistence.
9. They discipline themselves to always be saving money.
10. They treat everyone they meet like they want to be treated.
11. They commit themselves to constant improvement.
12. They commit themselves to quality.
13. They understand that happiness is not based on possessions, power, or prestige, but on relationships with people you love and respect.
14. They are generous.
15. They are forgiving of themselves and others.
16. They are self-motivated.
17. They are decisive even if it means they will sometimes be wrong.
18. They don't blame others. They take responsibility for every area of their life.
19. They are bold and courageous.
20. They take good care of those they love.
21. They don't do anything that wouldn't make their mother and father proud.
22. They understand that children need their presence more than their presents.
23. They know that nothing can replace a good night's sleep.

24. They give hugs and kisses and say "I love you" every single day.
25. They have traditions that keep their family tree alive and sprouting new branches.
26. They take time to recharge their batteries.
27. They need nature and take time to appreciate its beauty.
28. They practice unconditional love.
29. They all invest in real estate . . .

Each of these secrets comes from the heart and soul of someone who has become truly financially free. Each of these secrets can be learned. Let me explain.

In 1983, I sold a home to a gentleman named Bob Allen. At that point in my life, I had essentially no clue that there were other real estate investors in the world. I just was doing my own thing. I bought a property. I fixed it up. I sold it and made somewhere between $15,000 and $25,000. Then I did it again. I had bought this one particular property and done some minor cosmetic fix-up. I think that this was on a Saturday morning. I had just put up a "For Sale" sign in the window, and there came a knock on the door. When I opened it, I was greeted by this really nice guy. Almost before I could say "Hi," this man announced that he wanted to buy this home. He asked how much, and I gave him a price. He said, "Fine." We drew up a contract and he closed on the property within days. As I got to know this buyer, I began to notice that he really seemed to know real estate. Finally I told him that I had only owned this home for a few weeks. He replied, "I know." I then told him that I had just made about $23,000 on the deal. He said, "I know." I asked him if that made him upset. He told me that he had made a lot more on some of his deals. I asked him to show me, and we drove all over town. He finally told me that he was the author of a bestselling book on real estate investing, entitled *Nothing Down*. He gave me a copy that day.

As we got to know each other, Bob asked me if I wanted to share my own real estate investment story with some other investors. I said, "Sure." Well, Bob flew me out to Washington, D.C.

When I got there, I just about died. His "few friends" totaled just over 1,800 people. I don't think that I have ever been so scared in my life.

But once I got up in front of the crowd and started to tell my own story, something happened inside of me. I found some inner source of strength, and I soared. I loved speaking to this audience, and I found that I was able to share my story and teach my own principles of real estate investing with power and conviction.

I loved it.

From 1983 to 1986, I spoke almost every weekend at a real estate convention or workshop around the United States. I learned a lot. I grew a lot. But I also got frustrated. It was easy to get people pumped up at a seminar, but I started to notice that not a lot of people were able to go home from these courses and actually apply what they had learned.

That really upset me. I wanted something more real. Finally, while driving back to JFK International Airport with one of the other speakers, Jim Banks, I came to understand the truth of most real estate seminars. I had expressed my angst to Jim, and his reply literally changed my life. He said, "Marc, these real estate seminars are not educational experiences. They are just 'show business.'" I found that I agreed with him.

I thought back on my own learning experiences, especially on how I learned how to fly. First I completed ground school, where I learned the fundamentals, and then I got into a plane with an instructor by my side and learned hands-on.

I knew that I wanted to do just that with teaching real estate.

I soon quit speaking at the real estate "dog and pony carnival shows," and I focused on my own education, family, and personal real estate investing. I started trying out some new ideas for real estate investing that I came up with during graduate school.

I started investing not only in my back yard, but also in growth/boom/absorption markets all around the United States. My profits soared. And I knew that I could make my dream of teaching other investors "hands-on" come true. In 1986, I took a small group of fifteen real estate investors into Dallas with me. Hands-on, I taught these students the new tools for real estate investment today.

During those four days, this group made offers on more than 18 million dollars' worth of residential income non-owner-occupied income properties. I told that group where to buy. I taught them how to buy. And in the field . . . out of a classroom . . . on a bus . . . inside of actual properties . . . and through actual deals, I taught them all of the basics. I then watched the market and told them when to sell.

This type of real estate investing "learning experience" is available nowhere else—only through me. And it's something that I have essentially done every single month since May 1986. I limit each group to a small selection of fifteen members of the National Association of Real Estate Investors. Every single participant has either completed our seven-day "Challenge" real estate training program in person or watched our twenty-one–video "Challenge" course.

Our first BuyingTour group's success was beyond belief. In fewer than three years, they were selling their properties for 300 to 500 percent of what they had originally bought them for.

Since 1986 I have continued to teach one group of fifteen investors each and every month (with the sole exception of the time I had to take off in 1994 when I was seriously injured during a robbery attempt upon my family). If you add that up, you will find out that by now I have personally taught, hands-on, just over 2,500 real estate investors. No one else in the universe has ever done what I have done. All other real estate training programs are done in a classroom or via a book or audiocassette. But I broke that paradigm and taught these individuals real estate investing using actual deals inside real properties—hands-on, the same way that I learned how to fly a plane, and the same way (I hope) that your family doctor learned how to be a physician.

What I did worked; there has been no luck involved. As I've said: To date, more than 700 of the students we have taught have become documented self-made millionaires.

Take, for example, Howard Sklar. Howard came originally from New York City. I met him in Portland, Oregon. Howard signed up for one of our four-day BuyingTours. He came out into the field with us. We did a little classroom work, but we spent most of those four days in and out of a bus working on actual deals. Howard was hooked. Howard bought a property in one of our target markets. He temporarily left his wife and children in Oregon, moved into his property in Denver, and made things happen. Soon, Howard could afford having his family with him.

Howard worked hard, but he had a great teacher . . . me. Howard is now worth in excess of $3.4 million—and this is 100 percent thanks to what we taught him. His positive cash flow is more than $22,000 per month. What's really interesting about Howard is that he has tried to get all of his friends and relatives involved in real estate investing . . . but he has had no takers. Howard has come to me and asked if perhaps I could refer some potential real estate investors to him so that he could help mentor them and to teach them to do exactly what I taught him how to do.

I am humbled by the network of success that I have created.

You have no idea how easy life has become for me in terms of teaching new real estate investors. Imagine having an entire cruise ship full of students, all of whom you have taught during the past sixteen years, and all of whom have become self-made millionaires because of the real estate investing techniques that you taught them to use.

It doesn't take a rocket scientist to figure out that actually, I have learned more than anyone else during the past sixteen years. You should remember that all of the twenty-nine secrets of a self-made millionaire that Paula and I have discovered have come through our close association with our own students who have become financially independent for life because of their real estate investing with our mentoring.

I think of Tom Wieske.

I think of Pok Ward.

I think of John Stuart.

I have learned from each of them more than they ever learned from me. The greatest gift that I gave to each of these 700-plus students went beyond the mechanics of real estate investing. What I gave them was its heart and soul. During the rest of this book, I will teach you exactly what I taught to each of them.

Opportunity is knocking . . . and I have opened the door for you. But you are the one who is going to have to step through. My wife and I wish you and yours the very best. And if, after reading this book, you decide that you would like to find a mentor—one of my 700-plus documented self-made millionaires—and get personal access to this army of living and breathing real estate success stories, or even to work with myself and my wife on one of our monthly BuyingTours, just e-mail us at marcstephangarrison@narei.com or paulatripp-garrison@narei.com and we will tell you what it takes.

Onward,
Marc Stephan Garrison
Paula Tripp-Garrison

PART I

The Road to Success

CHAPTER 1
Becoming a Self-Made Millionaire

CHAPTER 2
Dreams Die Young

CHAPTER 3
Keeping the Dream Alive

Enthusiasm is the mother of effort, and without it nothing great was ever achieved.

—Ralph Waldo Emerson

Chapter 1

Becoming a Self-Made Millionaire

A RECENT FORTUNE MAGAZINE ARTICLE stated that 97 out of 100 self-made millionaires in America today have made their fortunes through real estate investing. However, most of the estimated 10 million North American real estate investors feel today like they are losing ground in terms of their real estate investment profitability and success. Why do the hundreds of thousands of today's potential real estate investors feel that they are just spinning their wheels? Why do yesterday's tools of real estate investing no longer work? Faced with unprecedented uncertainty in the economy and world today, why do so many people feel frozen, unable to act?

The answer to those puzzles, along with a clear step-by-step plan for creating unlimited profit and ultimate wealth through real estate investing in today's markets, is given in the very book that you are holding in your hands. It is a system that will work no matter what the economic conditions. Our real estate investing system is as certain as the law of gravity—it will always work because it is based on demonstrable economic facts.

My Own Story

My name is Marc Stephan Garrison. For the past twenty-seven years I have lived, breathed, and become wealthy beyond my wildest dreams because of real estate investing. To do so, I have always been willing to pay the price for knowledge.

At the age of twenty-two, as a young newlywed in southern California, I started investing in real estate to fund my college education. I was a self-made real estate millionaire well before I had completed my bachelor's degree. In 1985, I helped to organize and became president of the National Association of Real Estate Investors (NAREI). At that time I also became a member of the advisory boards for the National Association of Financial Planners and the American Congress on Real Estate. My involvement with these three organizations led me to begin speaking almost weekly at financial and investment conventions, seminars, and workshops across the United States and Canada. Also in 1986, my first hardcover real estate investing book, *Financially Free,* was published through Simon & Schuster. Since then, I have written seventeen additional books that have been published by Doubleday and Aspen Books. In 1991, a company I started, Gold Leaf Press, published the *New York Times* number-one bestseller *Embraced by the Light.* In addition to editing the book, I personally crafted and implemented its marketing plan based on concepts that I had learned through real estate investment seminars.

In 1994, during a robbery attempt upon my family in Hawaii, I had my neck broken, my back severely injured, my right optical orbit fractured, my left retina partially detached, and most of my eye muscles torn loose. Life sometimes isn't easy, but real estate investing has been an anchor during the uncertainties and the forced changes in my life's direction.

Real Estate Investing Then and Now

I wish that I could tell you that real estate investing is just as easy as it was during the 1970s and 1980s. But I just can't. I would be lying. The truth is that even though investing now involves a little bit more work, the profits are all that much more explosive. Also, the competition from other investors today in our target absorption markets (that is, regions of opportunity) is about zero. Most real estate investors I meet have given up in today's economy, leaving the real estate market wide open for you and me.

Please understand that the economy and its rules have changed. The old tools of real estate investment have as much relevance in today's real estate investment markets as an old vinyl record or a transistor radio in the new world of compact discs and personal computers. As a real estate investor in the mid-1980s, I was just like any other of the million-plus real estate investors in United States and Canada. I had made a killing in the 1970s and early 1980s, but now it seemed that my investment program had hit a brick wall. Properties weren't appreciating as well as they had before, and it was next to impossible to get any positive cash flow from them. The majority were still great investments in the respect that they were solid avenues for individuals investing for a retirement program, but for a fast turnaround capital investment, they were not producing at anything like the tremendous rate they did during the previous two decades. I guess that I had gotten spoiled.

It was lucky for me that I didn't put my real estate dreams on ice.

As Easy as Fishing in a Stocked Pond

I decided that, once again, the key to my financial future was knowledge. In 1983, I started graduate school at UCLA. However, I didn't go back to school to get a job; I was already making more money than any of my professors made just from my part-time real estate investing. Instead, I studied real estate economics and cycles and trends so that I could discover new ways to make money in real estate investing.

By the time that I started my Ph.D. program, I had developed several radical new paradigms of real estate investment, complete with new tools for how to make even more money in real estate investing than I had ever thought possible.

As I already told you, in 1986 I began applying these new tools.

The Garrison Cycle

Away from academia, I went back into the real estate marketplace, and, armed with my radical new approach, I completed my first "long distance" property acquisition within weeks. Using one of my nearly one hundred little-or-no-money-down techniques, I spent a total of less than $1,000 to acquire a rental property in one of my targeted absorption markets (also known as region of opportunity or recovery market). This was in a market that I had researched and found to be getting 67,000 new jobs in the coming twelve months because of industry that was relocating there from more expensive parts of the country (regions of obsolescence or decline markets). In fewer than two months of ownership, I had gotten my entire

"If you are wondering whether the Garrisons are correct about their markets, they are! If you are wondering whether these people have a genuine commitment to help you, they do! Can you achieve your goals with their competence and knowledge? You can! Is it worth the significant investment of your resources and energy? It is! Wondering whether you are the first to have these concerns? You are not!"

—Jim, New York, New York

$1,000 down payment back, plus an additional $600 monthly of positive cash flow. I have always had income-producing properties, real estate that generates a monthly income, but now I knew how to find the "hot areas." Within months, I had sold that property to an investor from another country at a $47,000 net profit. His new purchase price was based on his netting a 10-percent cash-on-cash return from this fully rented income property.

I used this same cookie cutter to do it over again and again.

On the next property I made $52,000 net. I did it again and again. On another property, I made $71,500 net. My profits continued to skyrocket. Making money in real estate with these new paradigms and tools became as easy as fishing in a stocked pond.

Teaching Others

I then decided to put my ideas to the test. I could make them work for myself, but could I teach others to do the same? I started with a group of fifteen members of the National Association of Real Estate Investors and invited them to spend a weekend with me in one of my targeted absorption markets to learn hands-on and for themselves my new methods of real estate investing. During that weekend, my first group made offers on over $18 million in income-producing real estate. Not one dime of this money was invested as a group effort. They bought only as individuals or in small partnerships. They had so many properties to choose from that they faced absolutely no competition from each other or from any other investor. During the next year, every member of that original group got not only every dollar of their original down payments back, but, in addition, they saw astronomical profits through the appreciation of their new properties and the positive cash flow they produced. This group continued to invest in our targeted absorption market and to follow its economic trends, which I taught them would indicate transitions. In fewer than twenty-eight months after those initial purchases, my technical indicators screamed out that it was time to sell our properties in that area. I immediately gave the "sell" signal to each member of that original group. It's funny, but when we went into that area and bought our properties, everybody there thought that we were crazy. The area had been depressed, and properties were a dime a dozen. However, by the time that we sold our properties, everyone from the cabdrivers on up was trying to get into real estate investing because of the now "visible" increased demand. Needless to say, we sold our properties at top dollar without one problem. The area was now thriving with new industry and the obvious population and economic boom it created. Within several months, every one of those original properties sold at prices ranging from 300 to 500 percent of the property's original price!

Spreading the Word

These original fifteen people told their family and friends about what they had recently done. Soon, through word of mouth, I had hundreds of people asking where they too could be taught these new paradigms and tools of real estate investing. In 1988, through the National Association of Real Estate Investors, I formalized this weekend training into a high-tech program that cost just under $8,000 per person. I called these hands-on training experiences

"The Garrisons expose you to everything you need to successfully conduct all aspects of a real estate business that works in today's market. Their demographic reports build your confidence in the market itself. They give you confidence in your local market because of the real estate investing team that they teach you how to create (brokers, attorneys, lenders, contractors, management firms, etc)."

—Dennis and Sandy, Sacramento, California

"This has been a big step to begin investing, and only by virtue of the extremely knowledgeable team you have taught us how to create have I been able to make sense out of today's market. The footwork Marc and Paula have done has been worth every penny!"

—Dawn, Chicago, Illinois

BuyingTours. I chose to limit each BuyingTour to a total of fifteen investors per group so that I could personally get to know each and every participant. With the three children that my first wife and I had then, and our own personal investment program, I figured that I could easily teach one group a month. I did this for eleven months a year. I would take off every December for extended quality family time and reflection to prepare for the year ahead.

Since that time, I have never taught or shared these new paradigms and tools in any forum other than on a BuyingTour to these small groups of investors. Over the years, I refined my techniques and became better and better at teaching both new, as well as seasoned real estate investors, how to make money in today's new economy.

The Perfect Avenue to Personal and Financial Freedom

At the young old age of forty-seven, I (along with my second wife) now have a combination of ten children—seven sons and three daughters. We even have two grandchildren. Since January 2001, I have been rearranging every aspect of my life so that I can have even more time with my children and family members. Real estate investing as a profession, even on a part-time basis, is the perfect avenue for personal financial freedom. With this freedom, the investor also gains the time for pursuing whatever personal dreams he or she may have. How many people are blessed with financial stability, but in exchange for it they are depleted of any extra time to enjoy the really satisfying pursuits this life has to offer?

This book teaches you how to prepare for your own personal "Social Security." We are all seeing that we cannot depend on our government's blindly reassuring promise of income for our "golden years." Even our own government in the last decade has responded to the reality of life for many of our seniors by stating that in addition to Social Security, Americans need to plan and prepare other retirement programs to be able to have even a humble home and money for basics like food and medical care.

The Fifth Migration

All over the world, both business owners and active and potential real estate investors desire to create wealth, but they are unsure about their financial futures. This book will teach you how to understand today's fifth migration (the flight of American business from regions of obsolescence to regions of economic opportunity) so that you can protect and ensure your financial future. Not only does the fifth migration tell a real estate investor where to invest for the highest profits, but it also tells a new generation of job seekers and business professionals where to look for the very best possibilities. This book is not a get-rich-quick program. It takes work to

"The Garrisons' BuyingTour made me realize how much more you all do behind the scenes, how much you do care about every individual participant. That really touched me and made the workshop that much more personal. I can't tell you how much that means to me. You all are a godsend and I feel like I have angels on my side now. Your techniques work today. My profits have proven that. Thank you!"

—Mark, Honolulu, Hawaii

"Learning the Garrisons' techniques has been a great experience. I can see your staff is dedicated to responding to my needs in an efficient, friendly manner. My mission is to tell my friends back home about this opportunity."

—James, Dallas, Texas

make money in real estate investing. *Unlimited Real Estate Profit* takes the reader by the hand and provides not only the information needed, but it also tells how to access, via telephone, an entire support system of active self-made real estate millionaires who have volunteered to work as mentors (we call this group the "Inner-Circle") for members of the National Association of Real Estate Investors. Members are also provided with the Web sites and e-mail addresses for select real estate investment organizations, newsletters, and local clubs.

I know personally that you can have both time and financial stability. To help you find this out for yourself, my wife and I have spent the majority of the past year putting each and every facet of my new paradigms and tools of real estate investing into an easy-to-understand, step-by-step hands-on action guide. This road map is the very book that you are reading now.

My Qualifications

You might be saying to yourself, "This all sounds great, but how do I know that you're the right guide to lead me to financial freedom?"

A fair enough question. Here are some of my qualifications:

- Twenty-six years of hands-on "street smart" real estate investing
- Master's degree in business administration

- Ph.D. in economics
- President, National Association of Real Estate Investors
- Advisory board member, National Association of Financial Planners
- Advisory board member, American Congress on Real Estate
- Eighteen published books
- Author of hundreds of real estate investing articles
- Three major book tours with hundreds of television, radio, and print interviews
- Former syndicated columnist
- Numerous appearances on Ken and Daria Dolan's CNBC financial show
- Featured article in *U.S. News and World Report*
- Featured article in *USA Today*
- Publisher, editor, and marketer behind the *New York Times* number-one bestseller *Embraced by the Light*

But, without a doubt, my number-one qualification is that I've traveled down this road myself, and I've already shown hundreds of people just like you how to achieve their dreams of financial freedom and security.

My wife, Paula, adds to my extensive experience with her own hands-on skill in the rehab and management of rental properties. Here are some words directly from her.

Paula's Perspective

As a young girl of nine, I vividly remember our first family real estate investment. Dad was a State Farm agent, but he always had many other interests. Real estate investing was certainly one of them. My parents bought a home in Ann Arbor, Michigan, that was in great need of basic repairs. Because of the general condition of the home, we were able to buy it with almost nothing down on a land contract directly from the owner. My parents always tried to avoid any unnecessary expenses, and a real estate broker certainly qualified as such! Working as a family, we all dug right into our new adventure. I was reared by parents who did not see anything as impossible, and what a blessing that was. When my parents did not know how to do something, they would just go to the library and read books and would educate themselves. I never remember having a professional repairman of any sort ever visit our home. Needless to say, we spent many Saturday mornings fixing the rental home ourselves and making it into a duplex. Dad figured out quickly that the real money would be made by splitting the living area and then collecting two rents. And, of course, this entailed putting in another bathroom and kitchenette. Ann Arbor is home to the University of Michigan, so he knew he would have an endless supply of college students needing apartments to rent. The lessons we learned were invaluable to the six of us children in a way we could not begin to appreciate at the time. Since that time, the buying and selling continued, and we have had many opportunities to learn everything from purchasing real estate with nothing down all the way through every aspect of maintenance and repairs.

Although I consider myself extremely capable in all phases of real estate investment, I have put my energies into the management and rehab portion of our real estate business. I really enjoy the interaction with our current and prospective tenants. Marc and I have meshed our backgrounds together, in order to fully utilize our individual strengths and to make our family business work as never before.

The Surest Road

Real estate investing is the surest and safest road to financial independence. In this book, Paula and I will introduce you to today's new economy and give you a specific step-by-step action plan for making unlimited profit and creating ultimate wealth for yourself and your family. If you have any questions whatsoever about anything

We are always getting ready to live, but never living.

—*Ralph Waldo Emerson*

Chapter 2

Dreams Die Young

THE FOLLOWING STORY IS HARD-CORE American reality. It is the true story of two of my students who were saved by real estate investing. It is a true story not just of this couple, but of hundreds of thousands of other American couples whose dreams never seem to materialize. The names have been changed at the request of those involved.

Jim was the all-American boy in high school, and Heather was his all-American cheerleader sweetheart. When they married, a year after graduation in the little white chapel on the edge of town, the entire world lay at their feet. Even though their goals were hazy and their dreams somewhat vague, there was no doubting that they would succeed. They knew one thing for sure: they wouldn't end up like their own parents, working all week to make ends meet and fighting all night when they didn't.

During the first few months of marital bliss, their plans were laid out and promises were made. Jim went to work immediately, the typical forty hours a week, and he was thrilled to be a thread in the fabric of America. He quickly picked up a couple of night classes at the local college while he dreamed of law school and a high-paying career. Heather decided to work as well; a lot of families need two incomes just to make ends meet, and my, they thought, look at all the money we're making!

Their dreams are fresh, and the sweet smell of potential success fills their home. Anything is possible, and the future holds incredible promise. There's no doubt that the Coopers will be living proof that the American dream is alive and well.

The honeymoon wasn't really over until the expenses finally caught up with them and then surpassed their combined income. Work suddenly wasn't so much fun, Jim decided, when you have no choice in the matter.

Before they were financially ready, the Coopers found themselves expecting their first child. Mixed with the initial happiness of becoming new parents was a little regret, a touch of worry, and the low-grade fever of envy, as they watched old high school friends climb the ladder of success. Somehow their young plans seemed to be getting derailed.

Heather had to quit working for a while to take care of the baby. Jim did get a raise, and they had some money saved, but without Heather's paycheck and with the expenses of a young family, the Coopers were sinking financially. Jim's father-in-law stepped in and offered him a few extra hours helping in the factory downtown. Jim still found himself awake at midnights, though, contemplating the future. He reasoned to himself that the factory job did pay well. Heather could be a full-time stay-at-home mother for their child and they could avoid child-care expenses. Besides, college seemed to be taking forever, and he really couldn't even remember why he ever wanted to go to school for years and years to be a lawyer. He thought to himself that this was a joke, at this rate it would be eighty years before he graduated. The truth is a foreman can make pretty good money these days . . .

So Jim and Heather lowered their hopes a notch or two, and they tried to ignore the growing discontent in their lives.

Unfortunately, reality has a way of slapping you right in the face.

Babies aren't free, and with Heather not working for an outside employer, Jim stretched himself even further and took on a little more overtime each week just to make ends meet. The extra hours at work were well worth the effort every time he picked up his little girl and held her close. But late at night, holding his gurgling bundle of innocence above her crib, he felt a stab of genuine fear, as their trainload of dreams was seriously jumping the track. Jim knew in his heart that any dreams that they had left were getting more and more unlikely to ever be a reality.

As time passed Jim and Heather, like many young families, found that they would spend a little more each month than they actually made. They reasoned with each purchase that they could still make the minimum monthly payments on the double-digit-interest credit cards they now possessed. Besides, they rationalized, it would be quite a while before all the cards were charged up to the limit, and surely by then Jim would be making even more money.

During this stressful time, they put off the plans for the cute little house with the white picket fence, the back yard garden, and all of the little extras. Soon going out to dinner meant getting a hamburger and fries from a drive-up window. Surprisingly, accepting their fate wasn't that hard now. They consoled themselves with the all too common idea that money can't buy happiness, and so they continued to blend themselves into the background of middle-class America.

Still, getting up late night after night, Jim sat at the kitchen table, trying to concentrate on the endless task of paying the bills. Often he would just push the stack of bills aside and rest his head on his arm and quietly listen to the stillness of the summer night. He was now a year on the job and was quickly promoted to foreman, and yet they were still just barely getting by. He felt like he was working like a dog, but Heather didn't seem to notice his unyielding efforts to stay afloat financially. He couldn't figure out what was wrong with his wife, as she spent all day drowning herself in watching talk shows, changing diapers, and eating. Her own self-esteem was zero, and the way she complained relentlessly made him tune her voice right out. He was sure he still loved her, but he felt a lot of resentment toward her. Once again, he dropped the pen, clicked off the light, and stumbled to bed.

The old dreams are fading fast, becoming ethereal fantasies. For Jim, dreams of law school, a home, and leisure time were finally put away in the same attic as his childhood dreams of growing up and being a fireman or a cowboy.

A few years pass, and the couple voted most likely to succeed now live the very lives they swore to avoid at all costs. The frustration that they both feel flares up at times, especially now with the credit cards all charged to the limit, a savings account that is empty, and a checking account that is overdrawn again and again. Heather sometimes reminds Jim of the promises and dreams he shared with her when they were first married. She often ponders and can't understand why her life has so little in common with the one she envisioned at the altar.

At the same time, Jim resents his family and views them as the reason he never made it through law school. Sometimes he sees Heather as lazy, and as someone who can't control her appetite or the children. Jim feels she is more of a nuisance every day. Besides, she's the one who spends all the money, isn't she? And the kids . . . It breaks his heart to watch them grow up from such a distance. He has tried to stay close to them, but there are only so many hours in a day. Somehow things and people got away from him. His little girl is ready to start school and he's hardly had time to even get to know her. He has a son now, too; he wants so desperately to take him fishing in a few years, but the little guy is almost two, and with work Jim never seems to have enough time to play with him for more than a few minutes. He struggles as he feels that his whole family are really strangers and are little more now than a financial ball and chain, keeping him from the success he deserves.

The dreams are dead.

Rewriting the End of the Story

This story could also be written in another way . . .

One of our recent students, Patrick Cook, followed a more traditional path. He graduated from high school and worked his butt off in college. He graduated with a technical degree and ended up working in marketing in the high-tech sector. His dreams were all coming true. He made a ton of money, and it seemed that he had it made. Patrick soon got married and planned on having a family.

Then came the dot-com collapse of the high-tech sector.

Patrick lost his job.

He got hired by another company.

He lost his job again.

He then got hired by yet another company.

Then, he was hired by Microsoft.

Patrick came to us to learn real estate investing. He became a member of the National Association of Real Estate Investors and attended one of our week-long "Challenge" trainings.

I have no doubt that he will make it.

As for Jim and Heather, they came out with us on a BuyingTour. Today they have no consumer debt, they own their home free and clear, and they have a $6,500-a-month positive cash flow from the ten homes that they ended up buying in one of our absorption markets.

The lesson here? Real estate investing with the right tools works.

I finally know what distinguishes man from other beasts; financial worries.

—*Jules Renard*

Chapter 3

Keeping the Dream Alive

THERE IS ONE ATTRIBUTE that we all share, one gift, one spark of divinity that separates us from all other creations: We can dream. For some of us, it is a dream of having a career that allows us to exercise our technical and intellectual abilities. Others may dream of impacting this world we live in by making new discoveries in science or medicine, while for some of us it could simply be teaching young children to read. Dreams are the foundation for all of the creative works of art and literature. For untold others, the dream is of being the best parent possible and serving in our churches and communities. The umbrella of dreams covers the entire scope from the simplest desires to have more time for family and friends, all the way to lofty ideas of financial wealth and owning a Rolls-Royce or Lear jet. Financial security paves the way for each of our own personal dreams to become a reality.

Whatever our dreams are, they certainly give zest and flavor to our lives. This ability to dream will be the catalyst for achievement, growth, and happiness in our lives—as long as we keep those dreams alive!

Dreams really don't die until reality sinks its cold, black claws into them and slowly starts to tear them away from us. Few of us, really, will fight very hard for very long to hold on to those dreams, preferring often to follow the example of everyone around us and acquiesce to a cruel fate. We don't even feel totally cheated; after all, that's life, right?

Wrong!

The all-too-common story of Jim and Heather is so familiar, isn't it? And, today Patrick's college graduate nightmare is commonplace. Millions of Americans are living—or seem to be destined to live—the same subtle nightmare of debt, layoffs, and their partner, despair. Hand in hand, debt, layoffs, and despair surely destroy many young dreams. If you recognize yourself anywhere in these stories, or want to be sure you never find yourself in that desperate position, we don't have to convince you anymore that you need more from life—that you can achieve your dreams by investing in real estate.

Why Investing Is for Everyone

But there are also thousands—maybe hundreds of thousands—of Americans for whom these tragic tales of Jim and Heather and Patrick simply do not hold true. They (you?) are perfectly happy with their work. And they (you?) are not laid off or threatened by a layoff. They enjoy every minute of work. They feel like they are accomplishing something worthwhile, and they are making more than enough money to get by on. If you are a member of this elite club, do you really need to invest? Why should you consider investing in real estate? First, because it is unlikely—in spite of how you feel right now about your dream job and personal satisfaction—that you really are as financially secure as you would like to be. If you were rich, you might not do anything differently than you do now, but you would have the security and satisfaction of knowing that you were independent from the need to earn a traditional living. You just might decide that the nine-to-five, forty-plus

22

hours a week, day-in and day-out routine could be eliminated from your personal satisfaction list. If you really think your work is fun now, imagine how much more you would love it if there were absolutely no financial pressure associated with it.

The second reason to consider real estate investing is that there is a dark cloud looming ahead that you might not have noticed: retirement. We'll talk about your future in more detail later, and I'll give you some statistics on retirement, inflation, and your future that should scare you into immediate action. Whether you love or hate your current vocation, whether you are flat broke or comfortable, your future is, at best, uncertain. Real estate investing can erase that uncertainty.

Even if you are financially exactly where you always wanted to be, and doing what you always wanted to do, don't try to tell me you don't have any unfulfilled dreams. As part of the human race, we have the unique ability to dream. I've found through personal experience that real estate investing is the tool that allows you to fulfill your dreams. I have seen it happen several hundred times with my own students.

What Are You Working For?

Let me tell you a little more of my own story. I already told you that after I had made some money in real estate, I immediately quit my job and went to college. This will show you how limited my vision was back then. My first degree was a four-year technical degree in electrical technology. I took my real estate profits to finance what I thought at that time would be my dream. After graduation, I took a job with one of the largest gas and oil companies in the United States. I soon found myself working as an electrical foreman on a major industrial construction project. Because of the demands placed on me by this wonderful high-paying job, I was away from my wife and children for weeks on end. This job required eleven to twelve hours a day, seven days a week. To say it was physically and emotionally taxing is an understatement!

Of course, not all jobs require your presence every day. But I'm sure you've experienced the same feelings that were driving me crazy and slowly destroying my family and my dreams. The bottom line was that my personal life was inconsequential to the company I worked for. Any mention of some (well-deserved) time off would guarantee the typical response, usually accompanied by a slight chuckle, "Sure . . . just don't bother coming back tomorrow." Often after work at night, I would call my family and just listen to their voices. I would feel tears of pain as I heard the small, distant voices of my son, my daughter, and my wife. It really seemed as though they were all a million miles away from me. I felt like I was imprisoned by "a great job." After hanging up the phone I would hate my life—or should I say the lack of it. I felt so unfulfilled. I had worked so hard to get a technical degree and an electrical license. I was making excellent money, but it wasn't enough to compensate for the sacrifice of family time and listening to my kids repeatedly ask Daddy to come home. It was during this time of sitting alone in the "man camp" (the live-in camp inhabited by a thousand roughneck men and a few even rougher women), night after night, that I began to seriously review my life.

I had been fortunate enough to be raised in an excellent family. What we did lack financially, my mother more than made up for with love. That might sound a little trite to the self-absorbed and somewhat cynical generation of young people today, but my mother inspired the kind of family closeness and pride that at one time set this country apart from most of the rest of the world and that no fortune or lack of fortune could destroy. My good mother taught me the values of hard work and personal responsibility.

I grew up in the Los Angeles area, in a neighborhood not noted for being a tourist attraction. I began working as an electrician for a member of my church the summer I was a young man of fourteen. One of the dreams I always had was to go to college and earn a degree. My own parents were not college educated, and I understood in a very tangible way the cost of not continuing my education.

However, the realities of my life made it very obvious to me that if I wanted to go, the only one who could raise the needed money for the tuition would be me, literally by the sweat of my brow.

In high school, I worked really hard to get good grades. After I served two years as a missionary for my church in Sweden, I found myself back in the work-full-time, go-to-school-part-time routine, catching only one or two classes per semester. Some rudimentary arithmetic told me clearly that at this current rate I would graduate by the time I was forty-five years old!

The Turning Point

Now, thinking back on that particular period of my life, I am very grateful for the bosses who allowed me to work and to study. I have to admit that without their patience and support, I might have quit school right then and there. But I know that I worked extra hard for them, so I think that they tolerated my studying during my breaks and lunch and my rushing off to class instead of staying after work to talk "with the guys."

It was right about this time that I reached a magical point, a turning point that all people must reach who want to be in control of their lives. That is the point where they pick up the reins and really decide that they want, and also are ready, to be the masters of their own destiny.

For me, this turning point happened when I was twenty-two years old. I had been married only three months, working full-time and going to school part-time. During one of those hectic days, I was involved in a car accident. It was really not anything especially traumatic, at least not physically. It was just one of those run-of-the-mill accidents, the kind a lot of people have, that don't even make it into the newspapers. But for me, it made me consider my own mortality and think very seriously about my life. At that point, I looked back at my life—what I had accomplished, the direction in which I was headed—and I didn't like what I saw. I had this dream of finishing college, of owning my own home, of having enough income so that my wife wasn't forced to work a job outside of our home if she did not want to. In addition, I had this boyhood dream of getting a pilot's license and—of course—flying a plane! Finally, like everyone else, I dreamed of having the freedom to do what I really wanted. I wasn't asking for an unreasonable amount of possessions or achievements, but no matter what the angle I looked at it from, the common denominator for each of these goals to become a reality was money.

At first I had tried working some overtime as a method of increasing our cash flow, but all that really ever seemed to do for me was to help me pay more in taxes. Oh, and let me state clearly how excited my wife and children were with the prospect of my working even more. Life just wasn't much fun when it meant getting up before the crack of dawn, dropping my overextended wife off at work, driving to my own job, working all day, picking up my wife on the way home, getting a quick bite to eat and a quick kiss, and then driving to a second job and working until the sun was somewhere in China! My life was like a marathon dance with no prize for the winner. Every Friday as we sat down together, going over our finances, we could see that once again we had spent every single cent that we had earned.

It was during this time that I began an intensive study of the investment world. I reviewed every type of investment that was open to us. I had previously met several real estate investors while working as an electrician, and from that experience I decided to include real estate investing in my studies. After several months, I began to realize that real estate was the perfect investment for someone like me who didn't have a lot of cash or credit to work with.

A First Step

I decided to get involved at first by going out and just looking at properties that were for sale. This was the initial learning period of real estate investments, the period people fear most, when I personally made at least ten mistakes a day just by trial and error. But my determination did pay off. Within weeks, I found a small home that needed a lot of cosmetic repairs. I negotiated a small down payment and did a simple assumption on the existing loan. The day that I closed on this house, I had the utilities turned on, and after work each night I anxiously tackled cleaning and repairing this home. I had a lot of family and friends who offered their help and advice. The toilet in this home had dark rings on the inside like a redwood tree. My grandmother guaranteed me that denture tablets would remove all of the stains. I put in a whole box and let it sit overnight. It worked. On one of the bedroom walls a young child had practiced his artistic skills with a box of crayons. My father told me that the spray lubricant WD-40 would take off all of those marks so that I could paint the wall. It worked. Within weeks I had completely transformed that house into something beautiful. I decided to put that home up for sale. On that home I ended up netting $16,272, after all expenses. So before very long, I was actually making money from my initial real estate investments. I couldn't believe it, so I did it again.

Before long I was making more money from my real estate investments than I was making from my job. With the extra income I was earning from my real estate investing I was able to finish a four-year technical degree and get a state electrical license and the dream job—or so I thought.

Now, as I sat alone in the man camp, I realized that my "dream job" was the job that was really destroying me. For years I had worked to get to the point that I had reached—electrical foreman (lots of power and prestige there, let me tell you) on one of the highest-paying heavy industrial construction projects in the nation . . . Big deal!

Making the Commitment

How did it really make me feel? I felt very disillusioned. I felt that all my work in college had been in vain. I saw that the dream I had worked so hard to achieve was nothing but an empty lie. The position, the pay, and the prestige carried with it a price that I was unwilling to pay.

My life as it was, day in and day out, seemed like walking down a dark road, a road that got further and further from any real light. It was the same road that most of my friends were also walking down, and maybe the same road you're on now.

I looked back once in a while and watched as my family became, in the words of Carl Sandburg, "far and wee." With all of the hours that I was working, I was losing the opportunity to invest actively in real estate. Real estate investing had been the vehicle to achieve my early dreams. I had one college degree in electrical technology and a home, but I wanted more for myself and my family. I knew that the way to do it again was through real estate investing.

Alone at nights, on the job, I began to plan so I would be able to do everything I had always wanted to.

I'll never forget the day I quit my job (yes, take this job and shove it!) and immediately went on a four-week vacation with my family, driving almost five thousand miles throughout the western United States. The trip wasn't just for fun though; it was also time to plan out my strategy. I was committing myself to a life where I would be able to say "No!" to a conventional job, especially one that I did not like or that violated my principles.

I began my plan by enrolling in school to finish another undergraduate degree and then an M.B.A. (master of business administration) and maybe even a Ph.D. During this period of rebirth, I would use my extra time to invest in real estate.

Once again, it didn't take long for me to see that I could make far more money as an investor than as an electrician, or even as a college graduate, and at the same time I could be my own boss.

The last year of my M.B.A. program, the career guidance counselor called me in to ask what the problem was; all the other M.B.A. candidates were scrambling for jobs. I politely explained that I already had enough work to keep me busy and that getting my M.B.A. degree was simply to fulfill my desire for knowledge. I'm afraid for a second that the counselor was ready to call security; she thought that she had a crazy man in her office. Interestingly enough, during this time I had two incredible full-time job offers come to me through my graduate research and work. One offer was a full-time position with the Central Intelligence Agency, and the other offer was from IBM. My wife and I flew back east several times to consider these two jobs, but in the long run we chose to continue on with our personal real estate investment program.

Imagine how I felt at that time. I was not yet thirty, and I was financially able to afford to continue my education without my wife supporting me with an outside job. I could get as many doctorates as I wanted or pursue any other endeavor I desired. I've found that school is a million times more fun when the pressure to succeed comes from within and has nothing to do with proving myself to IBM. Is that freedom? It sure is. It's the same kind of freedom that I want you to enjoy.

The income has allowed me much more than just school and survival. My family and I have traveled around the world. We have a vacation home in one of the most beautiful ski resorts in America. We have a summer home on an island in Sweden. We have been able to give our children opportunities—not advantages. And best of all, our wealth has given me time to be able to pursue my dreams.

More important than being able to enjoy my family by going on some great vacation, I don't find myself lying awake at night worrying about where I am going to get the money to fix the car. Instead, I have problems like what to do with the $83,500 check I will receive next week from the sale of a property. I know that through real estate investing, anyone can achieve his or her financial goals and live out their dreams.

29

What Are Your Dreams?

I get excited when I discuss the possibilities that real estate investing offers. I don't want to sound like a '70s housewife captured on a hidden camera in a Tide commercial, but investing really has changed my life. It has allowed me to fulfill dreams that I once thought were dead forever.

Let's talk for a minute about your dreams. What is it you really want? Would you really love to be independently wealthy, able to do whatever you want, whenever you want to do it? Do you want to join the ranks of the leisure class? Or would you rather have a little extra income and a secure retirement plan? Perhaps you really want nothing more than to have all the toys that money can buy. The first time I drove one of my new cars to graduate school it was a heady feeling. I have also enjoyed the comforts of a nice home that is owned free and clear, nestled away at the foot of a mountain. But millionaires eventually grow tired of toys, and you will desire something more someday. Having millions of dollars and being able to satisfy every whim may sound exciting now, but I have to warn you about something. If you eat prime rib for dinner every night, it soon loses its appeal.

Educated Persistence

U.S. News and World Report did a study about those people whom a lot of us envy, the one-in-a-million person who is the epitome of success: the self-made millionaire. No matter what your personal goals are, the self-made millionaires have an excellent lesson for each of us who has a desire to be something more than just "one of the crowd."

In interviews, these millionaires again and again stressed the same factors that had led to their success: drive, determination, and discipline; tenacity, readiness for opportunity, and educated persistence. I love the last expression—educated persistence—because it sums up everything else, wrapping it up and tying it with a bow paid for with sweat. It is an expression I try to live by every day. The combination of constantly educating yourself and never giving up practically ensures success.

If I can develop in you that one quality, any level of financial success that you desire will be assured, because everything else will fall into place if you refuse to give up and never, ever stop learning.

So let's work on education and then on persistence, you and I. Let's examine what you need to know to become financially independent, and then put it to work—every day, for the rest of your life.

If you stick with us to the end of the book, we'll give you a healthy dose of education. We will also teach you the new paradigms of real estate investment that work today and the new tools of buying real estate at pennies on the dollar in today's markets with little or no money down. And since we can't stand over your shoulder and coach you, if you contact me directly via e-mail, I will show you how you can gain access to one of my students, a documented self-made millionaire who can work with you as a mentor. Just send me an e-mail at marcstephangarrison@narei.com. I have contacts in most every state and major city in America. This list is worth its weight in gold if you are serious as a heart attack about real estate investing success.

Facing Your Fears

Now let's talk about persistence. Teaching you persistence is a bit tougher than giving you a list of contacts. We hope we can instill the right balance of desire for success and fear of poverty to get you going, but keeping you going will be the real challenge. Persistence is a rare quality; it's often the difference between success and failure. When Sir Winston Churchill, very near the end of his illustrious life, was invited to address the prep school he had attended as a boy, his entire speech—the sum total of all his experience—was this: "Never, ever, ever, ever give up!" We'll talk more about persistence as we go along—a lot.

Education, persistence, and . . . courage. Many eager would-be investors can't wait to get out and start making their fortunes—until they run headfirst into their own fears. If you are letting fear keep you from success, now is the time to develop the necessary risk-taking courage.

We would love to have a nice plaque in our office with these words engraved on it: "Fear is the greatest mind-killer." Fear paralyzes the mind and freezes the blood.

The first time you call a property owner about the ad they placed in the paper to sell their home, your hand is likely to tremble and your voice to quiver. That's okay; every single one of us has to go through the same experience when we start out. The first time you hand a written offer to a seller, the pages may be shaking like a fistful of drying autumn leaves. So what? There is no other way to succeed as an investor.

What Sets the Successful Apart

We know hundreds and thousands of very successful investors. Many of them, eschewing the life of the idle rich, have dedicated their lives to teaching others—through books, workshops, and seminars. They all have favorite stories about how they got started and how they overcame their fears.

Take a friend of mine, Bob Allen, author of the bestselling books *Nothing Down* and *Creating Wealth*. After graduating from an M.B.A. program near the bottom of his class, he hit the job market, ready for the exciting world of big business. It wasn't until the world of big business slapped him in the face that Bob encountered failure, frustration, and fear.

Today Bob is especially proud of one of his books. It is a leather-bound volume, appropriately entitled *The Many Failures of Robert G. Allen*. It contains rejection letters from nearly every major (and more than one minor) company in the United States. It is a unique collection, a slice of Americana, with samples from almost every state. Nobody, but nobody, wanted Bob. He had graduated from an excellent, highly regarded graduate program, and the business world was telling him that he was a failure—before giving him a chance to prove he could be a success. Yet he hung in there and finally found real estate investing.

So why is Bob Allen a multimillionaire today? Educated persistence and overcoming his fears. Bob's motivation for investing in real estate was simple—hunger. It was an unavoidable choice: Do or die. Make or break. Sink or swim. Pick your own expression; he simply knew that he had to make it on his own, and he did.

Bob had dreams. You have dreams. Bob educated himself. Have you? Bob persisted in the face of fear, fatigue, and rejection. What have you done so far? Bob set goals; he wrote them down on paper and concentrated his efforts on accomplishing them. With his dreams as a catalyst, Bob set goals that would turn those dreams into reality. Why should you do any differently?

There really isn't a special class of people destined for success. No one has ever had his or her dreams turned into reality by fate alone. But there are only a handful of people who are willing to persist, to educate themselves, and to overcome their fears and conquer their failures. And you can do every one of those things if your desire for success is strong enough, and if you have the right kind of education.

Dreams Drive Us On

I'm amazed, as I travel across the country talking to investors, that so many Americans feel sorry for themselves because they weren't born rich. They seem to be totally unaware that they live in one of the few countries in the world where desire and hard, smart work can mean success. I am glad that I live in America. I hope that in the future it doesn't take another terrorist act for us to wake up and smell the coffee about America. I am glad that the United States is the world's largest school of hard knocks. If it weren't so, I would still be working and living from paycheck to paycheck.

Do you know whom I feel the most sorry for? I feel sorry for the rich kids, born with silver spoons in their mouths. They have never known the hunger for achievement; most of them don't have enough motivation to blow out a match.

You envy their lifestyle? They have never had a dream, and their upbringing has been remarkably similar to the fat, fleshy pigs down on Paula's dad's farm. At least all of John's pigs serve some purpose (well, maybe not a certain one named Lucille).

It really doesn't matter where you are now, or whether you are happy or miserable in your work, or how fat your bank account is today. You still need to plan for the future; you need to find peace and financial security in a turbulent economy; and you have unfulfilled dreams that want so much to be reawakened and satisfied.

Be grateful for your hunger, for your unfulfilled dreams. Without them you would sit listlessly watching the world go by. Don't let them die just yet.

If you have dreams that are either dying or dead, or poisoned by reality, you can bring them back to life. Now is the time to be the master of your own destiny. If you aren't yet convinced that you need to invest, that you need to do something besides just work your job, the next chapter should do the trick. Whatever your dreams, turn the page. Follow us, and let us teach you how to create unlimited profit and ultimate wealth for both you and yours.

We forge the chains that bind us.

—Charles Dickens

Chapter 4

Golden Handcuffs
and Social Insecurity

YOU MAY HAVE HEARD THE EXPRESSION "golden handcuffs." You may be wearing a pair of golden handcuffs now, without even being aware that they are restricting your every movement. We are creatures with an incredible ability to adapt ourselves to our environment. We take jobs that tie us down for most of our lives and never seem to notice that they are keeping us from everything we ever wanted to do. We hope for a bright future without making any actual plans for extricating ourselves from a dismal present.

There are undoubtedly worse feelings in the world than realizing that you are trapped for life in a job that pays too little or is personally unsatisfying, but I am hard-pressed to imagine what they are. I suppose being sentenced to solitary confinement for life would run a close second, but at least then you would most likely have done something to deserve the sentence.

But when we've done everything society claims will bring success, how can we still seem eternally chained to a desk or a machine hoping to barely get by?

Golden handcuffs with velvet linings—a job that pays enough to take care of all the bills, with just enough left over for one or two weeks' vacation every year. A good job that offers excellent insurance benefits for the family and a company plan that assures a small pension upon retirement. What more could you want?

But they're still called golden handcuffs, because before you know it, you couldn't quit even if you wanted to. What would you do? Who would pay the MasterCard bill? What would you tell your in-laws; what would you tell your spouse? The golden handcuffs are now so securely latched that you are becoming numb to the American initiative and independence that you now only vaguely recall. Most of the time you don't even notice you're wearing them.

Do You Really Love Your Job As Much As That?

For some, these handcuffs are a blessing. These people absolutely love working for someone else and belonging to a large corporate family. They thrill at the team spirit and the enormous potential for major group accomplishment.

I am not anti-job, but humor my efforts to prove a point. The disadvantage of working forty years for someone else becomes obvious the minute you leave to go home with your paycheck. After a week of working—even in a career you thoroughly enjoy— you open the door of your eight-year-old station wagon with the McDonald's Quarter Pounder boxes scattered on your backseat and the spot on the carpet from the Big Gulp that spilled under your dashboard a year ago. As you pull away from the office, content with your work, you pass the executive parking lot and sigh as you gaze at the sleek lines of the CEO's new BMW.

Why is a feeling of oppression so common? For most people, it isn't the job itself but the lack of choice that depresses their spirit. It's the feeling that you're trapped, stuck in your job forever and always two weeks from bankruptcy. If you didn't have to work you'd probably love your job. But knowing that when the alarm clock rings, you have little choice but to get up and face another workday is bound to be depressing.

It's possible to keep your job and invest in real estate part-time. It is within your reach to earn unlimited profit and create ultimate wealth through part-time real estate investing. Or, what the heck, if you only did one deal a year, you could put a few thousand extra dollars in your pocket now and then. If you're among the minority of workers who love every day on the job, why not have the best of both worlds?

For the 99.9 percent of the workers who don't make it into upper management, the golden handcuffs that come with working for someone else are laced with a slow-acting poison. It's one that works its way into their skin and finds its way into their dreams, killing them gently and ever so slowly.

What You May Be Missing

My personal experience might be similar to yours. When I worked as an electrician on a job site, I met a lot of interesting people. Many of them had spent thirty years or more working one electrical job after another. They were wed to their work, and it was a rocky marriage at best. But it was life; what else did they have? They had no hopes and no dreams. All they had was an old, beat-up pair of golden handcuffs and a promise that was burned into their minds each day: that if they quit performing (got old, got weak, got sick) they would be laid off or fired. (Sound familiar?) That was it, no roses and no watch; they were canned and their positions filled by younger, quicker workers eager for their jobs.

And no matter how much you love your work, your time is just not your own; most jobs require that you be in a certain place at a certain time every day, Monday through Friday.

I compare that with the one-time-only experience I enjoyed with all of my children: their first day at school. For my youngest son, I was the only father out of the 153 parents who showed up for that special day. As I sat on a chair made for a six-year-old back-side and listened to the teacher, I noticed some of the women were pointing at me. As I left, I heard one of the mothers whisper to another, "He must be unemployed."

The experience of having the time to do something like I did that day may not seem like much, but think about it. You are either there, or you miss out forever. There is no second first day of school, just as there is no second first kiss or second first anything. If I had still been working at my high-paying job, I would have missed the experience. I might not have minded much. It would have been just one more pinprick in my dreams, draining them slowly of life.

How many people are able to go with their children on the first day of school? Just to be with them and see that little boy or girl start a new phase of life? Too many working parents are too securely attached to their desks and computers, to their cash registers and welding torches—fettered by golden handcuffs.

There are almost as many pairs of these shiny handcuffs as there are employed people in America. You are probably wearing a pair right now. Jim and Heather slipped into a bright and shiny pair one day and never got free until they started investing in real estate. Most people stop looking for a key, learning to enjoy the "security" the bracelets offer. They're just like the lifers in prison who, when released on parole at sixty-five, immediately do something—any-thing—to get back inside where it is safe.

Some of the shackles are twenty-four-karat gold. I know a man who is a well-paid and highly respected lawyer. Specializing in civil litigation, he has made a name for himself in the legal arena. What does he want to do? He wants to make tables and dressers and chil-dren's toy boxes. He loves wood. I have seen some of the beautiful, intricate works of superb craftsmanship that his skilled hands have produced. The man wants nothing more than to be a furniture maker. I asked him one day why he didn't pursue his love. His answer? He couldn't afford it. There were too many bills to pay. The kids needed braces, and his wife needed the new fur coat that he had promised her. He is wearing a twenty-four-karat pair of handcuffs, and he has thrown away the key. The way he could afford to do what he wants to do is through real estate investing. He could easily make furniture as he wished and rely on investing for the needed income.

I have helped a man who loves to design computer games get started in real estate investing. He quit his job working in a warehouse and formed his own company, which designs computer games. So far he hasn't made a dime off the games. How does he live? He invests in real estate. His program of real estate investments literally supports his dream. He is wealthier than most millionaires; he can do what he really enjoys doing.

Breaking Free

That is one of the main points of this book. To make money in real estate, you don't have to quit your job and invest full-time. Your job can continue to provide the basic necessities—the bills, the braces, the car payments—and at night and on weekends you can, with very little time and effort, realize fantastic financial benefits working just a few hours a week in real estate investing. If you've read other investment books, you realize that many methods demand seven days a week, twelve hours a day. Using the plan in this book, you will be able to achieve your financial dreams. And it's basic multiplication: if you increase by tenfold the time you put into investing, your results will be ten times greater. But it's all up to you.

Real estate investing isn't the only way to break free, but I sincerely believe it is the best way. It is safe, requires little starting capital, and is not shrouded by the impenetrable cloak of mystery that surrounds most forms of investment. Real estate is a basic and necessary commodity. As an investment it has worked better, for more people, than any other means of achieving financial freedom. In Chapter 5, you will compare real estate to other means of unlocking the golden handcuffs that bind you to your present life. When you see the possibilities there, you will be ready to learn the new paradigms and tools of real estate investment.

If you like working for someone else, that's great. But, there are alternatives to an eight-hour-a-day, five-days-a-week until-you-can't-work-anymore existence. You can have the best of both worlds.

Create your own wealth. Then, when you are lying on the beach on some tropical isle or relaxing by the fire in your cabin after a hard day on the slopes, you will know that you are not spoiled; you have earned your rewards.

Securing Your Own Future

"Marc," I can hear you saying, "You're way off base. I'm not wearing handcuffs at all." (That is you talking, isn't it?) "Not only do I love my work, but I also set my own hours and I make a good living. I live like a king or queen (or at least a prince or princess), and I put $2,000 into my IRA every year. I really don't need to invest in real estate at all."

Let me tell you something. You are on a cruise ship right now, on your way to a foreign land. You probably think that it will be paradise, and it may well be—if you plan well enough for the trip. Your destination: the Republic of Retirees. Your cruise ship: the USS Inflation.

Unfortunately, millions of people started out on the same cruise with the same plans. They thought that they had plenty of provisions for the trip, and the cruise itself was so much fun that they almost forgot where they were going. And they certainly didn't take into consideration the fact that the fare for the USS Inflation is very, very high. When they were dropped quite suddenly on the shores of their new country, it was a shock to find out that paradise wasn't such a hot deal when the only diet they could afford was bread and water.

If you are still working, you have time—ten, twenty, thirty

years or more—before your ship will pull into port. What are your plans for that day?

Most Americans have three sources of income when their working years come to an end: their savings, a pension plan, and Social Security. We all have a tendency to assume that the combination of those three will be enough to take care of us for the rest of our lives. But every shred of evidence points in the opposite direction.

It's shocking how few people even think about retirement in more than a wistful fashion before it hits them. It's too easy to imagine that when that someday comes, we'll all grab our fishing rods and knitting needles and enjoy a well-earned rest. The tragedies we see around us—hundreds of thousands of elderly people living in run-down, lonely apartments, kept company only by Bob Barker and Jay Leno; horror stories of retirees freezing to death in winter because the gas company shut off their heat, or eating canned dog food because they can't afford the price of a TV dinner—affect us in about the same fashion as a roadside accident. It's always someone else; we certainly won't end up in the same fix. It is terribly (and I do mean terribly) surprising that so many retirees are in such sad financial shape, when they should be protected by their savings.

Savings

How much will you be able to save between now and the day of your retirement party? Can you really put $2,000 into your individual retirement account every year? How about $1,000 or even $500? Here's an easy mental exercise to keep you awake: Decide at which age you want to retire. Subtract your current age—no cheating; if you're over thirty-nine, admit it. Now you know how much time you have left. Use your years-to-retirement figure to find out how much that savings account will add up to when you are ready to use it.

In this table, I am assuming that you are going to be earning 11 percent interest on your IRA. If you think 11 percent is too optimistic, and perhaps 4 or 5 percent is closer to the mark, get in touch with your local banker. He or she will be happy to show you what your account would be worth by the time you retire at whatever percentage you think is reasonable.

Compounded Values of IRA Savings Accounts at 11 Percent

YEARS TO RETIREMENT	ANNUAL DEPOSIT AMOUNTS			
	$500	$1,000	$1,500	$2,000
5	3,113.90	6,227.80	9,341.70	12,445.60
10	8,361.00	16,722.01	25,083.01	33,444.02
15	17,202.68	34,405.36	51,608.04	68,810.72
20	32,101.42	64,202.83	96,304.25	128,405.68
25	57,206.65	114,413.31	171,619.96	228,826.61
30	99,510.44	199,020.88	298,531.32	398,041.76
40	290,913.03	581,826.07	872,739.10	1,163,652.13

Here's an example. If you began a $1,000-a-year savings plan at age forty, with annual deposits until retiring at age sixty-five, you'd have twenty-five years to make your deposits. To calculate the value of your IRA at retirement, find the $1,000 annual deposit column, and go down until you come across the figure that corresponds to twenty-five years. This amount ($114,413.31) represents the value of your $1,000-a-year IRA with twenty-five annual deposits at 11-percent interest.

At first glance you think that's not bad at all; what's the problem? I've got a pension coming too, after all . . .

Pensions

Many employers offer some kind of pension plan, though many are also phasing them out and replacing them with 401(k) plans.

These pension plans vary greatly, and you should know what your company offers. As a general rule, your pension will be 25 to 35 percent of your ending gross salary. If, for example, you are earning $50,000 a year when you retire and your company pays 30 percent, your pension will be $15,000 a year for the rest of your life. (Be aware that very possibly your spouse will get nothing from your pension after you die if you happen to depart for the great beyond before he or she does.) Add that to your savings, and at first glance the picture still seems rosy. We know we can depend on our savings, pensions, and of course on Social Security.

Social Security

Good old Uncle Sam—bless his generous heart. Was there ever a more giving uncle born? He promises that if we will help out the elderly while we are young, he will make sure that our children and grandchildren do the same for us. Isn't that a wonderful promise?

The sad truth is that when the Social Security system was instituted, there were about a dozen workers for every retired person. The extra burden on each taxpayer was light, and the benefits were terrific. Today, as you are well aware, Social Security takes a big bite out of every paycheck. The problem is the shift in the population. We live longer, we retire earlier, and there are more and more retirees every year in relation to the number of workers.

You see, we had this thing called the baby boom. From the end of World War II until about 1962, there were a whole bunch of babies born. So many, in fact, that it caused quite a bulge in the overall population curve. We baby boomers are moving through time like a watermelon through a boa constrictor, and we are not putting forth much of an effort to provide a generation of workers to support us when the time comes.

According to current government statistics, there are presently five workers for every Social Security recipient. The same research shows that within fifteen years, the ratio of workers paying into the system to those receiving Social Security benefits will drop to two to one. Since Social Security is a pay-as-you-go program, that simply means that two employed members of the American work force will be responsible for paying the full bill for one recipient.

Projections show that, to maintain current benefits, as much as a 50 percent Social Security tax will be required on the gross monthly salary of each member of the work force. Other options include raising the eligibility age of Social Security recipients to seventy-two, or dropping the program altogether.

In light of such figures, I don't put much faith in the Social Security system. I honestly believe that when the burden finally gets heavy enough on the workers, they will revolt—politically, that is—and we will see the end of the program. This is especially frightening in light of the fact that for the great majority of Americans, the most important form of household wealth is the anticipated Social Security retirement benefits. You don't need to be a Rhodes scholar to figure out that there are a few major cracks in the dike. I prefer to call this program "Social Insecurity."

It's unfortunate that so many have put so much faith in such a weak system. In an article by Martin Feldstein that appeared in the *Journal of Political Economy,* it was reported that the anticipation of receiving Social Security benefits reduces personal saving by as much as 50 percent. People simply say to themselves, "Why save? The government will take care of me." And they go about spending almost every cent they have.

My advice is to assume, for safety's sake, that we are looking at the imminent demise of the Social Security system. I may be wrong, but please don't bank on it. It would be far wiser to plan on not having it and then be pleasantly surprised with some extra money for shuffleboard chalk or bingo if they happen to find a way to make the money presses turn that much faster.

The Real Culprits

Gee whiz, you might say, with savings, plus pension, plus (cross your fingers) Social Security, you will have it made, won't you? Well then, why are so many of our own parents having such a tough time today?

Low Savings

Here's one reason: We Americans are terrible when it comes to savings for a rainy day, aren't we? We believe firmly in the power of conspicuous consumption, and as a populace we sock away about 5 percent of our money in the bank. Compared with the Japanese (20 percent) we are incredible spendthrifts. The party on the cruise ship is so much fun that we simply forget to save for our final destination.

Inflation

This is the real monster. No matter how hard we are battered by inflation, we still fail to recognize just how devastating it can be in the long run.

Inflation has been likened to a pickpocket that quietly slips your wallet from your pocket, takes a dollar or two out, and then puts the wallet back without your ever noticing. But in the long run, inflation is anything but gentle. It kicks your legs out from under you, socks you in the jaw, knees you in the kidneys, and then takes your wallet, your watch, your wedding ring, and the fillings in your teeth . . . and then kicks your dog on the way out the door.

Yes, if you are frugal and put aside a thousand or more every year, you will have a half million dollars by the time you retire—but so what? By then a thousand dollars a month isn't much when a Big Mac, fries, and a Coke cost $45.79.

A Realistic Look at Inflation Past, Present, and Future

ITEM	1960	1980	2000	2015
Single-family house	$19,950	$69,100	$160,607	$373,298
Economy four-door car	2,900	7,100	11,350	19,585
Refrigerator	470	530	630	1,230
Man's suit	140	268	399	789
Car insurance premium	93	270	560	1,031
Electric bill	12	48	87	248
Dinner out (for two)	12	21	48	89
Paperback book	1.05	3.50	5.70	10.12
Movie ticket	.95	4.50	6.50	16
Candy bar	.05	.35	.81	1.89
First-class stamp	.04	.22	.34	1.19

Remember the IRA that you are investing in, and how much we decided it would be worth by the time you retire? Well, plug that amount into this table for an eye-opener. This is what your bank account will be worth in terms of today's buying power:

Present Values of IRA/Savings and Future Values in Real Dollar Terms with 7 Percent Inflation

	PROJECTED DOLLAR AMOUNTS OF IRA/SAVINGS DEPOSITS			
YEARS	$100,000	$250,000	$500,000	$1,000,000
5	71,298.62	178,246.54	356,493.09	712,986.18
10	50,834.93	127,087.32	254,174.65	508,349.29
15	36,244.60	90,611.50	181,223.01	362,446.02
20	25,841.90	64,604.75	129,209.50	258,419.00
25	18,424.92	46,062.29	92,124.59	184,249.18
30	13,136.71	32,841.78	65,683.56	131,367.12
35	9,366.29	23,415.73	46,831.47	93,662.94
40	6,678.04	16,695.10	33,390.19	66,780.38

Here's an example. The value of the $1,000-a-year IRA deposit ($1,000 a year for twenty-five years at 11 percent interest) would be a little over $100,000 in nominal terms. To determine the actual present value of that sum, look under the $100,000 column and go down to the number opposite twenty-five years. The value of that $100,000 twenty-five years from now would only be $18,424.92 in real spendable dollar terms today. In plain English, that means $100,000 will then only buy you as much as $18,000 will buy you now.

I am using an average inflation rate of 7 percent in this table. The actual rate may be higher or lower; only the future knows. If I had to make a guess, I'd bet that it will be even higher, but I don't want to be labeled a pessimist.

The Incredible Shrinking Retirement Account

Meet George. George is thirty-five. He's married, he's completely happy with his job as an engineer, and he has a couple of cars, a nice house, $600 in the family checking account, and 1.6 children. He now makes $49,000 a year. You can't get much more middle-class than George, and that suits him just fine.

George and his wife (Mrs. George, he sometimes calls her) are going to start putting away $2,000 a year into their IRA every year from now until they retire. George wants to retire when he's sixty-five. He wants to travel with Mrs. George. His company offers excellent benefits and will pay him 33 percent of his ending salary as a pension. Everything is right on schedule, and George is happy.

Lucky George.

George has thirty more working years. When he retires, here is what he has to look forward to:

Savings account/IRA $398,041.76

George has figured out that if he and his wife live to be eighty-five (she's the same age; they were childhood sweethearts), they can withdraw $49,984.35 every year for the last twenty years before they will deplete their savings, which they hope will still be earning 11 percent interest. That gives them the following annual retirement income:

```
Savings account/IRA  . . . . . . . . . . . . . . . . . $49,984.35
Pension plan . . . . . . . . . . . . . . . . . . . . . . . $41,360.88
```
(George's ending gross salary is $125,336—
too bad that he's barely getting by.)
```
Social Security . . . . . . . . . . . . . . . . . . . . . . . . . 0.00
```
(The program collapsed in 2015.)

```
Total . . . . . . . . . . . . . . . . . . . . . . . . . . . . . $91,345.23
```

That's not too bad at all, is it? In fact, they can really travel in style with that kind of money—that is, if there is no inflation for the next thirty years and none for the remaining twenty years after that.

But, if we experience a reasonable 7 percent average inflation rate, that $91,345.23 shrinks to $11,999.76 in today's dollars by George's sixty-fifth birthday, and all the way down to $3,100.97 by the time he reaches eighty-five. Remember that is only $3,100.97 in terms of today's buying power! Can you live on $258.41 a month today? If he is unfortunate enough to live longer than that, his entire savings will be exhausted—and so will he.

Poor George. This scenario is actually based on the highest possible return for an IRA right now. The facts are real, and the motivation and reason for investing in real estate are as serious as a heart attack.

By the time I move into the retirement home, I want to own it. How about you? I do not want to depend on welfare to support me. Savings, pensions, and Social Security just aren't enough. You must invest. Imagine if poor George had just bought one small rental property when he was thirty-five. Using the tools taught in this book, he could do it for little if no money down. With what he learned also in this book, he would have structured his payments so that he would have a positive cash flow from day one. The rents from that property would pay the mortgage payments for that property.

By the time George retired, that property would be paid for free and clear. With no more mortgage payments the entire income—less expenses—would go into his pocket. With rents today rising faster than the cost of housing, he would make a killing. Plus, he would have an asset with value that has appreciated over the next thirty years. Just that one income property purchase could make George a millionaire by the time that he retired. As I already said, real estate investing is the surest, safest road to financial freedom.

Taking Control

My advice for each and every one of you is to take control of your financial life from this very moment on. My first goal for you would be to pay off all of your consumer debt. Then to pay off your home. Then to work on acquiring at least ten rental homes and to structure their payments so that you would own each free and clear by the time you plan on retiring. My goal for you would be a $10,000 positive cash flow in today's terms by the time you want to retire. Real estate investing can easily do it for you. But you have got to learn the basics (that is, go to ground school). And then you need a mentor. I would love to help you get one.

And then you should start working on making your personal dreams come true.

If you are thoroughly convinced enough about real estate—then read on. If not, I have a homework assignment for you. Visit the nearest retirement home or the poorest section of one-bedroom apartments in town. Ask the residents what they think about real estate investing. Ask them if they could relive their lives, knowing what they know now, would they have done anything differently? Ask then what properties were selling for thirty years ago. Ask them if they wished that they had invested in real estate back in their working days. When you have the answers, come back and let's rock.

We do not see the lens through which we look.

—Ruth Fulton Benedict

Chapter 5

Analyzing Your Investment Possibilities

RYAN WAS BASICALLY A GOOD MAN his entire life. He worked hard to earn his reward, and as he drew his last breath he fancied he saw at the end of a long, dark tunnel a brilliant light—heaven. At last, after laboring for almost a century, he had broken the bonds of mortality.

When he arrived at the pearly gates, Saint Peter himself greeted Ryan and welcomed him graciously into a spacious room, decorated in sculptured marble and pure gold. Even the lighting was, well, heavenly. However, there was no indication where any door would lead.

Ryan turned and asked, "Where to now, Saint Peter?" "I don't know," was the answer, "I've never gotten beyond the gate myself."

It must be painfully evident at this point that you need to do something now to provide for your financial future in addition to working for a slave wage. The question is, what? If you are still not totally convinced of investing in real estate, then let's consider your other options. Let's consider which way you should go, which door you should open. How will you provide the income necessary to retire and comfortably fulfill your dreams? The doors to financial security are open and we will guide you, but that's up to you. Yes, there are a million ways to invest; we have tried about half of them ourselves.

All Those Choices

When we were ready to start our career as investors, like everyone else, we were faced with a plethora of choices. Should we invest in stocks, or bonds, or precious metals? Maybe we should invest in real estate, or in Cousin Eddie's yogurt-and-pickle shop.

What specifically makes any investment the best choice? The answer is the proper combination of risk and return that fits your personality and goals. The concepts of risk and return include, for any investment, the following factors:

- Loss of principal
- Loss of income
- Inflation
- Management
- Timing risk
- Liquidity risk
- Cash flow
- Tax shelter
- Equity buildup
- Control

Investing in a Denver-based family-run business or buying a stake in the future of a company called "Golden Glitter Movies" can often promise an incredible return on your initial investment, but the risks—such as loss of principal or, especially, management difficulties—probably outweigh the benefits.

Stocks and Commodities

The stock and commodities markets are only slightly less risky. Instead of three-piece suits, Wall Street brokers ought to wear visors perched on their heads and garters on their sleeves. They could stand in the pit and cry, "Hurry, hurry, step right up, folks, place your bets. Hey, hey, fella, step right up and buy some pork bellies, buy a little XYZ for the missus, it's a sure bet. Hurry, hurry; everybody's a winner!"

True, millions upon millions have been made on Wall Street, but millions upon millions have been lost as well. You simply have no control.

Precious Metals

All right then, what about gold and silver? At least the supply is limited, and rarity does mean value, right? True, but remember: Value is strictly a matter of collective personal opinion, especially today, when neither gold nor silver is used as a form of currency in our economy. And in a paper economy, the value of precious metals is never a sure bet.

Once I bought a considerable number of one-ounce silver bars as a hedge against our rising inflation rate. These silver bars were of the highest available quality. My purchase price was the best I could get "spot" (which is the going price of the metal at a given time if traded in large lots), plus a small commission to the trader.

I was guaranteed in several investment magazine articles that the price of silver was ready to skyrocket. The traders insisted it was a sure thing. In reality, the only sure thing that I had was a certainty that no one knows what the price is going to be next week. In fact, the price of precious metals is like the random movements of a three-year-old child; it just runs around with no predictability. I have personally found that the so-called "experts" really do not have any "inside" knowledge or, therefore, insight. They rely on luck about as much luck as a television weatherman or a government economist.

My "premium silver" is now worth less than what I paid for it. Why? What happened to lower its price? What can be done to increase the price? Could I possibly polish it, shine it up, and maybe advertise it to the right people? Or do I just have to sit and wait for some "mythical market force" to drive the price up?

The bottom line is that I really have no control. I have to just sit and wait. Obviously, I am not in the driver's seat with this one. You don't have to take my word for it; history is evidence enough for this "solid investment." The prices have never been predictable, and those who have tried to outguess the market have lost, sooner or later. Today's market for precious metals will find itself in tomorrow's history book—a book nobody can write just yet.

Mutual Funds

So you cannot control risk or return with stocks, precious metals, or other commodity markets. What does that leave you with? If you want to avoid risk almost entirely, you can always invest in a mutual fund or some "high-paying" savings account. They really are practically risk-free. But they are also practically return-free as well. Most of them seem only to keep pace with inflation at best.

Right before I totally quit my job, I did decide to jump onto the IRA bandwagon. I chose the "hottest," most secure mutual fund available at the time. (A mutual fund is a stock portfolio in which an investor buys shares of the portfolio. This entire portfolio is managed, along some established guidelines, by a managing committee for the fund.)

My particular choice was a mutual fund that had appreciated more than 35 percent each year for the previous five years. This looked really good, right? I couldn't go wrong. My stockbroker himself had this fund in his own personal IRA, and it was his "sure winning pick." The reality is that several years later, after fund expenses, fees, and so on, my investment was now worth about 90 percent of my original investment. How in the world could this be? It sure looked like it was a winner. Once again, the only answer is that I didn't have control.

Another good example of the power of real estate versus the roller-coaster ride that the stock market has become is that of Deming Shi. Deming came to the United States from Communist China in 1989. He had $40 in his pocket. Deming was a visiting scholar at the Colorado School of Mines. He saved every extra dime that he could and soon began investing in real estate. Now, Deming is worth just under $700,000. Last year he pulled $80,000 of equity out of one of his apartment buildings. He put that entire amount into a mutual fund. Less than a year later, his shares of that mutual fund are worth $20,000. I recently had dinner in Denver with Deming and his good wife. He and his wife not only manage their real estate, but they also maintain it. What a wonderful testimony of the power of real estate investing to make your dreams come true.

Small Businesses

I've left out one investment that has in rare instances turned paupers into princes: the sole proprietorship or franchise. Ray Kroc took a small hamburger stand in California and turned it into the largest fast-food chain in the world: McDonald's. Unfortunately, for every one phenomenal success there are a million failures. The failure rate for small businesses, according to the U.S. Department of Commerce, varies from 80 percent to 95 percent, each and every year. At least with this investment you are in control, but creativity is just not that abundant. To make it here you must have a new angle and a lot of luck to succeed.

Analyzing an Investment

Let me suggest the following format for you to use in analyzing any investment.

We will examine the ten risk/return factors mentioned at the beginning of this chapter and consider the proposed investment with each of them. Let's take a careful and detailed look at each.

Loss of Principal

With any investment, there is a possibility that you'll lose part or all of your investment. Buy gold at the wrong time, and you could lose most of your investment overnight. For example, the price might drop from $700 an ounce down to $320. Does that sound impossible? It wouldn't be the first time for a swing like that. Look what happened to the stock market after September 11, 2001.

An insured savings account, on the other hand, does insure your investment against loss as long as the government is financially stable. And buying a piece of real estate blindly—without a lot of consideration as to its true market value, ability to be rented, or salability—is certainly highly risky. However, real estate bought prudently, after a careful market analysis, will be sheltered from this problem. We will explain market analysis in detail in Chapter 8.

Loss of Income

Many investments do offer some income. Most stocks generally pay some dividends, and savings accounts pay minimal interest. Precious metals, of course, offer no income whatsoever until they are sold. Of course, the risk of losing any income varies with each investment. The stock market is very risky in regard to projecting income. With the savings account, the risk is minimal. Real estate usually depends on rental income and tax benefits. But residential real estate is a constant. People will always need a place to live, even during the darkest days of a depression. The need for residential real estate is a constant as certain as the laws of gravity.

Inflation

How much is your investment affected by inflation? A single year with double-digit inflation will ravage a savings account that pays 5 percent on your money. Remember, any investment that doesn't increase in value by at least the same percentage as the inflation rate for any given year is a losing proposition. If you understand the fifth migration (explained in detail in Chapter 7) and apply the lessons of the Garrison cycle (described in Chapter 9), our experience since 1986 has shown that your real estate investments will always beat the national rate of inflation. Real estate outshines all other investments if you simply do your research.

Management

How difficult will your investment be to manage? What are the hidden costs? Real estate is one of the few investments that does require some management, and for many potential investors this single drawback is enough to keep them from getting involved. Later in this book we'll take a look at property management and discuss ways to control this aspect of real estate investing.

Timing Risk

When you buy is often as important as what to buy. This is especially true if you have your heart set on commodities, stocks, precious metals, and real estate. In regard to real estate, the days of "buy anything and hold on" are gone. Timing is crucial with real estate investing. The trusty savings account is nearly immune to timing risk. Just remember that no matter when you open up your account, you'll earn the same low interest rate.

Liquidity Risk

Liquidity is a measure of an investor's ability to easily sell or transfer title of an asset. Investing in cold hard cash might have no other obvious benefit, but it certainly passes this test! A certificate of deposit will offer you a higher interest rate, but it lacks liquidity in comparison to a regular savings account. Real estate can be illiquid, depending on which stage of the Garrison economic cycle your property exists in. If you are buying in an absorption market, you should plan on at least eighteen to thirty-six months as your maximum length of ownership. Gold is highly liquid, as are most stocks.

Cash Flow

Does the investment offer you steady income? This is another aspect of the income factor examined above. Gold, as was pointed out, has no risk of income loss—because it offers no income! The savings account is essentially risk-free, but the actual cash accumulation leaves a lot to be desired. Residential income property is the winner here again. It can be a source of rental income, which often is substantial above and beyond expenses, and it also offers a tremendous source of real income in the form of tax savings.

Tax Shelter

Continuing on the subject of tax savings, real estate is one of the greatest tax shelters available. As a real estate investor, you join the ranks of the self-employed. Later in this book we will talk about the latest strategies, tools, and techniques for legally lowering your tax burden because of your real estate investments.

Equity Buildup

Also called appreciation, this is the consideration that mirrors the risk of losing principal. While there is little chance of losing the principal invested in a savings account, there is also zero increase in its value other than the actual interest the account pays. Gold may double, triple, or even increase in value ten times over. The chance of a remarkable increase is there, but determining its likelihood probably will require a crystal ball. Real estate's track record is excellent in this regard even given the changes in our economy. An extremely sharp investor can find a good deal in which the sellers are willing to walk away from part or all of their equity.

That means instant equity buildup. I can think of quite a few properties that we purchased that instantly added anywhere from $15,000 to $75,000 immediately to our net worth statement. The ways of finding such diamonds in the rough will be fully covered in Chapter 12.

Control

How well can you control the risk and return of your investment? With most investments you literally have no control. You throw your money down on the table and watch it closely. Picking a winner is still a hopeful toss of a coin. Even with the traditional safe investments, such as a savings account, you do not have any control. You only play by the bank's rules and will receive the interest rate they're willing to pay.

Stocks, bonds, gold, futures, and so on are even more out of your control. Yes, you can control when you buy and sell them, but you can do nothing legally to improve their price. Any real control that you have is a gamble at best.

Real estate again stands out. You can control the risk and return by learning the fifth migration and the Garrison market cycle well enough to buy only good deals in the right market at the right price at the right time. We also will tell you exactly when it is time to sell. For instance, if you can buy a house worth $135,000 for $75,000 in a market with 127,000 new professional jobs, you are surely controlling both. Remember that the risk and return factors are not dictated by 10,000 other people buying the same house.

Balancing Risk and Return

As you can see, the idea of risk and return with most profitable investments is really a double-edged sword. In most investments you sacrifice safety and security for the possibility of a high return. Some people can't sleep nights worrying about the risks involved, so they sacrifice any return above the inflation rate. I challenge you to run through this type of analysis with every investment you can think of: precious metals, penny stocks, futures, growth stocks. Then relate the results to your present financial situation. Precious metals or stocks are popular vehicles and can be an easy way for some people, especially if they have money to invest. In fact, eventually, we suggest having your eggs in several baskets—once you have several dozen eggs to work with. But for most people, whose balance sheets list desire as their greatest asset, diversification is simply not the avenue to financial security now.

However, there is an investment available to all of us who currently have many nonmaterial assets. Real estate investing offers both a high return and control of risk. The only investment that can provide all of the things that we have talked about as fundamentally being necessary—instant cash income, low risk, incredible tax benefits, and growth—is real estate.

Success occurs when opportunity meets preparation.

—Unknown

Chapter 6

Take Control of Your Money and Your Life

IF THERE IS ONE THING THAT certainly separates real estate from all other investments, it is the amount of control that you have over your money. Once you are educated with the Garrison cycle of real estate investing (don't worry—it will all be explained in the next section of the book, in Chapter 9), you control the risk and the return like a pro. Almost every variable that will affect your investment is now foreseeable, with enough desire and homework on your part.

You will learn to form a definition of value for your target investing area and how to make structured offers that guarantee you instant equity and positive cash flow from day one. If you choose to work in domestic absorption markets in addition to working in your back yard, you will learn how to buy in the path of progress and how to fast-track the appreciation of your real estate and know exactly when it is time to sell.

Compare that with stock prices, which are determined solely by the aggregate opinion of a fickle public or the manipulation of some Wall Street imp.

Immediate and Long-Term Return

I have many times received large checks for second mortgage payments on a property that I sold a while back. My initial investment into those properties was usually less money than most people spend on Christmas presents for their children.

I am thinking about one property in particular. When I first saw that property, it was really a mess. Actually, the family was apparently so poor that they couldn't afford a litter box for the cat, and since they also couldn't afford toys, the kids had used windows for target practice. Instead of looking at it as a complete disaster, I instead thought of it in terms of a couple of nights of major elbow grease! After negotiating an extremely favorable purchase agreement, my children and I went over and dug in.

At this very same time, I was running an ad in the local paper to sell it. Several days before the actual closing on the house for us, we had signed a purchase agreement with another young family. As it turned out, with this home we actually discounted our sales price to allow them to finish some of the painting so they could personalize it.

The bottom line is that after we closed on the property, we walked away with an immediate net profit of over 300 percent on the money we put into it just weeks before. Also, if we add in the annual second mortgage payments that we received, our return on our money was in excess of 1,400 percent—all within five years of our investment! And if we figure that we received our down payment back, plus several thousand more just within days of our own purchase, our return really has to be counted as unlimited.

Let us put it simply. Would you put up $1,000 if you could get $4,500 cash back within two weeks and $3,000 a year for five years? Well, it certainly beats selling cosmetics door-to-door.

Low Risk and High Return

The key is that you have got to learn to understand the fifth migration (also coming up very soon, in Chapter 7) and to be able to identify the exact cycle stage your local market is in. Then you have to follow through and use the right tools that work in your unique target market.

This is a legal and honest way to help other families get into homes of their own, and it is of course a fantastic way to provide for your own income, security, and retirement. When you finish this book you will know how to do this—no kidding.

As we get into more specific situations and talk about how to shop for wholesale bargains in each type of economic market (expansion, equilibrium, decline, and absorption), you will see the incredible returns that you can get while maintaining complete control of your assets.

Why is real estate such an incredible combination of low risk and high return? Because it is a basic commodity. (That means its price is not subject to the daily whims of a few powerful men or thousands of scared investors.) An old, battered house has more intrinsic value than a stack of gold. It has value, in and of itself, like a can of peaches in Grandma's pantry. For sure, a house's value is determined partly by how it sparkles when it is polished, but the bottom line is still measured mostly by its value in use and in the right type of market (absorption moving into expansion) and by its scarcity (a.k.a., supply and demand). And scarcity is assured; they just aren't making any more land.

Why Doesn't Everyone Do It?

Because of its unique place in the economy, real estate has rules all its own in today's market. You just don't play the real estate game the same way you play the stock market.

For a comparison, try this: Call a stockbroker and tell him you would like to invest. Be sure to insist that you must be allowed to buy your stock with little or no money down, and tell him you need to have your investment generating income every month. Also tell him that you want enough income from your stock to make the payments on your investments, with enough left over so that you can pocket $10,000 every month. And then, before you buy, tell him that you don't want to pay the market price. You will buy only stock at a price that is far below market value. Oh, yes, and tell him you want to be able to double your initial investment within the first month or two.

Immediately call 911. Have them send a couple of paramedics over to the stockbroker's office right away. Tell them there is a possible heart attack victim.

If we're making real estate sound like the ultimate investment for everyone, then you are getting the picture.

But you probably think, "If buying and selling a little dirt is so great, why isn't everyone investing in real estate?" We have often wondered about that, and we have come up with three universal reasons:

1. **Laziness.** Real estate investing takes more than a phone call to a banker or stockbroker—it does take work. It takes time to read and learn our techniques. It takes time to learn how to use the Internet, and possibly it takes several dozen phone calls to set up your real estate investing team and to form a definition of value in your target area. It can require Saturday and Sunday drives, and it may include countless disappointments, delays, and dead ends. Successful real estate investing will certainly cut into your leisure time—that is, if you do this part-time while you continue your full-time job. As with anything worthwhile, there is a price to pay.

2. **Ignorance.** Most people are totally unaware that they can buy a piece of real estate at a wholesale price and sell it at retail. They don't realize that enormous profits can be and

are enjoyed with a little judicious buying and selling—of course, when coupled with your educated persistence.

3. **Fear.** Nothing is more lethal to a promising career as a real estate investor than fear. Fear is the ultimate negative mindset. We've seen seminar junkies who attend all of the conventions, seminars, and workshops that are available for real estate investors. They actually know as much about buying and selling residential income properties and houses as most of the experienced speakers, and yet they hesitate and hold off that initial purchase. They are so paralyzed by the fear of failure that they never get to the point of making a single offer. They just can't take that first step.

If we can convince you to overcome your initial fears, to properly educate yourself, and to commit yourself to the work that real success requires, you will not fail.

The Fun of a Good Deal

Now that you've heard the boring details of investing and reasons why you should invest, let us tell you some personal real estate investing experiences that we had with our children in our own back yard in a full-blown equilibrium market—don't worry, we'll explain what that means in Chapter 9, too. Remember, this is by shopping in the wholesale housing market (which we will teach you how to do).

We recently purchased a home, putting only $1,400 down, and assumed an 11.5-percent FHA loan. We sold that home one week before we actually closed, for $14,500 more than our own purchase price. When we sold the home, we received a $5,000 down payment from the new buyer. Then, when we closed the deal, we put $3,000 in our pocket after paying the $1,400 to our seller and our share of the closing costs. And to top it off, for the next five years we will get payments of almost $2,000 per year on the second mortgage we hold. This one is fun—in fact, they all are! You just need to determine what cycle stage your back yard area is in and to use the right investing strategies, tools, and techniques for that unique type of market.

As president of the National Association of Real Estate Investors, I hear stories every day that put our best deals to shame. You'll read about a few of them as we go along, but what we would really love is to get an e-mail from you someday telling us a story like the one we just related. What we don't want to read is a letter from you saying that you're retired and living as more than 80 percent of our retired citizens do, dependent on their families and the government to support them and hopefully rescue them from poverty. No company, and certainly no government bureaucracy, can offer the retirement income that real estate can.

Find Your Courage

Before we leave this chapter, let's talk a little more about courage. If you never develop the risk-taking courage that is required, you'll never ever even make an offer on a property.

When do we lose that courage? You know we had it as babies, when we took those first shaky steps. Each of us slowly got up on our wobbly legs . . . and down we went. We think the difference then—why most of us didn't give up—was that our feeble efforts, and the initial failed attempts, were all met with enthusiastic praise from our loving parents. They knew what we were really capable of.

I know what you can do with investing in real estate.

You need to develop some risk-taking courage. Let us share four secrets we have discovered for overcoming those fears that are holding you back:

1. **Reward yourself for taking risks.** For example, you can make a written offer for a house (after we teach how if

you don't already know). Then make sure to treat yourself to something. Whether or not your offer is accepted. We all need the occasional pat on the back just for trying, even if it is our own hand that does the patting.

2. **List all the rewards that you might receive if you take the risk and succeed.** When you consider making that offer, think about the money you can make fixing the property up and reselling it. Listing the rewards will instill the confidence you will need when doubt creeps in.

3. **Realize that failure is only the first step to eventual success.** Thomas Edison burned up yards of filament, spending countless hours without sleep—until failure paid off. Every worthwhile success was preceded by many, many failures.

4. **Prepare for the worst and plan for the best.** List every problem that might possibly crop up if you take the risk, and prepare yourself accordingly. If the worst thing that could happen is a fire, then have a fire extinguisher handy. But at the same time, plan for the best. Preparing for failure is not the same as planning for failure. Plan for success.

With this newfound courage, you are now ready to be shown the road map for reaching financial freedom through real estate investment—the fifth migration and the Garrison cycle. These keys and tools have been discovered through a lot of trial and error, thousands of hours of study, a lot of investing, and many mistakes. This book has been written to help you get to your goal fast in today's market without having to suffer through the mistakes we have made.

A Tale of Two Investors

Several years ago, I spoke at two member workshops for the National Association of Real Estate Investors in the Pacific Northwest.

Before coming to speak, I had done a number of live radio shows in both the Portland and Seattle markets to publicize these two events. Out of the hundreds of people I met, I will never forget two of them.

I met Howard in Portland. He had heard me on the radio and came to the workshop. Howard was very cautious. He had tons of questions. I referred him to several of our past BuyingTour students, and I guess he decided to check us out. In Seattle I met Jeff. Jeff also had heard me on the radio and came to our workshop.

Both Howard and Jeff were new investors. It's funny how you meet some people and instantly connect with them. I liked both of these guys. Both were interested in the BuyingTour, but Jeff decided that he would rather invest strictly in his back yard.

That was in 1998. Howard used the techniques that we taught him on the BuyingTour and bought a great apartment building in one of our regions of opportunity. Jeff used his talents and bought a fixer-upper apartment building at a bargain price near Tacoma, Washington.

During the past three years, Howard's property has gone up 280 percent in price. His rents have more than doubled. Howard liked the absorption market so much that he decided to move his entire family there. Howard's positive cash flow from just that one purchase is earning him more money than he made from his job as a computer programmer. So Howard quit and is now doing real estate investing full-time. Howard recently called me to tell me that he had just bought a brand new custom home for his family. He told me that the positive cash flow from his rental is totally paying the bill. Congratulations, Howard!

Jeff still owns his property in Tacoma. That area has continued in the past three years to lose more and more professional jobs. Vacancy has increased, and he found out after buying it that there was a crack house next door. His property today will only sell for a fraction of what he paid for it.

Would you rather be Howard or Jeff?

Would you like to be the one who made $360,000 in equity

appreciation and an extra $6,000 per month in rental rate increases on a building that is now fully occupied?

Jeff could have successfully invested in the Seattle, Washington, area despite the fact that it is in the decline stage right now.

In Chapter 11, we will talk about building a definition of value for any and all areas that you invest in. We will share with you the way to find the highest growth areas to invest in in any given market (even in a decline) through a short series of phone calls. We will also teach you in Chapter 12 the tools that Jeff should have been using to find properties for pennies on the dollar.

Howard is now getting ready to move his investment capital into another absorption market.

Pray for Jeff.

Celebrate for Howard.

Real estate investing is not brain surgery, but it has to be done right today.

It is a pleasure for us to share the new paradigms and tools of real estate investing in the twenty-first century and beyond with you.

PART III

New Paradigms for Today's Real Estate Investment

Live where you want to live, but invest only where it makes sense.

—*Marc Stephan Garrison*

Chapter 7

The Fifth Migration

FROM MY INITIAL START AS AN INVESTOR in the 1970s through the early 1980s, it seemed like I could do nothing wrong. Every single property that we purchased was incredibly easy to rent out. When we would decide to sell, it was a cakewalk. Even our worst deals were like getting a bad haircut. Just give it a few weeks, and it will look just fine. In fact, we always had a stable of eager buyers for the homes and small rental properties that we bought and cleaned up. The properties that we held onto appreciated like clockwork. Life was truly good.

Little did we know that we were practicing what the big boys advocated in their bestselling real estate guides. They told all real estate investors that the key to their profits in any and all markets was to buy real estate and just wait. However, Jeff from Seattle is still waiting. So are hundreds of thousands of other real estate investors in North America. We were guaranteed that our properties would always appreciate, and we were surely on the yellow brick road.

Unfortunately for us—and for the hundreds of thousands of

"real estate guru" students—that "just-buy-and-wait" rule became obsolete in the early 1980s in a lot of real estate markets. You still could buy real estate quite easily in most areas. In fact, it became extremely easy to buy most real estate. There were tons of don't-wanters (people who wanted to dump their property). The fact of the matter was that income properties in most markets just about across the board had quit appreciating. All of a sudden, getting and maintaining positive cash flow and being able to do a quick flip (buy and resell) had become a nightmare. I was unwilling to give up on my real estate investments like thousands of other investors had done. I went back to school to academically seek the answers to the real estate puzzle.

While I was in graduate school, the value of our income properties was attacked even further. The 1986 tax reform act destroyed many of the tax benefits for owning investment real estate. In addition, the savings-and-loan disaster dried up most conventional sources of financing.

I felt lost.

Was I stupid?

What was I doing wrong?

Why didn't the buy-and-fly program work anymore?

A New Economic Model

During graduate school in my masters program and on into my Ph.D., I discovered not only a new trend in real estate but also an economic model that would literally rescue our real estate profits. Little did I know that this new way of investing in real estate would affect the lives of so many others.

This all started with my discovery of what I have come to call the "fifth migration." To be able to understand and forecast the future, I knew that I had to research the past history of all real estate investments literally from the beginning.

What I discovered has become the most radical revolution in

real estate investing since "nothing down." It all started with an understanding of what a migration is. A migration in real estate economics is a major shift or move of the population in any given area.

History documents America's first major migration as the initial colonization of the United States. Thousands of people relocated from Europe to America seeking economic opportunities and other freedoms that were not available to them in the old country. America was a land of seemingly unbridled opportunity. This original colonization and subsequent increase in population gave value to both the land in America's new cities and even to the seemingly endless tracts of land outside the cities that could be improved and farmed.

As in every economic model, change is inevitable. Over the years, as demand on the eastern seaboard increased, so did the value of its land and properties. As the price of the land and its improvements increased, the newly arriving immigrants were denied the opportunity of ownership because of the increased cost of real estate.

This increased demand led eventually to westward expansion. Westward expansion became the second major migration in America. Pioneers hungry for opportunity left the eastern coast and headed west with their dreams of land ownership still intact. Westward expansion continued through the end of the nineteenth century. By this time, the majority of the land in the continental United States that was arable had been homesteaded, granted, gifted, or purchased. A population that had always had opportunity just a little further down the road now found its new generation denied.

The invention of the steam engine and America's industrial revolution, which started in the 1870s, signaled the third major migration in the United States. Young Americans and farmers unable to adequately support their families flocked into cities where the new factories offered steady and stable employment. This migration continued to build through World War I. During the third migration, our inner cities were developed to house America's new workforce. Towns that had access to transportation by rail or water grew and blossomed.

The fourth major migration in America didn't start until after World War II was won. Prior to World War II, there was essentially no long-term financing available for home purchases in the United States. If an individual or family wanted to buy a home in America, they had to do so with all cash.

As a reward to World War II's returning veterans and to the nation that had supported the war effort, the federal government established the first long-term federally insured home loans. For the first time in American history, an individual or a family could obtain long-term financing and actually buy a home of their own with payments spread out as long as thirty years. These new loan vehicles gave rise to the invention of the single-family home subdivision. The very first single-family home subdivision was built in Levittown, New York, just outside of New York City on Long Island.

America's fourth major migration can be called "suburbia." This major migration was the movement of America's working class from the inner cities of the United States to the single-family subdivisions located within an easy short driving commute from the cities. This flight from America's inner cities created America's ghettos, as working families left the cities for the freedom and opportunities of home ownership.

If you think about it, each of these migrations makes sense. And each migration was caused by individuals seeking new opportunities and personal freedom.

The Latest Major Migration

America's fifth major migration started in the early 1980s. I call it "survival." When I first discovered it I was blown away. Understanding it told me exactly why not only I but also most of North America's estimated 10 million real estate investors now felt like we were spinning our wheels in our attempts to invest in real estate. I often use the analogy that today's real estate investors often feel like they are trying to fit a square peg into a round hole in terms of their real estate investment success. And back in the 1980s we truly were. Many of us were trying to invest in real estate markets that had enormous job cuts.

Think about it today. There is hardly a single day when you don't hear of massive job cuts from some company on the news. Later we'll teach you how to find out where those lost jobs are actually moving to and being re-created.

Underneath the economic surface—unbeknownst to the hundreds of thousands of real estate investors—corporate America had started to relocate. As I researched further, I was shocked to note that right in my back yard investing area, the net professional job numbers had started to drop exactly at the same time that my real estate investing program had begun to languish.

I also noticed that for each of the years that I did incredibly well in real estate, the net professional job base in my investing areas had been growing.

It doesn't take a rocket scientist to understand that supply and demand drives not only the price of rents but also the sale price of a piece of real estate. It made instant sense to me. As long as the job market was healthy and growing, I had done well because there was an optimistic group of potential tenants and buyers who were standing in line for my properties. Remove 50,000 jobs from my back yard and relocate them to another part of the country or the world, and you have a formula for disaster in real estate investing in that local market. I couldn't believe my eyes.

I then took a major step. I did a detailed investigation of cities in the United States with a population base of over 250,000. For every single one of those cities, I researched the net professional jobs created or lost from the end of World War II through the present.

It was wild. It all started to make sense.

I find that the harder I work, the more luck I seem to have.

—Thomas Jefferson

Chapter 8

Real Estate Market Analysis

ONCE I BEGAN TO ESTABLISH in which cities the "fifth migration" was taking place (see Chapter 7), I then went one step further.

I obtained the rental vacancy factors for each of those cities during those years.

It was really wild.

I then obtained the average real estate sales price for a basic three-bedroom single-family home for each city during every one of those years.

It got even better.

All three of those factors were linear. Each one of them almost identically followed the other when graphed out. As net professional jobs grew in a city, vacancy rates shrank, and real estate prices rose. As net professional jobs were lost, vacancy rose and real estate prices went stagnant or dropped.

I then contacted the economic development council of the mayor's office in each city that was currently experiencing job losses. I simply asked for an explanation of the job losses. One hundred percent of those cities named major industries that had closed up shop in that neck of the woods and relocated to another place in the country or in the world. I dug a bit deeper and asked them where these companies were moving.

I made a simple list of all of these cities where these companies were relocating.

I was shocked even more.

Every single one of those cities that I was given was registering strong job gains, decreased vacancy rates, and stable if not improving property values.

I couldn't believe what I was starting to understand.

Analyzing the Markets

I saw clearly that a fifth migration had begun. This migration, however, was not being fed by the choices of individuals, as those in the past had been. It was being fueled by the flight of corporate America from high-priced anti-business regions of obsolescence to inexpensive pro-business regions of opportunity. It doesn't take a brain surgeon to figure out that the restriction that I had placed on all of my real estate investing back when I started—that all my investing had to be done within thirty minutes of my home—was real estate investing suicide in today's market. And if it wasn't that, it severely limited my ability to continue to invest and receive the profits that I had become accustomed to.

As I talked with my local economic development council, I was told about the economic missionaries that other parts of the country were sending out to high-priced, anti-business regions of obsolescence like I used to live in. I was informed about the free building sites, tax abatements, low-interest bond financing, relocation assistance packages, free utilities, and more that other cities were offering companies in America's high-priced areas (regions of obsolescence) if they would relocate to their economically desirable city (region of opportunity).

I then contacted each of the top ten cities of job growth in

North America. I talked with their economic development councils. I told them that I was a real estate investor who was interested in investing in their city. I then asked if they could help me with getting answers to some very detailed questions about their city. I told them that I had a market survey form that I had prepared. I asked them if I could fax them my survey and have them answer my questions. They told me absolutely yes. They told me that it was their job to do this, as mandated by their mayor's office.

I got the fax numbers and sent off ten of the extensive market survey questionnaires that I had prepared. Within the week, I got all ten detailed packages back. Seven of them were sent back to me by overnight courier and contained not only answers to every one of my questions but also more detailed information, color brochures on the city, and even a video or two highlighting the advantages and best parts of having a business relocate there. I was blown away.

Here is the list of the questions that we have learned to ask the economic development council in each city that we are interested in investing in. Please note that these questions are worded in such a way as to help the economic development council take you as a serious real estate investor. Don't worry about the "big" words. The people that you send these surveys to will understand each and every one.

Marc Stephan Garrison
Real Estate Market Analysis Survey

1. **Description of the market area**
    a. Metropolitan area
       - Identification of entire area
       - Geography
       - Climate
       - General urban structure; location of facilities
       - Direction of city growth

- Commuting patterns (journey to work)
- Any major community developments and/or special features or characteristics germane to the market analysis

2. Demographic analysis

a. Population
  - Most recent estimate for total population
  - Past trends in population growth
  - Estimated future population
  - Distribution by age groups

b. Households
  - Most recent estimates for household formations
  - Past trends in household formations
  - Estimated future total households and average annual rate of growth
  - Current trends in household size (increasing, decreasing)

c. Schools
  - School districts in market area
  - District boundaries
  - Total annual K–6 enrollment for past ten years by district

3. Economy of the market area (demand-side analysis)

a. Economic history and characteristics
  - General description
  - Major economic activities and developments

b. Employment, total and nonagricultural
  - Current estimates
  - Past trends
  - Distribution by industry groups
  - Estimated future employment
  - Trends in labor participation rate
  - Trends in female employment

    c. Unemployment
- Current level
- Past trends

    d. Economic-base analysis
- Metropolitan area compared with national and state employment data
- Discussion of principal employers
- Payroll data (census of manufacturers, trade, services, governments)

    e. Income data
- Personal income by major sources
- Per capita personal income
- Family-income distribution
- Projections for growth in personal income

4. Construction and real estate activity (supply-side analysis)

    a. Building and construction industry
- Residential buildings by type (single-family, multifamily, rental, or sales)
- Nonresidential construction
- High-rise building activity (minimum height of five stories above ground)
- Heavy engineering construction

    b. Demand-and-supply analysis for properties other than residential
- General demand factors in metropolitan area
- Existing inventory, by property type
- Projected production, by property type

    c. Housing inventory, by type (single-family, multifamily)
- Most recent estimates
- Past trends including most recent census
- Principal characteristics

    d. Residential sales
- General market conditions
- Major subdivision activity

- Trends in sales prices (past ten years)
- Unsold inventory of new sales housing

e. Rental markets
- General market conditions
- Major activity
- Trends in rental prices (studio, one-bedroom, two-bedroom, and three-bedroom apartments)
- Trends in rental prices (single-family homes)
- Trends in rental vacancies overall (past ten years)
- Gross amount of available rental units
- New rental housing trends
- Residential units under construction
- Available government rental assistance programs
- Available government assistance rehab programs

f. Other housing markets
- Public and governmental subsidized housing
- Specialized submarkets for housing demand and supply

g. Real estate loans and mortgage markets
- Sources and availability of funds
- FHA, VA, FNMA, GNMA
- Interest rates and terms of mortgages
- Recordings of mortgages and/or deeds of trusts
- Foreclosures

5. Political and legal aspects (legal environment analysis)

a. Land-use planning
- Regional
- County (counties)
- Incorporated cities in market area

b. Zoning
- Review of present zoning ordinances for county (counties) and cities
- Zoning history and present attitudes of zoning authority
- Identify raw land presently zoned for residential income properties

c. Ordinances, codes, regulations
   - Special building codes for residential income properties
   - Special health and public safety concerns for residential income properties
   - Allocation of land for schools, recreational areas, open space
d. Municipal services
   - Public safety
   - Hospitals and health care
   - Utilities
e. Ecological
   - Environmental impact studies
   - Limited growth policies
   - Floodplains and flood control
   - Solid-waste disposal
   - Special lead paint laws
f. Property taxation
   - Tax rate per $1,000 valuation
   - Assessment ration as percent of market value

6. Sources of information
   a. Types of data
      - Population
      - Employment
      - Personal income
      - Planning
      - Building
      - Zoning
      - Other pertinent
   b. Sources of data
      - Secondary data sources
      - Primary data sources

The key purpose of my market analysis was to determine the expected demand for the market under consideration. Some of you might be thinking "Who would answer all of those questions for you for free?" The answer is simple: Each and every one of those original ten cities that I targeted was a possible area to invest in. Each of those cities was experiencing incredible job growth. They were hungry for the stability, population growth, and increased tax base that the new professional jobs would bring to the area. Their job is to help people like you and me, who are interested in doing business in their city.

I approached each of these economic development councils as a professional. I asked to speak to each of their directors. I directed my fax to that director. I asked them professional questions that they already had the answers to. Each and every one of them answered not only every single question, but most of them offered to meet me in that city so that they could show me around and introduce me to their contacts in the real estate investment community there.

Since our initial start in 1986, I have sent this survey to hundreds of cities to determine the economic health of major real estate markets in the United States and Canada. Real estate investing is defined as the sacrifice of certain outflows for uncertain inflows. Forecasting future income from an investment is risky. You, as an investor, must examine the factors influencing the possible income and formulate expectations from that analysis. To start, the investor must carefully analyze the market forces influencing any potential investment. This type of analysis is critical. Failing to identify the direction of market forces in your target investment area can be extremely costly and can result in huge losses today. Remember Howard from Portland and Jeff from Seattle? Howard did his homework; Jeff didn't. Howard was open to new ideas; Jeff wasn't. Which one would you rather be?

What You Need to Know

In "old-fashioned" real estate, the critical elements of an investment include the quantity and certainty of gross income, operating expenses, and net income over some future period of time. If you use the old tools, today's property value is a reflection of future income expectations. Hogwash! Such guesswork is risky. I believe that the only good insurance against risk is to do the following:

1. Determine the direction that your market is moving based on job growth, residential income property vacancy trends, and average property prices.
2. Identify the stage of the Garrison cycle that a market is in, and develop a game plan that "fits" that market. (We'll teach you that in Chapter 9.)
3. Form a firm definition of value in a market based on actual recent sales.
4. Identify the forces driving your target real estate market, and then choose the very best parts of that particular area to invest in. Identify any and all areas of growth. The very best indicator for what are the best neighborhoods to invest in is to study the kindergarten-through-sixth-grade enrollment statistics available through the local public school districts. Just call the local school district. It's free. You should try to go back at least ten years. You should focus your investing only in the areas of your market that have the highest elementary school growth.
5. Never buy a property based on any future appreciation or increase in rents. Buy only properties that give you instant equity and positive cash flow from day one. And always have a parachute in case your investing program develops engine problems.

If you diligently do these things, your risk will be greatly reduced, and you will gain faith in your ability to invest.

The Neglected Market Survey

Face the facts. Maybe you are from southern California, like I was. Net professional jobs where you live may be going down the tubes. You need to face that fact, and then limit your investing only to the very best areas of K–6 elementary growth in southern California if you want to maximize your profit in a region of obsolescence. You need to define value by getting information on all recent local sales of properties, and you need to know the rents. You need to know the vacancy factors. You need to know the trends. You need to know the local laws (like, is there rent control?). And you need to know the local crime problems. Is this a drug neighborhood? Does it have a bad reputation? I remember in Phoenix I was interested in buying a large residential income property. As part of my property purchase checklist, I always talk to the local police to learn about the crime in the neighborhood. While I was outside the property, a police officer drove by. I flagged him down and introduced myself. I told him that I was thinking about buying this property. I remember the police officer's telling me that I was crazy. He told me that this was a drug street that was controlled at night by gangs. I thanked him for his time and packed my stuff up and headed out to another property in a better neighborhood.

The bottom line here is that before you do any investing in real estate, you need to do a market survey on all potential real estate markets, with your principal thrust concerning supply and demand. Ironically, this market survey is the most neglected aspect of real estate investment today. I have read all the popular real estate investment books that are available. Never once has anybody even mentioned doing a market survey and/or forming a definition of value before taking the plunge into real estate investing. The focus instead is on the mechanics of investing. They all seem to ignore the underlying foundation of the economy where they invest. The purpose again of the market survey is simply to reduce the risk associated with real estate investing. Remember, a real estate investor today needs to consider factors such as these:

- National and local economic trends, such as unemployment or recession
- A deteriorating economic base
- Economic obsolescence, perhaps due to a changing neighborhood
- Functional obsolescence, lack of quality construction, or age
- Legal restrictions, such as rent control and zoning laws
- Population and demographic trends
- Changes in income levels, tastes, and preferences of tenants

Finally, remember that I have never once been turned down for this essential informational help from a city that is benefiting from the fifth migration.

The Greatest Opportunity

Each year now, we survey the top 300-plus real estate markets in the United States. We now contract out with a professional research company to do this work for us. The results of this analysis direct us into future regions of opportunity for that particular year. Up until now, I have only shared this research data with our BuyingTour students. These demographic studies give you confidence in your real estate investing. The results from our data have led thousands of our students into the most profitable real estate investing areas that they ever could imagine. Our students have done incredibly well.

Since 1986, we have quietly worked real estate investing almost exclusively in these regions of opportunity. Since 1986, I have also taught these principles to an exclusive group of serious students. My wife and I have created hundreds of self-made real estate millionaires since 1986. We have been content to teach this program to a limited group of individuals. But the events of September 11, 2001, changed all of that. Since that date we have seen a major reversal. Economic development agencies all over the United States are being inundated by American corporations who have manufacturing facilities around the world. Because of the sheer instability and insanity of today's world, the leaders of corporate America are scared. They are afraid of being subject to acts of terrorism taking place outside of the United States of America. Companies are scrambling. Corporate America wants to come back home. They want the safety and security in their manufacturing that the federal government of the United States of America has taken a stance to provide, no matter what the cost.

You are sitting on the greatest investment opportunity of your lifetime. That opportunity is buying real estate in the path of progress. This opportunity cannot be based on gambling or blind speculation. You invest in real estate only based on demonstrable facts.

It really is legal insider trading through real estate investing.

This opportunity will take some work on your part. You just need to ask the right questions, which we are providing you. The market survey questions that we shared with you not only show you where to invest, but can help you open up sources of capital from outside investors and lending sources to fund all of your real estate investments. The results from these surveys also help us to resell our properties at incredible profits as we share copies of this information with our potential buyers.

A Typical Market Survey

Let's take a closer look at the market survey form and share with you the answers that you would typically get from a region of opportunity (absorption market) and a region of obsolescence (decline market). There are six basic sections. Let's look at each one individually.

Marc Stephan Garrison
Real Estate Market Survey

1. Description of the market area

The answers to these questions will give you a quick picture of the basics of any given city. For example, when we chose to move into Oklahoma City, the answers to this section told us about the new River Walk section of town, the new baseball stadium, and the focus on urban renewal. In decline markets, there typically are no major community developments.

2. Demographic analysis

This helps you to understand the vitality and overall health of a given real estate market. In regions of opportunity, you will see a strong steady growth pattern in not only population but also a vibrant K–6 rate increase in student enrollment. These answers cannot be viewed in isolation, however. For example, Los Angeles, California, recently registered some of the highest population gains while at the same time showing some of the highest job losses. An in-depth analysis through their economic development office showed that their population growth was due nearly solely to an increase in welfare and other public assistance programs. In recent years, California has become the welfare capital of America.

3. Economy of the market area (demand-side analysis)

The real estate market can be defined as a mechanism by which real estate goods and services are exchanged. This is a mechanism that is influenced by the demands of the participants in a market. Demand on residential income property is a function of the stability and growth in any given market. It just makes sense. In a region of opportunity, you are going to see new job growth. You are going to see new companies moving in. You are going to see local companies expanding. In regions of obsolescence, you are going to see a flat if not negative job market. You are going to also see rising unemployment rates compared with national averages.

And you thought that economics was hard! It really is just plain common sense.

4. Construction and real estate activity (supply-side analysis)

In regions of opportunity that are at the beginning of the absorption stage (defined in the next chapter), there basically is no new construction at all. In many cases, when that market was in expansion years earlier, the area was overbuilt. Typical absorption markets have a high inventory of unsold new housing. Typical regions of obsolescence have some new construction activity, but the trend in sales prices has dropped and there is an increasing amount of unsold inventory.

In rental markets in regions of opportunity, vacancy rates are shrinking, while in regions of obsolescence vacancy rates are growing or staying flat. In regions of opportunity, rents are typically lower than national averages and have been flat for the previous years. In regions of obsolescence, gross monthly rents are falling and foreclosures are typically increasing.

5. Political and legal aspects (legal environment analysis)

In regions of opportunity, there is an increasingly pro-business climate. Allowances are being made, and variances are being given to builders and developers. Typically, building codes are lax in regions of opportunity, and there exists a partially unused infrastructure of available public services such as roads, utility distribution lines, schools, and parks. A good example would be Gilbert, Arizona, where we now live.

During Arizona's boom of the late 1970s and early 1980s, local cities thought that their growth would never end. Hundreds and thousands of new roads, schools, and utility distribution lines were built for the seemingly unending demand.

When the market quickly cycled through equilibrium and into decline, these improvements were left for the most part unused. Typical regions of obsolescence will have vacant land with developments waiting to be completed.

Markets typically absorb in regions of opportunity until the available supply of existing services is fully utilized. By that time rents rise high enough to justify new construction, which leads to higher values and, once again, almost inevitable overbuilding.

6. Sources of information

This is just for your information. It's important to always be able to double-check all of the facts you are given. Be an intelligent consumer.

A Reality Check

I think it's time for a real estate reality check. Before we move on to the moneymaking possibilities, let's see if you fully understand the fifth migration.

Think about this. Would you rather buy a fifty-unit apartment building at 16 percent under market value in a region of obsolescence that is losing 147,000 professional jobs in the coming thirty-six months, or would you rather buy a fifty-unit apartment building at 10 percent below market value in a region of opportunity that is gaining 87,000 new jobs in the next eighteen months?

Next question. Would you rather open up a McDonald's franchise in a market area that is losing 87,000 professional jobs in the next year, or would you rather open up a McDonald's franchise in a market area that is gaining 93,000 new jobs in the next year?

Last question. If you were currently unemployed, would you rather try to find a job in a market area that is losing 93,500 professional jobs in the next year, or would you rather look in a market area that is gaining 57,349 new jobs in the next year?

It's obvious, isn't it? You'd have to be dumber than a box of rocks to choose the market that is losing jobs. We'll talk about the specifics of creating a complete market analysis and turning it into a full-blown demographic research project farm report later. Right now, though, we want you to think about the implications. We want you to think about the regions of opportunity that are begging companies from around the world to relocate there. Think about being a CEO and being able to move your facility from New York City, or San Francisco, or Los Angeles, or Chicago, and move into a Memphis, a Syracuse, a Kansas City, an Oklahoma City, or a Tulsa.

There are dozens and dozens of hot growth markets today. I would list them all in this book, but they are constantly changing as new markets rise out of the ashes of the decline stage and rebound into an absorption market. If you are interested in finding out how you can obtain our current list of the very best regions of opportunity, e-mail me directly at marcstephangarrison@narei.com.

The Ripple Effect

Why would Hewlett-Packard have moved their corporate headquarters from the San Francisco Bay area to Idaho? Why would American Express leave the Big Apple and relocate to Salt Lake City?

The answer really is just good business management. You can cut probably as much as 70 percent off the cost of your facilities and as much as 50 percent off your labor costs. Here's the really wonderful thing: Even though you are paying your employees less, they will have a better lifestyle. An identical brand-new average home in Orange County, California, that costs in excess of $250,000 can be purchased today in Memphis for just over $90,000. The overall cost of utilities is less. The commute is a fraction of the time. The pollution and crime are almost nonexistent.

Understand?

I think that you do. Now for the cherry on top of the cake. It is a little-known fact that I found out through my research. An area doesn't lose just one professional job. An area loses that job plus an additional 4.2 jobs in the service sector that once supported that professional job. Those are people like butchers, bakers, candlestick makers, teachers, gas station attendants, UPS drivers, policemen, government workers, car washers, and on and on.

This ripple, or ancillary, effect takes about three years to fully play itself out in the marketplace. And this effect works both ways. A market that is gaining 50,000 new professional jobs will realize an additional 210,000 service sector jobs for a total of over 250,000 new jobs. In the same way, a market that is losing 100,000 professional jobs will lose an additional 420,000 service sector jobs for a total of over 500,000 lost jobs. I like to call each of these new service sector jobs a new tenant. Do you want your real estate investment areas to be losing or gaining new tenants?

Another Moneymaking Example

Understanding the fifth migration can make you money. Let's give you another example. Let us share with you the story of two of our students, Steve and Eric, from southern California.

"We made $170,000 within thirteen months of getting started with Marc and Paula Garrison. As Marc says, 'You can make money or you can make excuses, but you can't make both.' Go for it. If you ever need help, feel free to get our e-mail address from the Garrisons. We would love to assist you on your road to financial freedom the same way that they helped mentor us."

Discovering the fifth migration led to my personal development of a radical new approach to profit in real estate investing. It is an entirely new paradigm or set of assumptions and beliefs based on cold, hard facts. In terms of real estate economics, I call it the Garrison cycle. We will teach you this in Chapter 9.

By understanding this program, you will be able to turbocharge your investments in real estate today and protect yourself from the typical economic risks.

Welcome to success.

The ancestor of every action is thought.

—*Ralph Waldo Emerson*

Chapter 9

The Garrison Cycle of Real Estate Economics

ARE THERE ANY GOOD DEALS left anymore?

What would you give to buy properties right now between $10,000 and $15,000 per unit that have a stronger positive cash flow than if you paid between $50,000 and $80,000 per unit? The traditional dilemma in residential investment-grade real estate has always been, "Should I buy for appreciation or cash flow?" My wife and I refuse to buy any property unless it has both. And you should do the very same.

A New Way of Looking at Market Cycles

During graduate school, my discovery of the fifth migration led me to a new way of looking at all real estate markets from the beginning of time. After developing my theory of the fifth migration, I chose ten real estate markets that represented everything in the spectrum, from the markets with the highest job growth to the markets with the highest job losses. I was looking for an economic model that I could use to identify the economic health of each unique market. I was not only looking for a definition and an explanation of how I could make money in any market, but also a way to identify the most profitable time to buy in a region of opportunity and when to sell before that market became a region of obsolescence.

Over a period of almost a year of hands-on study, I found that all real estate markets are always—without exception—in one of four market cycle stages. I defined those stages as:

- Expansion
- Equilibrium
- Decline
- Absorption

I saw this circular economic cycle as the explanation of why my real estate investing profits had hit a brick wall in the mid-1980s. I had been investing successfully in an appreciation expansion market that had quickly transitioned straight through equilibrium and was now in a free-fall decline due to job cuts and local government anti-business policies and practices.

It made more than sense. But did it work in hands-on practice?

To solve that puzzle, I defined each of the four economic stages as follows—and then I made a plan. During the next year, I would leave the world of education and focus on perfecting the analysis of an investment area and timing signals to maximize real estate investing profits. To do this I chose one expansion market, one equilibrium market, one decline market, and one absorption market to work in.

Little did I know then that the understanding of this circular cycle of real estate economics would essentially and practically eliminate all my future risk in real estate investing and guarantee me profits on every transaction.

No longer would I be subject to the whims of my local real estate investment market, job cuts, rent control, or government policies and practices. Acts of God and national tragedies such as September 11 would be my only risk. But I would protect myself with proper property insurance and the assurance that my investments were placed in a needed asset that wasn't merely paper as the stock market is. The bottom line is that I knew that people would always need a place to live. I set out with confidence. If you can master these economic realities, you can have that same confidence to proceed in your real estate investments. Your profits can be predictable again. You can be in control.

As I began my experiment, some areas of the country were booming; armed with an understanding of the fifth migration and the Garrison cycle, I felt confident that I would continue to be able to make real estate investing financially profitable.

One point is important to remember at the start: All markets begin in expansion.

Expansion

As I went into the market, I noticed that demand structures due to new job growth forced the absorption of all available housing. A market at the beginning of absorption could have as much as a 26 percent vacancy rate. New professional job growth and the ripple effect in the service sector would quickly absorb all vacant rentals.

It made sense. If you put 129,000 new professional jobs into Dallas, Texas, there would instantly be an incredible demand in the service sector. More butchers, bakers, teachers, gas station employees, UPS drivers, and candlestick makers would be needed. In economic terms, that ripple effect is 4.2 new service sector jobs for every new professional job. So, in essence, you were not just looking at 129,000 new jobs, you were looking at about 600,000 new tenants.

I also saw that as a market absorbed residents, its rental rates exploded. As I researched, I saw markets where rents had raised as much as 250 percent in fewer than two years. I have seen rental rates go even higher. Landlords aren't stupid. They are, however, slow to react. Information transfers very slowly in the real estate investment community.

I noticed that in each and every expansionary market, the property owners had typically lived through some very dark days during the past decade. During that time there were not many buyers for their real estate and hardly any potential tenants. I also saw that—unbeknownst to the landlord—new professional job growth and its ancillary ripple effect in the service sector was going to entirely change the picture.

I saw opportunity.

An Example of Expansion

A great example would be Salt Lake City, Utah, in 1988. Property prices had been stagnant for years. Landlords had been lucky just to keep their units filled. When we first started investing in Salt Lake City, it was just starting to absorb. (Absorption is the most profitable economic cycle stage for the real estate investor.)

At that time in Salt Lake City, there was a minimum new job forecast in excess of 85,000. Combined with the ripple effect in the service sector that would be about 400,000 new jobs.

I had done my market analysis research. When we started buying in Salt Lake City, the rental market was about 18 percent vacant. When we started investing in Salt Lake City, the real estate investors and real estate professionals thought that we were crazy. We were—crazy like a fox, that is.

Before we started investing, we knew that the companies that were relocating to Salt Lake City were coming from more expensive areas of the country. It was like fishing in a stocked pond. We made rock-bottom offers and got nearly all of them accepted. Our sellers felt they were lucky to just dump their real estate. I remember on one rental property we bought, we were getting only $185 rent per month for a two-bedroom apartment. Within eighteen months of buying that residential income property, we were getting $750 for the same unit. It was simply supply and demand. The housing market became so tight that a city ordinance was passed that you could actually convert your garage into a rental unit.

For a developer to secure any construction financing, they have to prove to a lender the financial viability of a project. That means that if you build a residential income property, you are going to have to demonstrate a positive cash flow. Rents had to go up almost 400 percent in Salt Lake City before any new construction would be feasible via traditional financing.

Crazy?

Rents were so low that no banker would feel confident about giving a new construction loan on a piece of residential income property. Even so, as the demand increased, landlords would put an ad in the paper and get seventy-five phone calls from potential tenants. Soon, landlords began to figure things out. At this point, rental rates in Salt Lake City began to skyrocket.

Earlier in this book we talked about Steve and Eric. These two brothers from southern California were students of ours on a BuyingTour in Salt Lake City. We taught them about the fifth migration, the Garrison cycle, and the tools for investing wisely in real estate today.

Their first real estate investment after being taught by us was a small residential income property. In fewer than two years, that small rental property not only produced a positive cash flow every single month, but it also appreciated to the point where they sold it for a $170,000 profit. It was just cause and effect. The Salt Lake City market had transitioned from the absorption stage into the expansion stage.

The Best Time to Sell

In these expansion markets there is an incredible job growth. The expansion stage of the Garrison economic cycle of real estate economics is accompanied by new construction. In other words, supply catches up to and (in most cases) exceeds the demand. Because growth places heavy demand on materials and labor, this condition is also depicted as an inflationary phase. We found that it's great to be a seller early on in this stage of the cycle. The bottom-line definition for an expansion market is that the rents have gone up high enough to make a banker believe that a new construction loan to a developer of residential income properties is justified.

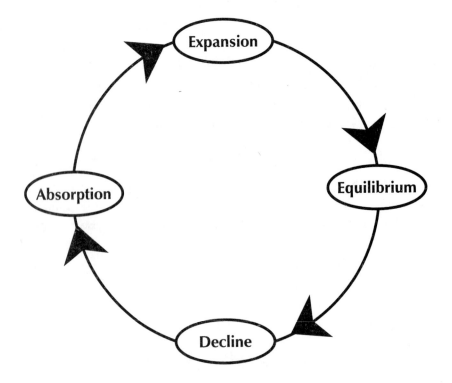

Equilibrium

As demand pushes new construction in the expansion stage, the cost of housing dramatically rises. The value of any property is a function (product) of its ability to earn income, its replacement cost, and a comparison of recent sales of comparable properties.

When you buy a property in the absorption stage, replacement cost and comparable sales are thrown out the window. You focus almost entirely on a property's ability to earn income in today's market. Remember that rents in absorption markets do not justify replacement cost. There also are typically no comparable sales.

It's your understanding of job growth trends that allow you to purchase with confidence. Understanding that a property boom is just beginning to happen is like frosting on a cake. Remember that you don't buy based on speculation. You buy only at prices below market value with payments structured to give you an instant positive cash flow after all expenses.

And you thought that economics was boring in college! Just remember that by applying it to real estate investing today, you can make a fortune.

The new job growth that was the catalyst for this demand continues until the cost of housing reduces the incentive that a company has to relocate to a given market. In economic terms, the market imperfection, or "low housing price," incentive disappears because of the very same demand that it attracted. We have watched this happen in market after market after market.

Here's the point: It becomes apparent that buying properties at the cycle stage before expansion (absorption) is the only viable approach today for earning explosive real estate profits. As you are starting to see, market timing is really everything for today's successful real estate investor.

An equilibrium market is a perfected market where new job growth and residential income property appreciation have slowed to national averages. In an equilibrium market, buyers are looking for deep discounts on the purchase of real estate investments because they realize that the current property price appreciation will barely beat what they could do on their own with investing their money in a normal passbook savings account.

Decline

Because the previous phase of the market was characterized as a period of high prices, the market becomes less attractive to businesses looking to relocate or expand. Also during the equilibrium stage, local and state governments become increasingly anti-business. This "lack of humility" is easily apparent in California and most other traditional major market areas. During the latter stages of equilibrium, many jobs are lost to other domestic and foreign markets who are aggressively seeking businesses to relocate there due to the high cost of living in equilibrium markets. With job losses and predictable overbuilding, there is far more supply than demand, resulting in declines in occupancy levels, rents, and values, and new construction of residential income properties.

The negative attitude or group-based "psychological hysteria" of a down market feeds upon itself. To the owner of a residential income property in a decline market, there seems like no hope or way out. If only they had sold years before, while their market was in the expansion stage of the Garrison cycle of real estate economics and was filled with buyers. Hindsight is twenty-twenty.

Absorption

Because the previous phase of the Garrison cycle was characterized by declining values, this stage of the economic cycle offers a lower cost of housing than national averages and an extremely pro-business climate. This low cost of living and doing business, combined with new governmental incentives offered to businesses looking to expand or relocate, is like throwing gasoline on wet wood. When struck with a match, it simply explodes. The same thing happens in absorption markets as the economy starts adding jobs, which then results in increased demand, increased occupancy levels, rising rents, and skyrocketing property values. Investing early on in this

106

stage of the Garrison cycle is like hitting the mother lode of a gold mine. You essentially can do no wrong.

Getting in at the Right Time

Brad came with us on a BuyingTour when Kansas City, Missouri, had just started to recover from its decline. The minimum new professional job growth estimates were well above 50,000, which translates into a quarter-million new tenants when you factor in the ripple effect into the service sector. Brad invested in several properties using our nothing down and low down payment techniques for absorption markets. On just one of his buildings, he made enough money to completely pay off his family farm in Nebraska.

John from New York State also came with us into Kansas City, Missouri. John is still investing in Kansas City as we write this. He just e-mailed us that he had just bought a duplex for $26,500 with nothing down. He estimates that he will put $9,000 into it in rehab money. When the repairs are completed, the market analysis that we taught him how to do (and we will teach you how to do the same) tells him that he will have two rental units that will generate a $750 per month positive cash flow. He will also have a property that he can instantly sell in that market for a profit in excess of $30,000. John is a young man. He is single. He is a born-again real estate investor since we rescued him from wage slavery. He has invested with us in several absorption markets now. He is a testament to the validity of our strategies, tools, and techniques for investing in the twenty-first century and beyond.

As you get more and more involved in real estate investing, you will come to realize how incredibly nice and friendly most real estate investors are. They are down-to-earth real people who are not looking for handouts. They are willing to learn. Successful real estate investors are humble and teachable. They don't know it all. They listen, learn, and then dig in and work hard.

We would love to help you make money in today's absorption

markets. But remember this. You really need to learn to walk before you run. We would encourage you to first determine the exact stage of the Garrison cycle that your back yard investing area is in. We would then refer you to Chapter 12 to learn the strategies, tools, and techniques that work in your specific market. It doesn't matter which stage your local market is in because we have discovered methods that can make great profits in any market.

Once you have mastered some of the basics of real estate investing, you should begin your research of absorption markets. These markets are where the truly incredible real estate profits are to be made because job growth fuels population increases, which in turn support increased occupancy and rental rate increases.

We would love nothing more than to meet you one day in one of those goldmine absorption markets.

Making money certainly makes real estate investing a lot of fun.

You can make money or you can make excuses, but you can't make both.

—*Marc Stephan Garrison*

Chapter 10

Live Where You Want, Invest Only Where It Makes Sense

IMAGINE ALL THE MONEYMAKING OPPORTUNITIES if you could just turn back time. Imagine turning the clock back to 1978, which is when I first got started in real estate investment. Might you have invested a little more heavily in real estate? Since discovering the fifth migration and defining the Garrison cycle of real estate economics in 1986, I have successfully chosen the very top absorption markets in North America.

Don't believe it? Then I double dare you to do your research on every major absorption market that I have targeted since that time.

- Dallas, Texas—1986
- Las Vegas, Nevada—1987
- Boise, Idaho—1987
- Salt Lake City, Utah—1988
- Denver, Colorado—1988
- Phoenix, Arizona—1990

- Kansas City, Missouri—1993
- Fort Worth, Texas—1995
- Tulsa, Oklahoma—1997
- Oklahoma City, Oklahoma—1999
- Memphis, Tennessee—2001
- Kansas City, Kansas—2001

Do your homework on these markets.

Check them out.

Find out the vacancy rate per unit when we started to invest in those areas. Find out the average residential rental rate for a studio, a one-bedroom, a two-bedroom, and a three-bedroom apartment then. Find out what actual sales per unit were in those markets at that time.

And then finish your homework by seeing what those factors were about three years after we went in. Our typical buy-and-hold period is about thirty-six months. You will quickly realize that we nailed each market perfectly. You will find out that vacancies dropped to zero within the first couple of years after we went in. You will find that rents went up through the roof. You will find out that the prices have skyrocketed, then leveled off after they reached a level that would justify new construction.

Getting Started

Those property booms are just starting to happen in other markets across the United States of America. To take advantage of those absorption markets, you need to gain some experience as a real estate investor first.

As we've said, the very best way to gain experience as a real estate investor is to get started in your own back yard. Each of the chapters in the next part of this book (Part IV, Level One Investing: Buying in Your Own Back Yard) has been meticulously crafted to give you all the basic tools.

We start off with teaching you the basic principles of real estate investing. Then we teach you the tools for finding deals in real estate in expansion, equilibrium, decline, and absorption markets. We then teach you how to buy a piece of real estate right, and we tell you all you need to know to negotiate the best deals.

In Part V, you'll learn how to prepare a property once you have purchased it for rental or resale to maximize your profit. We then teach you the basics of property management.

You'll need all of these tools to successfully invest in your own back yard, and they will prove even more valuable when you decide to move to Level Two, and you begin real estate investing in the best absorption markets around the country.

Reaching Your Goals

Harry and Dorothy from Northern California first came with us on a BuyingTour in Denver, Colorado. Both were retirees who were desperate to be able to supplement their retirement income and to allow themselves the opportunities that they had always dreamed of. Their first acquisition was a building in Denver. They then went with us on a BuyingTour in Phoenix, Arizona. They then went with us on a BuyingTour to Kansas City. They then went with us on a BuyingTour to Tulsa. In each market they used our tools to invest in domestic absorption markets. They have done incredibly well and are now able to afford the lifestyle that they had only dreamed of. They are now selling their home and relocating to an incredibly beautiful area near where their son lives. Dreams can come true through the new paradigms and tools of real estate investing.

Tom from Northern California tried and tried to make real estate investing work near his home. He learned the basics of investment, something that he now calls his real estate apprenticeship. He then came with us into three different absorption markets on several different BuyingTours. He bought residential income properties in each market with little or no money down. On just one building, he made $194,500. Tom is now worth well over $2,000,000. Tom is an incredible gentleman, a great father, and now a good friend to our family.

Pak, who is also from Northern California, came with us on a BuyingTour into Salt Lake City. Cautious, she bought only one single-family dwelling. Within the first eighteen months, she made $37,000 on that property. She then rolled those profits over into a medium-size apartment building in Denver. Within two years, she sold that building at a profit of more than $200,000. She then rolled those profits over into a larger apartment building in Kansas City, Missouri. She made even more money on that. She then went with us on another BuyingTour into Tulsa. She bought several properties this time and walked away with almost $700,000 in profit. She then went with us on another BuyingTour into Oklahoma City. Her anticipated profits from these new transactions will net her over $1,000,000. Real estate investing has changed the life of this mother of five children. Imagine this: Pak has only worked real estate investing part-time. She has never made a dime off real estate investing near her hometown of San Jose, California. And she started out with less than $5,000 cash invested.

We are proud to call Pak a friend. We are proud to call all of our students friends.

Are you ready for financial success like Pak, like Tom, like John, like Steve and Eric, like Harry and Dorothy, and like the hundreds of other students at our BuyingTours to whom we have taught these new paradigms and tools?

Then turn the page, and let's go.

The fun is just getting started.

PART IV

Level One Investing:
Buying in Your Own Back Yard

CHAPTER 11

The New Principles of Real Estate Investing

CHAPTER 12

Tools for Finding Deals in Real Estate

CHAPTER 13

Buying Right

CHAPTER 14

Making Money at the Kitchen Table

Every expert started out the same way—by learning the basics.

—*Ryan Marc Garrison*

Chapter 11

The New Principles of Real Estate Investing

WE ARE GOING TO BE LOOKING AT real estate as the ultimate investment. But before we can look at the details of a real estate transaction, or even discuss any type of property in detail, we need to understand the subject of real estate itself. What is real estate? What laws govern its sale, or its lease? This is dry, admittedly boring stuff, and if you already understand it thoroughly, jump ahead. No, on second thought, stay with me—the review can't hurt, and it can always help.

Let's start with the obvious question: What is real estate? Understand first that real estate, unlike most other "investments," is more than a store of wealth; it is a tangible asset, a worthwhile usable commodity. Real estate is a commodity in the same sense that a stereo is. It is purchased, used, enjoyed, and sold. Unlike the stereo, though, real estate is comprised of two major components: the land itself and man-made improvements affixed to the land. And, of course, the legal aspects of real estate ownership are slightly more complicated than the ownership of a stereo.

Real Estate Basics

The land consists of the surface area of the real estate purchase and, when legally specified, the mineral rights and air rights. The mineral rights are the rights of the owner to use and enjoy the space below the surface of the earth. Theoretically, this space is like an inverted pyramid that starts on the surface and extends to the center of the earth (about 4,000 miles), but in practice mineral rights generally extend no more than 50,000 feet. (Do you need more than that?) The air rights apply to the legally specified three-dimensional area that extends 1,500 feet above the property. The federal and local governments may limit the height of air rights by enacting and enforcing building height restrictions and by designating certain airspace as public property for use by aircraft.

Improvements include the buildings, structures, and other man-made additions such as driveways, irrigation canals, and fences. These improvements take two forms: improvements *on* the land and improvements *to* the land. The first category includes all types of permanent man-made structures; improvements to the land are changes made in the physical condition of the land itself, such as grading, utility lines, and the construction of access roads that make the land suitable for use.

The laws governing the ownership of land dictate that the owner has a "bundle of rights." These rights include the right to possess the property, use the property, enjoy the property, exclude others from using it, sell the property, and give it away. These rights are intangible factors that pertain to the land and on-site improvements and are guaranteed by law. The government, through its police powers, can enact laws that not only protect the landowner from the rest of the public, but the public from the landowner—what the law giveth, it can take away, and the law can give and take any rights it deems are in the best interest of the public. That means if Farmer Brown wants to change his new suburban home into a slaughterhouse, he may be prevented from doing so by local government zoning ordinances.

Legal restrictions on a person's rights to a property are generally placed so that the property owner and the neighbors may each enjoy the "highest and best use" possible from their properties. Other restrictions on ownership include easements, which allow properties to be purchased by the government at a fair market value to allow for improvements deemed advantageous to the public interest.

Property and Ownership

Property is possessed in two basic forms: freehold and less-than-freehold estates. A freehold estate is what you think of as ownership; the property is held for an indefinite period of time by the possessor. The less-than-freehold estate is common in tenant-landlord relations, where the possessor is given the right by the owner to possess and use the land for a period of time. It is also called leasehold.

Stop here for a second and review. Make sure you understand the vocabulary presented so far. Reread if necessary because we are about to tackle another string of new terms, and every one of them may be important to you shortly.

Forms and Rights of Ownership

The ways of holding property in freehold estate are sole ownership, tenancy in common, joint tenancy, community property, tenancy by the entireties, real estate investment trusts, partnerships, corporations, or a combination of the above. A basic knowledge of these forms of ownership is absolutely necessary for anyone interested in real estate investing.

Sole Ownership

When one individual owns the property, without any co-owners, he or she is said to have sole ownership. He can buy, sell, trade, or do anything else that he sees fit—within the limits of the law. He alone is responsible for the debts of the property and the taxes owed on the property and any income from the property.

The alternative to sole ownership is co-ownership, in which more than one individual shares a freehold estate. They may hold the property as tenants in common, as joint tenants, as a trust, partnership, or corporation (as explained in the following sections). The method of ownership chosen will determine the tax consequences and the right of survivorship for the owners.

Tenancy in Common

When two or more persons own a property, they may choose to do so as tenants in common. Under this arrangement, each person owns an undivided interest—a fraction—in the property. Each owner has the right to sell, trade, or give away his interest in the property, without the permission of the other owners.

If one of the owners dies, his ownership interest passes on to his heirs.

This is an important consideration. If, for example, you owned a piece of property with your best friend as tenants in common, and your friend died, you would suddenly be faced with a new co-owner—one you might not get along with too well.

Tenants in common do not necessarily share the property equally. They can agree to hold any portion they choose. Three partners can each hold one-third, or one partner may own half and the other two share the remaining half, or any other division they may agree to.

Since each partner owns his own share separately, he is also responsible for a proportional share of property repairs, taxes, mortgage payments, etc. And he is entitled to a proportional share of any income derived from the property.

One problem that tenants in common face is the possibility of disagreement among the partners. If the difficulty cannot be solved outside a courtroom, any one of the partners may file a suit against the others, demanding that the property be physically divided or sold. Also, if one of the partners files for bankruptcy, the bankruptcy court can sell the property to satisfy debts. Each of the other partners will receive his proportionate share of the proceeds, but they have no say in the matter of the sale.

Joint Tenancy

When two or more persons own a piece of property as joint tenants, they have equal rights in the property, and they all have the right of survivorship. They have an equal voice in the disposition of the property, and they share its income equally.

For a joint tenancy to occur, four "unities" must occur: unity of time, unity of title, unity of possession, and unity of interest. Unity of time means that every co-owner acquires his ownership at the same time. Unity of title means that there is only one title to the property and that each owner has a share of it. Unity of possession means that each owner has an equal share in the possession of the property. Unity of interest means that each owner has an equal interest in the property. If there are two owners, each has a one-half interest; if there are four owners, each has a one-fourth interest.

Joint tenancy is popular, especially among married couples, because of the right of survivorship. If one owner dies, his or her rights are extinguished, and the property ownership goes directly to the surviving owners. This eliminates the problems that are encountered in a tenancy in common when one owner dies, leaving his share of the property to heirs.

Community Property

Some states apply the law of community property to husbands and wives. California (my old home state) is one such state, and the community-property fights around Beverly Hills and Hollywood are staggering. Some of the other states that are governed by the rules of community property are Arizona, Idaho, Louisiana, Nevada, New Mexico, Texas, and Washington. Check with a local attorney to see if your state has a community property law.

Simply put, the idea behind community property is that each spouse is entitled to one-half of everything acquired during the marriage. Unlike tenancy by the entireties, the rights of survivorship vary from one state to the next. You should find out the laws in your own state when you are considering the purchase of real property.

Tenancy by the Entireties

This is similar to joint tenancy in that the co-owners have the right to survivorship. But only a husband and wife can be tenants by the entireties. It is a doctrine applied in the states that do not recognize community property. In this form of co-ownership, the husband and wife are considered to be one legal entity, not two separate owners. As long as they are both alive, they act as one owner. Both of their signatures must appear on the deed in order to convey title.

A tenancy by the entireties faces a problem when there is marital trouble. This form of co-ownership can only be severed by agreement between the two parties, and in the case of divorce both must agree on the division of the property.

Real Estate Investment Trusts

REITs are formed by groups of investors (usually more than a hundred), who put their money into a common pot, called a trust, which is managed by trust officers. The investors are called beneficiaries, and their interest in the investment is similar to that of shareholders in a corporation.

Partnerships

Co-owners may choose to form a partnership for the purpose of buying a property. They may do so as a general partnership, in which case each partner has say in the management of the partnership. But each partner also has an unlimited financial responsibility to the partnership. He may be sued for every last dime of his own personal wealth to satisfy the debts of the partnership.

The alternative is a limited partnership, in which the general partners have full control over the property, make all of the management decisions of the partnership, and accept the full financial responsibility, while the limited partners only provide investment capital and share the profits. The advantage to the limited partners is easy to see: They have little or no management hassles, and their losses are limited to the extent of their investment. The only problem that plagues limited partnerships is that it is difficult to ensure the honesty of the general partners, and the limited partners can easily be taken for a ride.

Corporations

A corporation is a separate legal entity in the eyes of the law. That is the most important difference between a corporation and a partnership: it exists independently of its owners. They can come and go, trading and selling their interest (in the form of stock), but the corporation goes on. It is responsible for its own taxes and its own financial obligations. The shareholders cannot be sued for the debts of the corporation.

The problem with a corporation is that it must pay income tax before distributing profits to the owners, who then must pay taxes on their income. The double taxation takes away profit that would have been shared by the owners in a partnership.

Before You Buy with a Partner

If you are considering purchasing property with another person, check with a real estate attorney first. You can find them in the Yellow Pages under Lawyers, or get a recommendation from a title officer, a banker, another investor, or your local bar association. It is vital that you understand the laws in your own state before you make such a decision.

A Quick Review

I know that studying page after page of definitions isn't nearly as much fun as, say, reading this week's issue of *TV Guide*. But then it's unlikely that anything you read in *TV Guide* will help you invest in real estate, right? Before we continue, read the following list of terms. How many can you define for yourself? If you need to review, do so now.

- Land
- Air rights
- Mineral rights
- Improvements to the land
- Improvements on the land
- Zoning
- Easements
- Eminent domain
- Freehold estate
- Less-than-freehold estate
- Leasehold
- Sole ownership
- Tenancy in common
- Joint tenancy
- Community property
- Tenancy by the entireties
- Real estate investment trusts (REITs)
- Partnerships
- Corporations

In the back of this book there is a reference guide to terms that you should know as a real estate investor. If you come across any terms that you are unfamiliar with, please take time to look them up.

The Best Investments

You now understand the basic rights of ownership and the forms such ownership can take. Let's consider next the different types of real estate investments. You can claim to be a real estate investor whether you buy an acre of swampland in Florida or the Taj Mahal. But which is the best investment for you and why?

Real estate includes all of the following:

- **Raw land:** Undeveloped real estate. Examples would be rangeland or, in a city, empty fields that don't have improvements such as utility hookups or curb and gutter.
- **Developed land:** Land that has been improved and is either already built on or ready to be built on.
- **Apartments:** A building with rooms or individual dwelling units that people live in but do not own. The tenant makes payment to the landlord (the owner or his representative), usually on a monthly basis.
- **Mobile home:** A personal residence, considered to be private property, which is not permanently attached to the land and may be moved to another location or mobile home site.
- **Condominium:** Typically, condominiums are multi-unit housing complexes where individual apartment-like units are purchased instead of rented. Each condominium owner has his or her own deed or mortgage. Typically, owners of these housing units are required to pay a monthly common fee, which pays for all outside maintenance, lawn care, and common utility fees.

- **Co-op:** Similar to a condominium, but ownership exists in shares of the total building, not in one specific unit. As a member of a co-op, you are assigned to one specific living unit within a complex.
- **Residential property:** Property or land that is zoned by the local government agencies to be used for single-family homes or other living quarters.
- **Hotel or motel:** A property where individual sleeping rooms or suites are rented by the night.
- **Commercial property:** Property that is specifically zoned by the local government authorities for commercial uses such as shopping centers, stores, and laundries.
- **Industrial property:** Property that is specifically zoned by the local government authorities for industrial uses such as manufacturing and processing plants.

Of these many types of investments, only two are really ideal for the beginning investor: single-family homes and apartments. Mobile homes and raw land rarely if ever return even the original investment, and commercial and industrial properties are expensive and very complicated investments.

The Advantages of Buying Single-Family Homes

Nearly 80 percent of all real estate transactions take place in the lower-middle range of house prices. Specifically, the average home in this range is a three-bedroom, two-bathroom house with a carport or garage and approximately 1,100 square feet. Why are these bread-and-butter houses such hot sellers? Because they are the transition houses for people moving up and down the financial ladder of life. They are usually the starter homes for up-and-coming couples, and they are the lifelong homes for the blue-collar backbone of America. Later we will talk about the specifics of how to find these bargain properties.

This area of real estate investing has several advantages. First, these units represent the bottom end of the housing market. The sale prices are low, the down payments are usually low, and the demand is high. These homes can be diamonds in the rough. By putting in some minimal fix-up and cleaning, you can resell them at fantastic profits.

One good example today would be of John Stuart from Long Island, New York. John has been with us on several BuyingTours. He first invested with us in Phoenix, Arizona, in several multifamily units. John is now focusing in on one of our target markets and doing nothing but singles. In that market, John has never paid more than $15,000 total for a single-family home. John renovates those homes and is renting them out at in excess of $850 per month. If you run the numbers, these homes are being paid for free and clear in fewer than two years. John, though, is renting out these properties at top dollar and then flipping these single-family homes to other investors at a $35,000 to $50,000 profit per house. It is a pleasure to see John find this niche and to watch him work it so well. Next summer John is going to help us host a group of investors in his market for a BuyingTour teaching fifteen of our other members how to do just what he is doing himself.

The Many Advantages of Rental Properties

Rental properties—small apartments and single-family homes that you rent out—are good investments because there is always a shortage of housing, and there are always people who can afford to rent but cannot afford to buy a home. Because of the high price of home ownership, and the fact that it is generally undertaken with borrowed funds, there will always be renters, those who are afraid of the financial obligation or unwilling to leverage themselves into ownership.

The main advantage that real estate offers is leverage. Using a small amount of money—or even no money, in a few cases—you can buy real estate worth tens or hundreds of thousands of dollars. In this book you will learn the basics of using leverage: how to find the deals that allow you to invest little or none of your own money and yet reap tremendous rewards.

The second advantage is the price appreciation that occurs in real estate, whether it is through inflation, or fixing up, or just the fact that buyers and sellers are working in an imperfect market, usually with only a hazy knowledge as to the real value of property. This is even truer in absorption markets where the job growth is filling every single vacant rental property. The house that you bought yesterday for $60,000 may be worth $65,000 to another person. Find that person, and you've made $5,000.

Price is also boosted by the simple law of supply and demand. The supply of housing is growing slowly, and the population is mushrooming, through both the constant flow of immigrants looking for the Promised Land and our reliance on the old-fashioned way of enlarging our own families. As long as demand for housing continues to outrun supply (and do you see it doing anything else?), prices will keep going up.

Other factors that affect the price of real estate are the general economic condition of the community, the condition of the surrounding neighborhood, the actual condition of the property, the terms (this includes the available financing, the time period involved, owner financing, down payment, and other factors), the legal rights inherent in the transfer of the property, and its perceived future value.

Comparing Real Estate Investments

One of the most interesting characteristics of real estate is the concept of "fixity." Unlike two cans of beans, two similar real estate investments can't be compared side by side. The investment is fixed; it is permanently attached. To compare two similar real estate investments, you need to use some specialized valuation techniques. A system of determining value in real estate will be discussed later.

Tax Advantages

The tax advantages of real estate are staggering. You can own a rental unit, collect rent, pay operating expenses and loan payments, and come out with a positive cash flow, and then still get a tax break on the fifteenth of April. When you own rental real estate, or even if you just do what John Stuart is doing, buying and selling properties, you are classified as being self-employed. You are also allowed to deduct operating expenses, which further reduces your income (for tax purposes). Being self-employed is one of the greatest tax savings tools that exist. You are able to shift a lot of your regular living expenses into the area of legitimate tax deductions.

Of course, along with the advantages of preferred tax treatment, appreciation, and leverage, there is also monthly income that can be made, using a few simple methods of buying, renting, managing, and selling that I will be showing you throughout the book.

You now know what real estate is, how it is owned, what rights an owner has over his or her real estate, the different types of real estate, which real estate investments are the best, and the advantages of owning real estate. We can begin the next part of your education: how to buy real estate.

Educated persistence—one step at a time.

—Hunter James Garrison

Chapter 12

Tools for Finding Deals in Real Estate

I REMEMBER THE FIRST TIME that I was introduced to the word "paradigm." When I heard it for the first time I almost laughed, as the word sounded so "funny," but when I caught the concept I was floored. It made so much sense. This word became popular in the last few decades as a way to describe a person's "belief window" or their "view of the world." It was first used to describe scientists who were so ingrained in their "core beliefs" that it was almost impossible for them to recognize and be open to new scientific discoveries and ideas.

The paradigms that I had been taught to believe in through my own experience as a young real estate investor were these:

- I had to always invest within thirty minutes of my home.
- All properties would appreciate and create cash flow.
- Real estate agents were taboo.
- The only way to make money was to buy "fix-up" or "rehab" properties.

By 1986, each of those beliefs had been shattered.

I want this chapter to be very direct and to the point.

This is not 1977, when I started investing in real estate.

And this is not 1986.

We are living in the twenty-first century, and we are facing an entirely new real estate investing market.

Let me illustrate through example how my basic paradigms of real estate investing had been shattered and revealed to be mere illusions.

Illusion #1: You always have to invest within 30 minutes of your home.

This concept is kind of like fishing. If you spend all morning without even getting one nibble or hit, then you probably should pull up your anchor and move your boat to the other side of the lake. I think of Steve and Eric, who were from southern California— two brothers who couldn't make any sense of their back yard. I think of David from New York City, who spent days and weeks and months caught in traffic trying to find good deals in real estate in and near the Big Apple. I think of Tom Wieske from San Jose, California, who tried for years to find good deals that he could buy in real estate in the San Francisco Bay area.

Each of these people spent more time in rush-hour traffic just going across their hometowns than they spent on a plane flying to their first BuyingTour. These individuals and almost 2,500 others since 1986 have broken free of their Level One back yard-investing paradigm. The results have been nothing short of incredible.

But I don't want you to misunderstand me. I want this point to be very clear. All real estate investors should start in their own back yard. Take the example of Kyle and Tara from Denver. Denver was an area that we went into in the late '80s and early '90s. Within a few years of our going into Denver, prices in the area skyrocketed. So many new jobs came into the Denver metroplex that there were bidding wars on vacant rental units. This demand caused rents to soar. As rents escalated, the values of rental units boomed. As this market moved out of decline into absorption there was tons of opportunity. Unfortunately, 99.9 percent of the locals never figured it out. And by the time that they did, it was too late. It has become a common factor in all of our absorption markets that the locals never figure out the opportunities in real estate investing in their market that is in "absorption" until rents have risen high enough to justify new construction. By that time we are ready to sell. And who do you think our buyers are? You just have to remember that when we go into a new market, we do so based on demonstrable research. "Legal insider trading," in other words. We go into markets at a time when the locals think that we are crazy.

Remember the cycles:

- Expansion
- Equilibrium
- Decline
- Absorption

Your job as an investor is to do these things:

- Determine the economic cycle stage of your back yard.
- Use the appropriate tools for real estate investing.

You can make money in any market. But unfortunately, you are severely limited in expansionary, in equilibrium, and in decline markets. Kyle and Tara are going with us on a BuyingTour next month. Together we have determined that their back yard market is swiftly moving into the decline phase. Thousands of new rental units are flooding the market today to fill the demand that most people thought would never end.

Kyle and Tara have been taught that they can make money in their Level One market—even in a decline—but to do so they are going to have to focus on properties that have glaring, blatant cosmetic problems. In other words, they are going to have to buy the worst property on the best block. Kyle and Tara have already decided that they are not interested in doing major rehab projects and doing flips. Instead, they have chosen to buy good stable properties in absorption markets and to sell as the market transitions to expansion.

But they—just like you—still have to start at home in their back yard. Even if it's just for practice, we all have to start with the basics, just like Kyle and Tara. What follows is a step-by-step checklist that every investor today needs to follow, regardless of the economic cycle stage of their target market:

1. Contact every one of your local school districts and obtain all annual elementary school enrollment statistics and projections.
2. Get a city map, and locate all areas that have the highest K–6 (kindergarten through sixth grade) growth rates.
3. Focus your investing efforts on those target areas of growth.
4. Contact your local title companies and have them do a "farm report" on each of your target neighborhoods. This farm report will list the exact address and sale price for any and all properties within your requested areas. This report typically is done free as a service to real estate investors and professionals who are or who will become the title companies' customers.
5. Drive by and photograph and make a record of each recent sale in each of your target markets. This is called "forming a definition of value." One of the things that we have already talked about is how improved real estate has site-specific value. In other words, a three-bedroom house in one part of town can have a totally different value than the exact same three-bedroom house in another neighborhood of town. There is no other way to form a definition of value.

6. Now drive each and every street in each and every neighborhood and take good notes on each and every property for sale. If you have a cell phone, take it out and instantly call and ask about the property listed for sale. If you find a property that looks vacant, write down the address and instantly call your title company and have them do a search to find out the owner's name, what they bought it for originally and when, and what the owner's telephone number is. As soon as you get that number, be sure to follow through.

7. Pay attention to each real estate agent that calls you back about a listed property, and try to pick out the very best for that area. Ask that Realtor to start focusing specifically on that area and to tell you about any and all properties that they can find that are for sale in that area.

8. Follow through on each and every lead that you generate or that is provided to you.

9. Work your Sunday real estate for-sale listings in the local paper religiously.

Kyle and Tara have no intention of buying properties in Denver right now, but right now, as I write, they are working Denver. I truly believe that every single real estate investor needs to constantly work their back yard. Not only are there lessons to be learned, but it also keeps you abreast of your local market and puts you in place to find potential deals that may just entice you to invest in your back yard.

Illusion #2: All properties will appreciate and create cash flow.

When I first started investing, I was in a market that was on fire with growth. It was a hot market of opportunity that was moving out of absorption into full-blown expansion. For six years I could do no wrong. But when the pendulum swung, and jobs started to move away, it seemed that I could do no right. We have been raised on the paradigm that real estate is just like the stock market. We are told almost daily by the national news that there is an average price for a home and that all real estate markets move the same—that they are all up, or that they are all down. The truth today is based in hard-core reality. Some markets are hot because of job growth and their underlying low prices, low cost of living, and pro-business attitude as expressed through their state, county, and/or city governmental agencies.

Right now we are working five different markets that are all up. We tax-free exchanged into these markets from other markets that had just run the complete absorption cycle, and we will move into still other fresh markets after our current markets are played out.

It couldn't be simpler.

In the old days, I used every trick in the book to find good deals. I worked probate. I used tax sales. I used foreclosures. I worked the classified ads. I passed out fliers. I sent out letters to property owners in my target areas—the address labels were furnished by my title insurance agency free—and I nailed and posted up professional signs that simply stated:

"I Buy Houses."

I made money. But it was a horribly large amount of work, and it seemed like I was always trying to form a definition of value. Over the years I learned to use elementary school enrollment statistics to point me into markets of growth. I formed definitions of value for those areas, and then I could instantly recognize a good deal based on the research that I had already done for that area of growth.

In 1986, when I first ventured out into Level Two absorption markets, I kept trying to do it all myself. It was then that I discovered the law of human leverage. It was then that I found out just how valuable a real estate agent could be for me as a buyer.

Illusion #3: Real estate agents are taboo.

When I first started investing in real estate I did not have a lot of money. I found rather quickly that if I was using a real estate agent to buy a property, that the agent's commission was typically buried inside of my down payment. Not having much money for down payments, I became very adept at avoiding real estate agents like the plague. In my first book, *Financially Free* (published by Simon & Schuster in 1986), I taught tool after tool after tool for finding deals in real estate in your back yard without ever having to come close to using a real estate agent.

I now must admit that this paradigm was wrong. In the late 1980s, I discovered a type of real estate agent called a "buyer's broker." This new breed of real estate agent came out of a landmark ruling in the state of Hawaii. This ruling allowed, for the very first time, real estate agent to represent the buyer. In the "old days," all real estate agents represented the seller, and they had the legal fiduciary responsibility to do nothing but get the very best price and terms for the seller. A buyer's broker is just the opposite. Their job is to get the very best deal for the buyer—you and me. It is because of this change that I have never bought one single property since 1987 or 1988 without using a buyer's broker. I use buyer's brokers to find me good deals in all areas of real estate. I find professionals who work my target areas who know all the tricks of the trade and who are motivated to find me the very best deals available so that I will keep working with them as their client. Makes sense, doesn't it?

Using a buyer's broker has freed me up from chasing deals, and it has allowed me to focus like a laser beam on being the very best real estate investor that I possibly could be. The real key is finding the buyer's broker who really performs and who specializes in that area of town and in that type of property that you want to invest in. As I already said: Drive your target area. See who is active. Make phone calls, and see who returns them in a timely manner and who seems to know what they are talking about. Be aware that most multifamily apartment buildings do not have "For Sale" signs in front of them when they are for sale. If you are interested in larger income properties, first build a team of professionals from the ground up, starting with a great buyer's broker who works that area almost exclusively. Have that agent find you the right multifamily real estate agent to get you the deals that you are looking for.

The Advantages of Having a Broker on Your Side

Traditional real estate investing doesn't teach you a thing about the new paradigms of real estate investing today. Traditional real estate investing is focused on finding the deals that are nothing down or that give you great terms. Just a few minutes ago, as I am writing this, I talked on the phone with a new student of mine. Carlos bought two resort condominiums in Park City, Utah, with nothing down. Sounds great, doesn't it? Not to me. Most "nothing down" deals that I have ever seen or heard are delayed time bombs for personal financial disaster. Don't believe me? Let me tell you more about Carlos's deal. In writing, Carlos was told that this brand-new condo would give a neutral cash flow and build equity from day one. Since the day he got his "nothing down" deal on these two condos, Carlos has paid out almost $3,000 per month in negative cash flow to maintain his two mortgage payments, which do not even include his condominium association fees. Upon further investigation, I found out that Carlos has never even visited these two condos, which were out by the Park City Outlet Mall. If you know Park City, you would know that this location is nowhere near central Park City, Utah, or any ski resorts. It's rather like planning a trip to Disneyland in Anaheim, California, and getting booked into a motel in gang- and drug-infested Compton, California, near where I lived as a youth.

Carlos made this disastrous deal about one year before he got involved with us.

Making mistakes is nothing new to those who are on their road to success.

I have a fairly open door policy to my students, and I spent almost an hour tonight talking with Carlos and giving him a concrete plan for "cutting bait" or getting rid of this problem—and how to make sure that nothing like this ever happens again.

This is where the real power of using a good buyer's broker comes about. My wife, Paula, is a great judge of character. Some of us, like myself, would rather look on the bright side, and we have a tendency toward being taken advantage of. If you are married or have a partner, be sure to develop yourselves into working as a team. Let each of your individual strengths rise to the top. Working with Paula, I focus on research, property acquisition, and sales. Paula does all of the business deals, the property rehab, and the maintenance. We both have made tons of mistakes. But we do not let our mistakes cripple us or hold us down. Hindsight is twenty-twenty. We focus on our future and work hard to learn from our mistakes.

Choosing a Buyer's Broker

When you are choosing a buyer's broker, let their track record and performance with you be your guide. Talk with their other clients. Start slow. Take everything step by step. Double-check everything.

I cannot stress the importance of checking with a real estate professional's other clients. If they refuse to give you referrals, let that be a warning. Immediately cut off that relationship, and go on down the road to someone who is willing to earn your business.

As a side note: If you ever feel inclined to get involved with any investment advisor, mentor, or coach, ask first to talk with some of their current clients. I have made it a rule since 1986 that I refuse to sell any of my programs. I have chosen instead to simply give the details and then refer the potential student on to other students who have worked with Paula and me and our programs. I believe in referrals. I don't like marketing pieces or telemarketing salespeople. I don't believe in coaching programs that aren't taught by someone who has not actually made the program happen in their own life. My wife and I prefer to practice what we preach.

Illusion #4: The only way to make money is to buy "fix-up" or "rehab" properties.

During my early years as an investor, the only way that I ever made money on a property was to buy a dump and to make it pretty. Fortunes have been made using such a program, but the reality of real estate investing profit in the twenty-first century is that there are really far better ways. I am thinking of a property that one of our students bought in Salt Lake City for about $10,000 down and sold fewer than three years later with a profit of well over $200,000. The property was bought through a buyer's broker. The property was clean. The property was not a foreclosure or a "nothing down" deal. The property was listed for sale in a market that made financial sense. Several hundred thousand jobs were moving into Salt Lake City, and a rising tide lifts almost all boats.

Since we started our BuyingTours in 1986, I have found that most of the very best deals that our students are making today are just simple bread-and-butter deals like this eight-unit apartment building. The investor comes in and targets several micromarkets through research. The investor then builds a team that will bring deals to him or her on a regular basis from that market. When a deal comes in, the investor compares that asking price with other recent comparable sales in the neighborhood. The investor runs some basic numbers and evaluates the property's cash flow after all expenses, including full property management. The investor then follows through on that deal, even if he or she is not interested in it as presently represented for sale. In other words, if you want to become a successful investor, you need to learn that if someone brings you a property, then you are honor-bound to respond to that solicitation for sale. If you think that a deal has too high an asking price, then respond back with an appropriate offer price. If you are not interested in a deal that is presented to you, then call that agent back and tell them why you are not interested. Most phone companies have long-distance plans with rates around five cents a minute. Following through via phone, fax, and/or e-mail will separate you from the rest of that market's investors, and it will do nothing but build trust and respect from any real estate professional who you are working with. In essence, that is really what this business is all about.

When I was talking with Carlos on the phone today, I told him the story of two other investors, one from Portland and the other from Seattle. You know them from the story at the beginning of this book, Howard and Jeff. Both of these investors came with us into Denver on the very same BuyingTour. One of these BuyingTour participants jumped into Denver and started doing research. The other investor chose not to buy in Denver and instead invested in some low down payment properties in a rundown neighborhood near Tacoma, Washington.

The investor who jumped into Denver did his research and found out where the families with children were moving to in that area. He then followed the steps—he formed a definition of value; he developed his real estate team; and he saw beyond the obvious. Through research, he clearly understood his future.

The investor from Portland bought a great building in Denver. He was unemployed at the time, so he temporarily left his family behind and moved into his Colorado property and immediately went to work. Having never done any real estate before he faced a big learning curve, but through our inner circle he had an entire network of mentors and real estate professionals to help him out step-by-step.

Today that investor from Portland now has a net worth of several million dollars. He lives in a home of his dreams. He has an incredible positive cash flow. He works hard, he plays hard, and he now lives a life that others can only dream about.

I remember meeting that young man in Denver in front of his building. I told him that if he worked several years like other people won't, then he would be able to live the rest of his life like other people can't.

That dream has come true not only for him but also for hundreds of our other students.

Correct principles . . . applied.

What about that investor from Seattle?

His low down payment, nothing-down back yard dream deal was bought in an area that he had done not a dime's research on— just like Carlos with his Park City property. Great terms suckered him in. Unfortunately, all the families who could were moving out of that neighborhood in droves. The people who lived there knew that once it got dark, that neighborhood was taken over by gangs and drugs. Today that story is still the same, and that property is not worth a dime more than he paid for it. Do you think that he wished he had bought in Denver instead of his back yard?

Not Just "Diamonds in the Rough"

Finding good deals in real estate today to me is a combination of factors. I think I have seen all the "get-rich-quick" real estate gurus on television that hawk "nothing down" formulas and parade a half dozen of their "success stories" on each show. But have you noticed that they never feature any of their students who have become self-made millionaires? Why is this? Because they don't have any. They would if they could.

I recently checked out one of the biggest television real estate gurus through their list management company. Their list management company reports that they have well over two million people who have bought their program. It doesn't take a rocket scientist to figure out that with over two million sales, some of your "nothing down" students would have gotten lucky and made a deal or two work out. But what about the rest? What about all their failures?

Some people aren't good at fixing up properties. Other people are. Some people love chasing down deals; other people do not. What I want you to realize is that real estate investing works. You don't have to find only "diamonds in the rough" and tear the property apart and then put it back together again to make a dime in real estate. That is, you don't unless you are investing in expansion, equilibrium, or decline markets. In an expansionary market, new product is coming online that is going to draw away most of your decent tenants into their newly developed apartments. In an equilibrium market, there is no significant property price appreciation. And in a decline market no one knows just where the bottom is— most likely, it is a property's loan amount. In those three types of economic cycle stages, you had better darn well know:

- Which direction each neighborhood is heading.
- What other properties are selling for in that specific market.
- How much it is going to cost (under the worst scenario) to rehab and renovate your target property.

There will always be good deals in every market.

Find the Right Market First

I hope you realize by now that every real estate investment strategy that is currently being taught or that has been written about is doing it all backwards.

They focus on finding the "deals."

Then they spend the next few days or weeks trying to figure out if that property is worth investing in. Unfortunately, like Carlos with his Park City condos, and our student from Seattle, tens and even hundreds of thousands of American real estate investors simply assume that all real estate markets will equally appreciate. They falsely believe that all areas within their target community will

The man, who insists upon seeing with perfect clearness before he decides, never decides.

—Henri Frédéric Amiel

Chapter 13

Buying Right

THE BIG SCHOOL CHRISTMAS PARTY included a gift exchange. Every guest brought a gift, and the presents were stacked on a table. One stood out easily: larger than the rest, it was magnificently wrapped in gorgeous paper, bedecked with ribbons and bows. Every eye was on the same box as the guests drew numbers. The girl who got number one lost no time in selecting the gaudily wrapped package. Holding her breath in anticipation, she shredded the beautiful paper in her hurry to get at the gift. Inside the box was a single scrap of paper with this note:

"I only had enough money to buy the paper and ribbons. Sorry, no present."

It took me several years of real estate investing to reach a point where I generally knew what I was going to find under the wrapper. Even now I'm sometimes initially deceived by outward appearances. Everything looked great right up until closing, when suddenly there were little surprise charges tucked neatly away between the lines of the contract. That didn't mean they weren't great deals, although I have backed out of one or two at closing.

You must know exactly what you are getting into before you buy a property. You have to be able to analyze your investments, and that means knowing every hidden flaw. Part of that, of course, is learning how to recognize the value of a deal without being deceived by outward appearances.

In the last chapter we looked at tools for finding good deals. But when you've found what appears to be good, how can you be sure? What do you look for, and what do you look out for? How do you cover yourself legally, and how can you get the best deal possible? This chapter answers all of these questions and more as we investigate some of the dangers in buying, how to write an offer that covers your assets, and what to expect at the closing.

Dangers to Avoid

There are a few dangers to be aware of when you look at a property for the first time:

- Nonassumable loans
- High mortgage rates/payments
- Negative cash flow
- Adjustable rate mortgages
- Short-term balloon mortgages
- Large down payments
- Overpriced properties
- Properties needing major repairs
- Properties in bad areas of town

As you can see, there are many factors that could increase the risks of buying a property far beyond the benefits. However, there are many ways for an investor to lessen or even entirely eliminate these risks in the search for a good deal. Most properties that seem to have a great many liabilities may actually turn into good deals, if you can avoid in advance the problems described below.

Nonassumable Loans

If you are new to real estate, you may not know what the word "assumable" means. Quite simply, if an existing loan is assumable, the buyer can take over the payments from the seller and assume responsibility for the loan. If it is nonassumable, the buyer is stuck finding a new loan at current rates. Since interest rates on older, assumable loans are usually lower, it makes sense to look for them.

There are legal manuals to help you work around the nonassumable loans that you may come across. But why hassle with them? All that takes is a lot of time and trouble. Assumable loans are much easier to find and to use, especially in our target absorption markets.

For example, loans through the Federal Housing Administration (FHA) or the Veterans Administration (VA) are ideal. The cost for an investor to assume one of these loans is only $45, and the qualifications are easily met. The conditions of these loans were probably best stated by the Rice brothers when they said, "The only qualification to assume one of these loans is to hold a mirror under your nose and be able to fog it up." Of course, the process may take slightly longer than that, but the point is a good one. Why tangle yourself up in a nonassumable mortgage when there are so many of these better loans available?

About 1978, most banks found themselves in a horrible position. They were forced by the money market to pay higher interest rates on savings accounts than they could collect from their old real estate loans. To put an end to such a catastrophe, they began to include a "due-on-sale" clause in every real estate loan. This clause states that the full amount of the loan may be called due upon sale of the property. Such a loan is automatically nonassumable, and therefore one to avoid. If you are considering a purchase, find how old the existing loan is. If it is pre-1978, chances are good that it is assumable.

For the bank, calling the loan due is merely an option, but if the interest rates have risen since the loan was written, the bank will probably ask you to qualify for the loan—if it doesn't call for complete repayment—and then adjust the interest rate upward in order to increase the bank's earnings.

High Mortgage Rates/Payments

Is the property that you are interested in able to pay for itself? If the property is a single-family dwelling, is the mortgage payment affordable to people in the middle-income range? If the property is a rental unit, does it already have a positive cash flow after all expenses? The more attractive the property is, the more likely that it will prove advantageous for you to own it.

With the advent of graduated payment mortgages (GPMs), which start with a very low monthly payment and then increase every year, many people who could not afford to buy a home were suddenly able to make the first- and second-year payments. They tied themselves into a GPM, thinking that in three or four years they would—thanks to raises and cost-of-living increases—be able to afford the higher payments. But when the expected pay increases didn't materialize and the house payments continued to rise, they ended up in serious trouble, many times in foreclosure.

The temptation for the investor is to think that these distress properties are excellent deals. They can take over the loan and buy the property with nothing down. And the owners are willing to walk away without anything for their equity, so what could be better? The payments are a little high, and due to get higher next year, but the price is right, and it's a nothing-down deal.

Don't be fooled. When time comes to sell, who is going to buy the house from you? If you can't offer low monthly payments, price is meaningless.

Negative Cash Flow

There is only one way to lessen the risk that a negative cash flow can bring to an investment: Avoid it like the plague! If you are going to have to take money out of your wallet every month to keep the property afloat until you can sell it, you are not finding a good deal. There are too many positive cash flow properties out there to waste your time asking for trouble.

Yes, I've heard the argument that if you can withstand a negative cash flow for a year or so, you'll more than make it up in tax savings and in profits when you sell. But I have never had to invest in negative cash-flow properties to make money, and you shouldn't have to either. And you'll sleep better at night if your properties are breaking even or making money each month, rather than costing you precious cash.

Adjustable Rate Mortgages (ARMs)

Use caution in deciding to accept this method of financing. You should be aware that as interest rates in the country go up, your mortgage payment will go up, too. Before you commit to an adjustable rate mortgage, be sure that the payments after the increase in interest rates are still reasonable.

Let me give you some guidelines concerning adjustable rate mortgages:

There are hundreds of different types of ARMs. Some are much better than others. The two most important areas to scrutinize are these: What protection do you have against large increases in monthly payments, and how will these increases (or decreases) be handled? To find out, ask your lender the following list of questions:

1. On what financial index are changes in payments based?
2. Can this index be changed during the course of the loan?
3. Does the loan have a cap (maximum amount of interest or

highest payment that can be charged)?

4. If this cap is on the payment, how is the negative amortization handled?

5. Is this cap for the life of the loan?

6. Is there an annual cap?

7. What happens if the index decreases?

8. What are the reverse caps?

9. How often is the index reviewed and the payment adjusted?

10. How much more would this ARM cost than a fixed rate loan under a worst-situation scenario?

11. Can this loan be assumed?

12. Can the loan be refinanced?

13. Are there any prepayment penalties?

The things I especially look for in ARMs are assumability, the ability to convert the loan to a level interest loan, low annual and lifetime caps on the interest rate that avoid negative amortization, and a tie to a longer-term index. My best advice concerning ARMs would be the wise adage *caveat emptor,* meaning "Let the buyer beware."

Short-Term Balloon Mortgages

You should almost always try to avoid balloon loans (loans that come due in a large final lump sum). However, there are occasions when you might consider assuming a balloon. In those situations, you should require that the loan has at least seven years of low payments until the large balloon payment is due. The reasons behind this requirement are simple. If you decide to hold on to the property for two years before selling it, there will remain a five-year period of time before the loan comes due, and to a buyer, five years is much more attractive than three months.

Avoid a short-term balloon (less than five years) for yourself.

There is too much of a chance that it will backfire. But there is a way to use a balloon loan to create a good deal. Instead of taking one out yourself, look for someone who has a short-term balloon coming due. Here you will find a distressed and flexible seller.

Here's a word of caution: If you do take on a balloon mortgage, it is never too soon to start examining your options in the event that you do not or cannot sell the property. You may be stuck with the balloon payment after all, and it would be best for you to be prepared. Whatever you do, don't let that balloon pop in your face!

Large Down Payments

Leverage . . . what a beautiful word. Use leverage correctly, and you can move yourself into a position of financial freedom faster than you would ever believe possible.

There is no question that large down payments can be a problem. The more you must pay in a down payment, the sooner you will run out of cash. A large down payment will also make it harder for you when it comes time for you to try to sell the property. A good rule of thumb is this: Whenever you sell, always recover the full down payment that you originally invested, plus a little extra.

You should set a standard for what you expect out of a sale. For example, whenever you buy a house, you could set a limit of 6 percent or less of the asking price as the down payment you would be willing to pay. Later, you would be able to sell the house asking for less than 10 percent of the price down and still make a healthy profit.

Overpriced Properties

An overpriced property is not a good deal. If you are paying more than the property is worth, you are defeating the purpose of real estate investing. When you buy an overpriced property, you will have to hold on to it for a long time in order to build up the equity that will enable you to make a profit by selling it. As trite and overused as this statement is, it still contains an ageless truth—buy low, sell high!

Properties Needing Major Repairs

I'm not saying that these properties can't be profitable. Some may be very beneficial to you, but they will always be costly. The price that you could pay to renovate a broken-down property could even exceed the price of building a brand-new one! And this is ignoring the cost of professional labor, if it is needed to bring wiring or plumbing up to local building codes, as well as any inspection fees you may need to pay.

If you are planning on doing the renovation yourself, ask this question: Would it be more profitable for me to spend my time buying and selling homes or renovating homes? Buying a property needing extensive repairs is a very different thing from buying a lower-priced property needing a bit of fixing up. Buy that home in need of a little cosmetic work; forget the one that will require a face-lift. In this area, as in every other, let common sense be your guide. Use caution; above all, be realistic!

If you are not sure before your purchase how much rehab a property will require, you should invite over several different rehab companies to give you a prepurchase inspection and estimate. Use experts. Check their references. Make your offer subject to a satisfactory inspection of all records and the physical condition of the home or multifamily income property.

If you have trouble recognizing just what you should be looking for when you analyze a property to see if it needs major repairs, please see Chapter 15. There you will find a complete description of a property analysis system that includes an on-site physical checklist. If in doubt about a property's physical condition, always seek expert advice. In this case, an ounce of prevention is worth a lot more than a pound of cure.

Properties in Bad Areas of Town

Just because a property has a low down payment and small mortgage installments, it is not necessarily a good deal. Any benefit that you may get from buying a property cheap will pale in comparison to the disadvantages of having to sell below market value or being forced to rent at a negative cash flow. If you are in an area that does not rent well, your vacancies will cost you money—a lot of it.

Before you buy, do a property analysis. Remember, there are more factors that define a "bad area" than trashy streets or vagrants. The considerations of safety and cleanliness are, of course, important, but you should also think about the way that you will be using the property. Is the area right for your purposes? If you are planning to sell a property soon after you buy it, look for an area with stable property values in a reasonable price range. An analysis such as this should help you a great deal when you are deciding what and where to buy. Fill out an analysis form on each property that interests you. If a property fits within the guidelines that you have set, buy it!

At all costs, avoid these nine problems that we've just laid out, especially when you're just getting started. By doing so, you will avoid some of the snares and pitfalls that cut a lot of investors' careers short.

Positives to Look For

Next are a few things you should look for, ask for, and (whenever possible) insist on when buying real estate:

- Low payments
- Assumable loans
- Instant equity
- Escape clauses

Low Payments

At the bottom line of every mortgage is the monthly payment. If you cannot afford the payments, or if rent won't make the payments, you are buying an alligator (the buzzword in real estate for a property with a negative cash flow). The name is accurate, because these negative cash flows can be very powerful animals, and they are only safe as long as you can feed them. But the minute you run out of green stuff to keep them fed, they will eat you up. Maybe you can afford to feed a whole alligator zoo, but I would rather pass up what appears to be a great deal if I can see that it is an alligator in disguise.

Structure every deal so that your payments are within your budget. Instead of giving a seller $2,000 down and $300 a month for five years, offer the same down payment with $150 a month for ten years. Keep your payments low, and all potential alligators under control. If you cannot structure low-enough payments, I would strongly suggest that you look elsewhere; you are only looking for the best deals.

Assumable Loans

I've already mentioned assumable loans. But the fact that a loan is assumable doesn't mean the seller will be willing to let you assume it. And your only alternative is to visit your local bank and get a new loan.

Whenever you have to go to the bank to get a conventional loan, just try to get out paying only the charges they told you about when you sat down. By the time they are through with their "origination fees" and "points" and this and that other charge, you will likely walk out feeling as though you have been professionally fleeced. Every time I close a bank loan, I want to call the police and report a robbery.

To gently coerce the sellers into letting you assume their loans, you must convince them that you are a good credit risk. One of the best ideas is to put together a biography—a short history that shows your ability, accompanied by recommendations from respectable people, such as a minister, an attorney, or a local politician.

If the sellers still seem unwilling to cooperate, explain that, with the extra cost of a new loan, you will have to lower your offer substantially if you can't assume their loan. If that doesn't work, you probably aren't working with motivated sellers.

Instant Equity

Go for the instant equity, if there is any. Instant equity is the difference between what you pay for the property and its actual market value. If you find a property worth $100,000, should you buy it for $110,000? Of course not! What about $100,000? No way! You need to buy equity; $80,000 is more like it. The same holds true for any amount of money. If someone wants to sell you a baseball card for fifty cents, should you buy it? Well, if you want to sell it and made money, you need to have some idea of the card's market value, don't you?

I recently got a call from an investor who needed advice. He told me all about the property he was considering—about the new paint, the 13.5-percent VA loan he was to assume, and what a great price he was paying. He said he was getting this home for only $78,000 with $15,000 down. I asked if the property had been appraised, and he assured me that it had: it was worth $90,000. Then I asked him the question that he should have asked long before calling me. "What kind of appraisal was done?" He wasn't sure, but he thought it was an accurate appraisal. I strongly suggested that he find out more about the appraisal: was it a formal appraisal, prepared by an accredited appraiser, or was it a market appraisal done by a Realtor? In this case it was neither; a neighbor down the street had suggested that the house might be worth "around $90,000."

When he following my suggestion and insisted on a professional appraisal, it turned out that the property was actually worth $72,500—a far cry from $90,000 and well under the $78,000 price he was prepared to pay. Determine the true market value of a house as part of your analysis, and only buy properties with built-in equity. Remember that different areas of a town have totally different price ranges.

Escape Clauses

In every offer you make, include at least a couple of escape clauses. What are they? They're clauses that allow you to back out of the deal without suffering any consequences if something should go wrong between the acceptance of the offer and closing.

Always include a lifeboat when you set sail. I hate to tell another war story so soon, but this important lesson was driven home only a few days ago, when I got a call from a desperate man in an eastern state. He had retired there, taking his $25,000 savings with him "to invest in real estate." He had heard how much money could be made with a few shrewd investments, and he could hardly wait get started.

P.T. Barnum would have said that there is an investor like him born every minute. In his first deal he was required to turn over $16,000 cash earnest money to the sellers. When he went to the bank to apply for a loan on the property, he put "unemployed" in the blank that requested employment information. The application was immediately rejected. When he returned to the sellers to ask for his $16,000 back, what do you think they told him? They said that he was breaking the contract, so he would have to forfeit his earnest money.

I agonized to think of this man's lifetime dreams shattered by a few too many weasels and not enough weasel clauses (another name for escape clauses). I advised him to seek the best legal aid he could afford. Other than that, there is nothing he can do; he is an adult, capable of entering into a contractual relationship the same as you or I.

Where did he go wrong? Well, first he gave cash earnest money to the seller; second, he made that earnest money for more than $500; and third, he failed to include an escape clause.

An escape clause is a clause that every buyer should include in an offer; it allows him or her to wriggle out of a contract should anything unforeseen (such as a loan rejection) come up that will make a deal infeasible or impossible. It is a lifeboat that should be on every investor's ship, so that when the Titanic deal hits an iceberg, a safe escape is possible.

Let me give you a few escape clauses. Don't ever make a written offer without including at least one of the following:

1. "Offer subject to partner's approval."

   If you don't have a partner, find one. You do need a second opinion, and even if your partner is only your best friend or your spouse, you are able to change your mind any time between the time your offer is accepted and the day of the closing. You can simply say, "I'm sorry, but my partner will not approve this deal, so I cannot go through with it."

2. "Offer subject to satisfactory inspection of loan records and rental records."

   This is another case of not taking anything at face value. Just because you were verbally promised that every unit in the fourplex was rented out at $450, it does not mean that you will ever see $1,800 in rents. And when the owners assure you that the payments are only $450 a month, don't be surprised to find out that they made a little mistake and that they meant to say $540. With this escape clause, you are free to cancel your offer if you do not approve of the past records—no matter what was said.

3. "Offer subject to purchaser being able to obtain 30-year

permanent (conventional/FHA/VA) financing at an interest rate less than _____ percent, with no more than $_____ being paid by buyer for total origination fees, points, and closing costs."

This is a big one. If you are unable—for any reason—to obtain satisfactory financing (the problem our friend faced), you can back out of the deal with your earnest money in hand.

4. "Seller to provide a complete inspection and written report of all mechanical systems by an appropriate licensed contractor. Inspection to be at the expense of the seller. Offer subject to buyer's approval of the completed written inspections."

With this clause you are forcing the seller to help you appraise the entire house, and if the inspection does not produce a clean bill of health, you are free to walk away without losing dime one.

You can also make each offer subject to having the home inspected by the local county or city building inspector and certified that it is up to code. The fee for this inspection is usually $10 or less. The inspector will go through and warrant that the property meets the city housing codes. If it doesn't, they will note on a rejection card which items need to be brought up to code.

Your offer can state that any deficient items must be brought up to code by the seller before closing. This wording can save you thousands in repairs.

Put In As Little Money As Possible

While it is true that there is more aspirin in the world than headaches, think a minute about the man who failed to include the proper clause in his home purchase. I believe that some headaches—when they get into the $16,000 range—would require an aspirin the size of Mount Everest.

You should understand the function of the earnest money itself. In any legally binding contract, consideration must be given for a promise to be binding on the promisor—the one who makes the promise. This consideration must be of some value, and money will do just fine. It does not, however, have to be $16,000, as was offered by the man in Florida. I try never to give more than $500 as earnest money.

You should not give cash if you can avoid it, and if the seller absolutely insists, do not make a check payable to the seller. Instead make it out to the title officer, real estate attorney, real estate sales company, or closing agent to hold in escrow until closing. Once that money is gone, even if you have to back out of the deal and are covered by a good escape clause, you may have to take the seller to court to recover it. Always make the check payable to the title company that is handling the transaction, or give the seller a promissory note. Not all sellers will accept a promissory note as sufficient earnest money, but most will, so you should at least try.

The closing itself will present you with some costs you need to be aware of when you are analyzing a transaction. Here are a few of the typical expenses that will be involved in a closing:

- **Assumption fees.** Usually about $45, but check with your bank; they can vary greatly.
- **Processing fees.** This is to pay the title officer or attorney for closing the loan.
- **Recording fee.** This is to pay for recording the new deed.
- **Title insurance and abstract examination.** While the seller usually pays for this, there is no firm or fast rule other than making sure it gets done!
- **Appraisal.** You may want to make your purchase offer contingent on having the property's value formally appraised. When you think about it, this is some very inexpensive insurance to guarantee that you are getting a good deal when you first begin.

- **Credit report, loan points, origination fee.** All of these are fees charged by the lending institution when you have to get new financing to buy. They vary widely in every situation, and you must know exactly what you are going to have to pay before you go to closing. Check with your banker about these frightening fees.

Whew! All of this is a lot to think about. It's almost like chewing two wads of gum while drinking a pop, eating a sandwich, playing the piano, and reading a book. But I sure bet you could find a way to do all of those things at the same time if you knew you would make $30,000 for your trouble.

The Value of a Partner

When you are starting out, consider taking on a partner for your first investment. I have had a lot of good experiences with partners. I have also heard a lot of war stories about some of the perils and pitfalls. The best advice I can offer is to get to know your partner well before you get hitched, so to speak. By doing this you can save yourself a lot of grief.

However, there is one partnership I recommend highly. Find an experienced investor, and work out a one-time partnership. You can work together, and with your brawn and the other investor's brains (experience), you can share the work and the profits.

Buying right includes everything you've read so far, and more. You must use the tools for finding a good deal; you must actively seek motivated sellers and yet avoid problem properties; you must structure your offers so you can enjoy positive cash flow and instant equity. Next we'll look at negotiating with the seller and actually making a written offer. That's not really the hard part, but for first-time investors, an attack of sweaty palms at this stage often holds them back from actually making an offer.

Lack of willpower has caused more failure than lack of intelligence or ability.

—Flower A. Newhouse

Chapter 14

Making Money at the Kitchen Table

UNLESS YOU CAN TALK THE OWNER into seeing things your way, you will always end up paying more than you need to. I have learned—usually the hard way—what works best with home-owners who are selling their houses.

First of all, understand that they are not investors. They are doctors, grocery clerks, housewives, househusbands, and every other stripe of citizen imaginable. They will only be involved in two or three such transactions in their lifetimes, and most of them are afraid when it comes time to talk terms. Their fears are based on a lack of knowledge. Why? Because most real estate terms are hard to understand, and few people take the time to study even the basics.

Imagine how many times that fear is multiplied when they are trying to sell the home without the help of a real estate agent, and some know-it-all investor starts talking about "negative amortizations" and "escape clauses."

Try a tactful, helpful approach. I always introduce myself as a family man interested in buying their home as an investment. I don't pull out the HP-12C financial calculator, and I always discuss terms on their level. If it is apparent that they don't understand what I am talking about, I back up and explain myself carefully. A well-structured deal should satisfy all of their needs and mine as well, and I know that I can structure just such a deal in every case.

Ten Basic Negotiating Strategies

Whether you know it or not, you begin the negotiating process the moment you meet the seller. You both automatically size each other up, trying to figure just how much to give and take. In many ways this is the most crucial aspect of buying real estate. If you are to negotiate a good deal with the seller, face to face, it's usually a simple matter of writing up the offer and signing it; after that it's all red tape and formalities. The sale is actually made at the kitchen table, not at the closing.

Here are a few basic negotiating strategies to keep in mind, whether you are buying or selling.

Strategy #1: First Impressions Count

Before you stop by to visit the sellers, take a look at yourself in a full-length mirror. Are you looking at someone you would want to sell your house to? As an investor, you will often want the sellers to take equity on an interest-bearing note. Do you look like a good credit risk? Their impression of you when they first open the door will often make the difference between a sale and another disappointment. In real estate, you want to look clean, pressed, honest, wholesome, and not extreme in any way. You do not need to put on a three-piece suit, but you should wear nice, clean clothing that reflects the lifestyle of someone who takes care of his property and possessions.

Strategy #2: Establish Rapport

Your first task once inside the door is to make the sellers feel at home—which is exactly where they are. Find common ground. Talk about your interests, or show an interest in something of theirs, such as a picture on the wall or a piano in the living room. Forget about the house and the price for a minute, and get to know the owners.

Strategy #3: Talk Price Last

Don't jump into a discussion of price and terms just yet. As you walk around the house, talk about features and faults, but leave the price tag out of the picture. Talk about dollars after your cursory inspection is finished, and then get the seller to name a price.

Strategy #4: Never Give Unless You Get

Start with the assumption that you will get everything in the house, from the Tupperware to the wedding albums, and work from there. I'm being a little facetious, but if you start there, then every time the owner takes something away from you—as in, "No, our three adorable children are not included in the deal"—you can expect a concession in return. If they want to keep the refrigerator, say, "Fine, but I assumed that was included. Of course that will be reflected in the price."

Strategy #5: If They Say Yes, Keep Working On It

Both parties to a negotiation establish negotiating ranges. If they accept your first offer instantly, you obviously were near the top end of their range, and you can always ask for more. For example, if they accept your first offer of $50,000 (and they were asking $56,000), continue your offer with, "Of course, that includes the cars out front and your firstborn." Now you're more likely to find yourself somewhere closer to the bottom of their range, and the real negotiating can begin.

Strategy #6: Ask Open-Ended Questions

I always lead the conversation with open-ended questions. For example, when a clerk in the drugstore approaches and asks, "Can I help you?" you are perfectly free to say, "No, thanks." If on the other hand the clerk asks, "How can I help you?" your "No, thanks" isn't a workable answer. The second question is almost the same as the first, but it doesn't allow a simple yes-or-no answer. Start your questions with "how" and "why," and avoid questions that can be answered with a simple "yes" or "no."

Strategy #7: Ask for Agreement Often

The second trick of guiding a conversation is to ask questions that begin with a statement and end with a request for agreement. An example is, "This bathroom does need a lot of fixing up, doesn't it?" The question only allows two responses: agreement ("Well, yes, I guess it does") or defensive disagreement ("No, not too much work"). In either case, you are directing the flow of the conversation. Comment on every room in the house. Not all of your comments should be derogatory; if you like something, say so, but if there is something that you dislike, attach a "Don't you agree?" question to your comments.

Strategy #8: Establish Your Negotiating Range Before You Talk Price

You will often know the asking price before you actually sit down and make an offer, and you will be expected to have a specific dollar amount in mind by the time your tour is finished. If you know the sellers are asking $60,000, how much should you offer? And how high will you actually go? That's the basis for your negotiating range.

If you've been doing your homework, you shouldn't have too much trouble estimating a fair market value for the home. As an investor, you should not be willing to pay that price, unless a minimum fix-up investment will substantially raise the value of the home.

In the example above, where the owners are asking $60,000, you have determined that the real value of the home is between $56,000 and $58,000: that's what you could resell it for. Now you must decide how much to offer, and how much you are actually willing to pay. There is no set rule for determining your range, but in this case, you might decide that you will offer $52,000 and pay no more than $55,000. If the sellers are unmotivated, your offer will likely be rejected out of hand. If they really want to sell, however, they will probably reject it but show an interest in continuing the negotiation.

Another important factor in setting a range is that by offering less than you actually expect to pay, you are inviting the sellers to negotiate, and they will have the opportunity to save face when you begrudgingly give ground and raise your offer. Many new investors, in an effort to make a fair offer, start the bidding at the top of their negotiating range. Then they're surprised when the sellers don't accept the first offer. They have no more room to give, and they lose the deal.

Strategy #9: Be Willing to Negotiate

An offer made with a "take it or leave it" attitude—especially an offer at the bottom of your negotiating range—will often be left, and the sellers will shut you out mentally. If that happens, you might as well take a walk, because you will have lost the rapport you established at the beginning. Always make it clear to the owners that you are willing to negotiate.

Strategy #10: Don't Talk Price and Terms Until You Are at the Table

As they say, there's a time and a place for everything. While you're walking around the house, that's the time for looking at the features, such as the peeling paint on the outside trim or the broken railing on the stairs. Look at each room carefully, without allowing yourself to be sidetracked by a discussion of price and terms. Wait until you are sitting down with a legal pad, a pen, and a calculator. That's the time and place for money talk.

Talking Terms

We all come to that dreadful moment of truth when we must sit down with the seller at the kitchen table and come to terms. And here is where we seem to have the most difficulty. It really shouldn't be that much trouble.

Sit down with the seller and talk to him or her, face to face, in plain English. Discuss what you like and dislike. If you seem to be faced with an impasse on one subject, such as the price, put off further discussion for later, and agree on some of the minor points.

Avoid the confusion of legalese. Talk about monthly payments, the assumption of the existing loans, and the price as though you were haggling over the price of a toaster at a garage sale. Keep in mind that your best bet is to assume the existing loans (if they are assumable) and give the seller a contract for his equity. As you discuss a contract, remember that the payments are a function of price and interest. You can offer a higher price if they will lower the interest rate and your payments will stay the same. This will affect their tax consequences, but in a positive way, since more of their profit will be in the form of long-term capital gains and less in the form of interest income. (Check with a real estate attorney or a CPA about current tax laws.)

If you don't know how to figure out what your payments will be, buy and learn to use a financial calculator. They can be found for under $30, and they are absolutely indispensable. I use Hewlett-Packard's HP-12C and recommend it highly. It can tell me almost instantly what my monthly payment will be on any kind of loan I can imagine.

As you talk to the seller, write everything down. Take a legal pad with you, and every time either of you makes a suggestion, write it down. As you come to agreement on this point or that, circle it and initial it. Then, when you have agreed on every point, write up your offer on an earnest money and purchase offer form, available in any stationery and office supply store.

If you don't know how to fill out the offer properly, have an expert help you. Your title officer, real estate attorney, or an experienced investor can help you translate the terms you have agreed on into legal mumbo-jumbo.

Once you have come to terms with the seller and your written offer has been accepted, you are pretty much done. Your title officer will explain how to close the deal, and all you have to do is show up at the closing, pay the closing costs and down payment, and sign a few papers. That's it—you now own your first investment property!

We must walk consciously only partway toward our goal, then leap in the dark to our success.

—Henry David Thoreau

Chapter 15

Preparing to Sell or Rent

HAVE YOU EVER SEEN A CAR after it has been detailed by a car dealer? Talk about miracles. A friend of mine traded in his old junker for a new car recently. If all the old, beaten-up cars in the world were laid end to end, his old car would still stand out like a sore thumb. Later that week I drove by the lot where he had traded it in, and I saw a car that resembled his clunker—but this car couldn't be the same one; I didn't think anyone could resurrect my friend's dinosaur. Curious, I stopped for a closer look.

There was just enough resemblance to convince me that this was the same car my friend had turned in only a week before. The tires were that glossy black that tires only are for the first fifty miles or so, the chrome shone like new, the stains in the upholstery left by uncounted spilled Big Gulps were gone, and the carpet had been ripped out and replaced.

By this time, the dealer's C.A.R.S. (Customer Approach Radar System) had alerted him to my presence, and he was on his way out to sell me one of his beauties. I asked what had happened to the bomb that had existed only a week before. He laughed and explained "detailing." It was my turn to laugh; that's exactly what I had been doing to my investment properties for decades.

How Much Should You Invest in Fixing Up?

When you are preparing to sell a property, what is your first consideration? It should be the buyers you will be looking for. What can you do to convince them they should pay top dollar for the property? And what is top dollar? How much fixing up is enough, without being too much?

There is an idea so universal and true that economists have even given it a name: the law of diminishing returns. According to this law, each dollar invested in production will produce a greater return than the previous dollar, up to a certain point. At some point, the return is the same as the investment, and thereafter it is less than the investment.

The law can be applied to almost anything. If you buy one Popsicle and eat it, your enjoyment will be greater than the price invested in the Popsicle, or you wouldn't have bought it. That might hold true for the second and third Popsicle as well, but at some point your enjoyment—the return on your investment— would not exceed the cost, and you would quit eating.

Here are some of the levels of investment that you might put into any property that you were preparing to sell. They will give you an idea of where the line is that indicates you have crossed over from an investment you will get back to money you are throwing away.

1. A small investment would mean cleaning up the yard by mowing it, trimming the plants, edging the grass, and pulling the weeds. It would also include going through the home or rental unit and taking care of minor cleaning. Things to include on this list would be to clean or have the carpets cleaned, wash the windows, wash down the

walls, clean the bathroom and kitchen and all appliances.

2. A moderate investment would mean doing the basic items plus painting some walls, replacing some cracked windows, exchanging the burner trays on the stove, and doing some minor home repairs, such as fixing the doorbell.

3. An extensive investment would mean fixing the home up so that it looks like new. New carpet, new cabinets, a new furnace, water heater, and complete landscaping and sprinklers. You now may have to move in, because no one will be able to afford to buy your property.

Essentially anything that you do to a property up to the level of a moderate investment would give you a return that is greater than the investment. And typically, with anything that falls into the "extensive" investment area, the return is less than the investment. Too many investors jump zealously into fixing up a property, pouring dollar after dollar into points beyond moderate. I never invest a penny beyond moderate, and I usually stop before that point.

Remember that if you put $10,000 down on a property and have $7,000 tied up in closing costs and fix-up expenses, you will have to charge at least $17,000 when you sell it to return your original sunken investment. Every time you buy and sell a property, you have to at least get your original investment returned; otherwise, your investment capital keeps going down and down until you are no longer an investor. Ask yourself this question: "How many $3,000 checks do I have lying around the house?"

Hidden Treasures

One of the best investments you can make—especially as a beginning investor—is in "fixer-uppers," those run-down houses you wouldn't consider living in. I consider these homes to be hidden treasures. With a little bit of polishing, you can reap great rewards. You should also note that single-family homes are very easy not only to buy, but also to rent. In one of our areas right now, we are exclusively buying just single-family homes. The rents being paid through several government-assisted housing programs are so high that it is almost insane. (Later, we will talk about the importance of developing a portfolio of at least ten single-family homes that you need to pay off in full before you hit your target retirement age.) Single-family homes also are very easy to rent. Almost anybody would rather live in a home than in an apartment. And single family homes are fifty times easier to sell should there come a crunch than multifamily apartment buildings.

The rewards are a result of homebuyer mentality. When people are looking for a place to live, they want a home, not a run-down, secondhand house. They may be fully aware of how little work is really needed, but that's beside the point; they are looking for a place to live.

Most of the houses we see today that we are buying for pennies on the dollar could be easily sold if someone would take the time to mow the lawn and slap a coat of paint on them. That someone is usually one of our students—a smart, trained real estate investor who is not afraid of a little work. Smart because they looked beyond the overgrown lawn and peeled paint; rich because they bought it at a bargain price, fixed it up for a couple of thousand dollars, and sold it at a $35,000 profit.

Fixing Up Can Be Fun

We look into such properties all the time. Recently a seller called me and left a message. The long-distance telephone number clued me in to the fact that I might be dealing with a motivated seller, so I called back right away. The woman who answered said that she and her husband had rented out their three-bedroom house for a few months after they were transferred, but the tenants had been hard on the house, and it was simply too difficult for them to manage so many miles away. The house had been appraised at $52,000 (an FHA appraisal) only three years before, and she would consider selling for $50,000 with nothing down: they didn't need any cash at all.

Picking up the key from the neighbor, I took a look inside. She had underestimated the destructive powers of a tenant. The place looked worse than a teenager's bedroom. There were holes in the wall the size of a fist, and in the carpet were globs of gunk the color and texture of overcooked oatmeal. Nobody looking for a place to live would even consider buying this mess. But I could see that with a little of my money and somebody else's work I could easily do enough detailing to turn this clunker into a beautiful home. The carpet could be cleaned, the lawn could be mowed and watered, and the holes in the walls could be easily patched and painted over.

The total fix-up costs would be under $1,000, and I knew I could make $15,000 or more in profit.

Whenever I buy a property, I know exactly how much fixing up I will do, and I know exactly how long it will take and how much it will cost. In this chapter I'll give you some specific tips on exactly how to make these judgments.

Very rarely we will buy a house with the sole intention of renting it out for more than two or three years while the market absorbs; the real money is made in selling after the rents jump up high enough to justify new construction. I do keep the occasional single-family home that offers positive cash flow and tax write-offs, but in today's absorption markets those are the exceptions to the rule. If you are working expansionary, or equilibrium, or decline markets, then you are going to have to forget about appreciation and instead focus on looking for the instant-equity properties that can be bought wholesale and sold quickly for a profit.

I enjoy working on renovating homes. It's a great family project. My wife, Paula, started doing this with her family when she was nine years old. You just have to remember that when painting the trim on a home you are getting paid as a painter, and when you are out investing you are getting paid as an investor. Keeping that old law of diminishing returns in mind, I estimate the cost and return of alternatives, and then we get to work.

What to Fix Up

The condition of some aspects of a house will affect a buyer's opinion more than others. When you are evaluating a house you intend to fix up and polish, consider everything, and then put your efforts into the places where you will get the most added value for the least time and money.

The Exterior

The first place to concentrate your efforts is in the front yard. If the house isn't selling because of its poor "curb appeal" (how it looks as a prospective buyer drives up), you must start there. When judging curb appeal, pay particular attention to the following:

1. **Yard condition.** If Tarzan would be comfortable in the front yard, few homebuyers will be. Start with the lawn—does it need water, or a mower, or both? If it needs a good cutting, rent a mower, and put it to good use. I always rent, and I always pay extra for the insurance waiver; no sense in chewing up old dog bones with my own mower. Second, pull the weeds and trim the shrubs. Third, if the front looks really lifeless, buy a few instant flowers (bedding plants); they will return a hundred times their cost.

   The yard doesn't have to be manicured down to the last blade of grass, but the front should be attractive, not repulsive, if you want to sell to Mr. and Mrs. Homebuyer.

2. **Paint and trim.** Look closely at the exterior paint and

trim. If it is peeling and chipped here and there, you can usually scrape it down and touch it up with matching paint. One or two gallons should be enough for a nice detail job. If the entire house needs to repainted, then beware; an average two-bedroom house will cost a lot more to paint than you think, and the law of diminishing returns begins to set in.

I suggest that you go out and buy your paint in five-gallon cans. You should choose one basic trim, exterior, and wall color. By buying paint in the large cans and staying with the same colors, you will save a lot of money in the long run. You will never get to that point of having a dozen half-filled cans of paint around your home.

3. **The roof.** Take a close look at the roof from the outside, and look at the ceilings carefully on the inside. It's surprising how many homebuyers notice the condition of the roof, and if there is a leak, you will have to fix it before selling. It's also surprising how much a little roof repair will cost, so beware here as well.

The Interior

Let's walk inside and take a look at a few simple, inexpensive repairs. Replacing the entire carpet is rarely feasible, but there are a few things to look for:

1. **Holes in the wall.** Toothpaste (the regular white kind) can be used to fill in the little nail holes. Just put a dab on your finger and wipe it over the hole, then clean the excess off with a wet rag. The bigger holes may need some plaster or other repairs.

2. **Dirty walls.** Many homeowners, especially those in a "must sell" situation, will walk away from minor cleanup jobs. They are sick and tired of the house, or time is

pressing and they can't take the time to scrub the walls. Few of them realize that it is the splotches of peanut butter on the kitchen wall that are preventing the sale of their homes.

If paint is needed, match the paint and touch up the worst parts. You don't have to repaint every wall in the house, and if a touch-up will do the trick, why invest beyond the point of diminishing return?

3. **The bathroom.** This is one of two rooms that will be the deciding factor in a sale. I'm not crazy about scrubbing a toilet bowl any more than the next person, but the slightest stain in the toilet, bathtub, or sink will scare off most homebuyers. Remember, they are considering the purchase of a home, not an investment property.

4. **The kitchen.** This is the other room. Extensive studies done by real estate sale researchers indicate that it is the wife who ultimately makes the buying decision. This fact may be losing credibility every year, as we move away from traditional sex roles, but for now it is still the norm. For hundreds of thousands of homebuyers, the home will be the domain primarily of the wife and mother.

As a result, you as an investor must pay special attention to the one room that will sell the house for you—the kitchen. A dark, forbidding kitchen with peeling linoleum and burnt Formica will never sell. Here is where you can afford to invest a little money and expect big returns.

If you are just starting out with small homes in your back yard, most likely you will be selling the property yourself. There are a few tricks of the trade that every Realtor knows, and one of the best is to bake a loaf of bread in the oven just before showing the house. That smell will linger for hours, and the pleasant feelings evoked by the aroma of fresh bread will do more for the sale than all the sales talk in the world. And, of course, you get to eat the bread afterward.

Here's another little trick for those who can't bake bread: In a small saucepan, boil about a cup of water with cloves and cinnamon sticks in it. By the time the water boils away, the entire house is filled with a clean sweet-spicy smell.

Make sure the kitchen is well lit. Replace any bulbs that have burned out, and use 75- or 100-watt bulbs wherever it is safe. That rule holds true for every room in the house. A dollar invested in a couple of light bulbs may increase the sales price and decrease the selling time substantially.

Here's another hint for the lighting fixtures: Take down all of the glass covers on the ceiling lights, and wash away the accumulated dirt in warm soapy water. Rinse and dry the covers and replace them. Five minutes' work will do wonders for the overall appearance.

5. **The carpets.** Clean the carpets and sanitize them. A carpet will hold a lot of odors that detract from the sale or rental of a home. Few people will pay top dollar for a house filled with the odor of Fido and Fifi and Mr. Cigarette. The price you pay to have a thorough carpet cleaning done is well worth the cost.

Getting the Work Done

You know how much fixing up is needed, and you know how much you will spend for materials. Now you have to face a tough decision: Who will do the work? You really only have three choices: You can do the work yourself, hire cheap, or hire experts. A word or two on each is in order here.

My first suggestion is to do as much as possible yourself when you first start investing. I, for one, enjoy working with my family—scrubbing, painting, mowing, and so on. Recently my wife and children helped me fix up a condominium we had purchased. We had fun pitching in, putting our shoulders to the wheel and working together. I think the lessons my children learn about the value of work are invaluable, and my wife appreciates the profits all the more for her efforts.

The day will come when you just don't have the time to do the work yourself—I know, you can't wait for that day—but when you are starting your career, your labor will be well rewarded. I think the greatest advantage is in learning exactly how much time and effort is required to do a good job. You will have to judge someone else's work at some future date, and wielding a paintbrush all day Saturday should give you a little perspective.

When you have done enough of the work yourself, or when the task requires an expert (like a roofer or a carpenter) you will have to decide whether to use a high-priced, experienced person or an "inexpensive" teenage helper. Be careful there. A high school student is great for mowing and weeding, but when it comes to more skilled labor, such as painting the trim, the expert is usually the best deal.

You no doubt saw the ad for the dishwashing liquid that cost a few pennies more. Then, on hidden camera, Mrs. Housewife was shocked to find out that the bargain brand could only wash a fraction of the dishes that the name brand could when compared penny for penny. The same holds true when it comes time to have the roof repaired or the trim painted. I mention the trim twice for a reason: I learned my own lesson on a trim paint job. I hired a young man to paint the exterior of a house I wanted to sell. His prices were very reasonable, and he assured me that he could do a good job. (I was a little naïve at the time.)

During the next week, as he slopped paint here and there (occasionally getting some on the trim itself), the owners of the house next door hired professional painters to do a similar job. By the end of the week, when the pros had packed up and left, and the house next door looked like new, my own painter had managed to mess up three sides of my house and was ready to tackle the fourth.

During the next three weeks I ended up going over there dozens of times to teach my "painter" how to paint. I could have done it myself in half the time. When the job was finally done to my satisfaction I felt like I was the one who should have been paid. Live and learn!

Believe me, I've weighed the pros and cons, and when it comes to value for your labor dollars, one pro weighs at least three times as much as a con. Don't get conned into paying twice as much for half the work.

A Selling Checklist

Whenever I think about fixing up a property to sell it, I run through a checklist that helps me see it through the eyes of the buyers. First, before you put a property up for sale, drive up to it and do a little role-playing. Imagine in your mind that you are a buyer and are considering purchasing the property yourself as a home. Try to see your home or property as your prospective buyers might. Here's a checklist for you to use in considering what repairs to make on your real estate investments:

Seller's Checklist to Maximize Sales Price

OUTSIDE

Yard
- Look at lawn, curb, and shrubbery.
  To maximize your sales price:
  - ❏ Mow lawn; fertilize and reseed if necessary.
  - ❏ Weed and hoe flower beds.
  - ❏ Trim hedges and prune trees.

Exterior walls
- Look at masonry walls for cracks, and siding and exterior surfaces for weathered paint.
  To maximize your sales price:
  - ❏ Nail and caulk loose siding.
  - ❏ Paint siding and trim (especially in the front).

Roofs and gutters

- Look at the condition of shingles. Inspect flashings around roof stacks, vents, and chimneys.

  To maximize your sales price:
  - ☐ Clean gutters and downspouts.
  - ☐ Repair or replace loose or damaged shingles.
  - ☐ Repair any loose mortar or bricks on chimney.

Driveway

- Look at the condition of the asphalt or concrete.

  To maximize your sales price:
  - ☐ Repair the driveway surface. (Most asphalt driveways can be easily repaired and improved with an inexpensive new blacktop finish.)

Foundation

- Look at walls, retaining walls, walks, and patios for cracking, disintegration, or buckling.

  To maximize your sales price:
  - ☐ Replaster foundation wall. Repair any major cracks.

Garage

- Look at the condition of the exterior paint. Test electrical circuits.

  To maximize your sales price:
  - ☐ Lubricate garage door hinges and hardware.

Windows and doors

- Look at windows; check for smooth operation. Check the fit of the doors. Test doorbell, chimes.

  To maximize your sales price:
  - ☐ Replace broken or cracked panes.
  - ☐ Repair glazing.
  - ☐ Wash the windows.

INSIDE

Floors
- Check floors for squeaky boards.
- Check for loose or missing tiles and for worn linoleum.
  To maximize your sales price:
  - ☐ Nail down any loose floorboards or stair treads.
  - ☐ Glue down any loose tiles.

Bathrooms
- Look at the operation of toilet and plumbing fixtures. Check condition of painted or papered walls.
  To maximize your sales price:
  - ☐ Remove mildew.
  - ☐ Put a "blue" toilet bowl freshener in your water tank.
  - ☐ Repair dripping plumbing fixtures.

Kitchen
- Look at walls, appliances, faucets, cabinet structure.
  To maximize your sales price:
  - ☐ Repair any major damage to paint or wallpaper, clean all appliances.

Basement
- Check pipes for leaks. Inspect supporting beams. Check for signs of cracked or crumbling walls.
  To maximize your sales price:
  - ☐ Remove clutter.
  - ☐ Organize basement storage into neatly stacked boxes.

Electrical system
- Look at and test each plug and light switch. Inspect all exposed wiring for proper insulation.
  To maximize your sales price:
  - ☐ Label each circuit in the breaker box.
  - ☐ Repair any loose or broken switches and cover plates.

Plumbing system

- Look at system for any leaks. Turn each faucet rapidly on and off to detect any loose, banging pipes. Check each drain to make sure it isn't clogged or slow.

  To maximize your sales price:
  - ❐ Clear any clogged drains.
  - ❐ Repair any leaky sinks.

Heating and cooling system

- Look at system, turning on and checking for proper operation. Check filters.

  To maximize your sales price:
  - ❐ Change or clean filters if necessary.
  - ❐ Clean area around equipment.

Not everything on the list will need to be repaired, but a thorough review will aid you in selling your house for the best possible price. Make a copy of this checklist, and show it to your prospective buyers. Not only will they be impressed with your diligence, but you will eliminate most of their possible reasons for not buying your property.

Success is not a doorway, it's a staircase.

—Dottie Walters

Chapter 16

Property Management 101

IF I HAD MY WISH, this would be one of the shortest chapters in the history of real estate investment books. If you seriously want to make money in real estate, here's a good rule to follow: Never manage any of your rental properties yourself. Never! Since 1986, I have lived the belief that you should be able to live where you want to live, but invest only in the markets where it makes sense.

Finding a Property Manager

You might ask me, "How can one of your students who lives in San Jose, California, take care of his properties out-of-state in one of your target markets?" The answer is rather simple. You find the best professionally licensed and insured property manager in that town for your type of income property, and you hire that person to professionally manage all of your rental properties in that town.

Since 1986, we have worked eighteen different towns outside of our back yard. As part of our due diligence in getting a market ready for a BuyingTour, we literally contact every single real estate agent that works in residential income properties (always remembering to use a buyer's broker). We then ask these professionals for their very best referrals to the investing team that we are going to need to successful invest in real estate in that town. We find the best title companies, the best rehab specialists, the best real estate attorney, the best property inspector, the best maintenance man, the best painter, the best landscapers, and, yes, the very best property managers.

We then contact every single one of these referrals and get to know them. In choosing a property manager, you absolutely need to find one who will gladly let you talk with several of their current clients.

Let Your Property Manager Do the Work

Property management is really a weird science. Before you buy any rental property anywhere, you need to schedule a time for your potential property manager to give you a prepurchase inspection. You want to find out what specifically they can do for you and for your potential property. In exchange for a percentage of rent (typically 5 to 7 percent) your property manager will screen your potential tenants, perform credit checks on your potential tenants, collect your rents, baby-sit your property, and keep you posted on any problems or maintenance issues with your property.

When you are managing your own properties, you are getting paid the wages of a handyman. When you focus on investing in real estate, your time should instead be spent on research, finding the best deals, negotiating new deals, and timing the acquisition and sale of your real estate assets.

A good story to illustrate the need for professional management is the story of one of our students who came to the United States as an immigrant from Thailand. This woman (the mother of five sons) went on a BuyingTour with us to Salt Lake City back in the late 1980s or early 1990s. We told her where to buy and when to buy property in the Salt Lake City area. She put down all that she could scrape together ($7,000) and bought one small house. Before she bought the house, she had a local Utah property management firm do a prepurchase inspection on that single-family dwelling with her. The property management told her what she could expect to get in rent per month and exactly what they would charge her to keep that property filled with good tenants. (Remember that this is a science, not an art.) That property management firm practiced "fair but firm" property management on behalf of our student for a little over two years. Correctly, she had included the cost of professional property management into her decision to buy or not to buy.

For the next two years, this good woman had a property that was never empty and that was filled with tenants who didn't rebuild their motorcycle's engines on her living room carpet. Each month during her ownership, she got a property management report and a check. After two years we told our student that it was time to sell in Salt Lake City, so she did. After she took all her expenses out of the sale and repaid herself back her $7,000 down payment (plus opportunity cost interest), she walked away with a net of $40,000 in pure real estate investing profit.

This woman then, with our help, tax-free exchanged (a 1031 IRS property exchange) her $40,000 equity into our next market: Denver, Colorado. She didn't have to pay any tax on the money she made off her first real estate deal. This great woman owned several income properties that were bought with her Salt Lake City profit—all professionally managed, and all with a positive cash flow—and she walked out of Denver about three years later with over a quarter of a million dollars.

This woman didn't have to screen tenants. She didn't have to do credit checks. She didn't have to "show" her property. She knew up front what professional management was going to cost, and she negotiated deals (that included professional property management) and had nothing but a positive cash flow from day one. Today that wonderful woman from northern California owns properties in three different states. Her net equity is now $1.8 million. She has an $11,000-per-month positive cash flow. She is an investor in real estate and not a painter, lawn mower, carpet cleaner, or a slumlord.

Putting Together Your Team

Whenever we open up a new absorption market (recovery market) for a BuyingTour, we spend about ninety days putting together the very best real estate investing team that exists. Since 1986 we have personally introduced more than 2,500 investors just like yourself to a completely researched, professional team of the very best assets that you can have in our target market areas. We hear all the time things like "We could never have put this team together by ourselves, even after working full-time in this market for a year." But the truth is that if we can do it for our BuyingTour students, you can do it yourself. The golden key is referrals from your buyer's broker real estate agent who specializes in income properties. What turns the key and opens the lock for you is completing your own personal due diligence and talking with each and every potential real estate investment team member in your target market area.

Property Management Basics

For those of you who are brand-new at investing and who want to learn the basics of real estate hands-on, you really should do at least one deal in your back yard first before going out of town into one of our absorption markets. For those of you who are absolute beginners let me give the following advice for your first and only (hopefully) property management experience.

You've got the place fixed up; now what? Well, of course, you want to sell—at a handsome profit—as soon as possible, and we'll talk about the tricks of advertising and selling in more depth presently. But for now, let's admit a nasty fact: for a while, at least once, you might want to experience property management first-hand. And that means asking for trouble—a renter. Oh, I'm not that strongly set against renters. After all, didn't we all rent at one time? But I haven't met an investor yet who didn't have at least a few horror stories to tell about those renters who really went out of their way to destroy a house or apartment.

I've had my own share of experiences. I've made mistakes. I've been swindled, been driven nuts, and I've made a few good friends. To make your own landlording as painless as possible, I've come up with a list of suggestions culled from experts across the country—as well as a few tricks I've come up with myself to handle this necessary evil.

There are three main things to worry about with tenants. Take care of all three, and you may even enjoy the experience. The first is making sure you select the best possible tenants; the second is knowing what could go wrong and preventing it before it does; and the third is getting the tenants to take care of the property themselves.

Selecting Tenants

There are a few things to look for when shopping for good tenants. (Yes, you must do a little comparison-shopping—there are a million different species of renters.) The following factors will help you in your search:

1. **Occupancy period.** You should attempt to find tenants who want to rent as long as you own the property. This not only adds value to your property, but it also makes your job a lot easier. If you get a last month's rental deposit and security deposit, these long-term tenants can be worth their weight in gold. I met a lady who had lived in an apartment for eighteen years. Wasn't she a great tenant? Think how many "For Rent" signs never had to be sold to the owner of that property.

2. **Compatibility.** A close friend is ready to throw in his landlording towel. He is no longer in control of one complex he owns; he's a referee. And the problem could have been so easily avoided by choosing tenants who were compatible.

A warning is due here: Be very careful when you reject a prospective tenant. More than one landlord has been a forced lesson in discrimination law. Such laws vary from state to state, so you should check with a local attorney or apartment owners association for applicable laws.

Despite legal restrictions, you do have quite a bit of latitude in rejecting tenants, so be careful about tenant compatibility. Renting one-half of a duplex to a family with small children and the other to a motorcycle gang is not an example of perfect compatibility.

3. **Housekeeping ability.** If you have renters moving from a nearby area, try this: Have them fill out a rental application, and promise to get back to them soon. Then drop in at their current home to talk to them. Take a look at what your own property will look like in a few weeks with them as tenants. The effort spent performing this little private-eye routine may save you hundreds of dollars and thousands of headaches.

Use the same tactic when screening homebuyers. Stop by and talk to them about their offer. If you don't like what you see, think twice before accepting them as buyers; if they default someday, you will be the inheritor of their domicile—and their problems.

4. **Credit rating and employment history.** This is common knowledge, and every landlord should have enough sense to at least verify the creditworthiness of a prospective tenant. And yet I hear time and time again, "But she (or he) looked so honest . . . " Every rental application will have a place for credit rating and employment information, as well as permission for you to investigate the

validity of all claims. Make the calls and do the necessary checking before making a final decision. Don't forget to call previous landlords. Call the landlord before the current; if they are lousy tenants, the current one may claim that they are excellent, just to get rid of them.

Avoiding Problems

Problems with tenants are like summer colds. They aren't fatal, but they are extremely irritating, and they are inevitable. Sooner or later you'll have one. There is one all-important preventive medicine, which will stop about 99 percent of the problems before they exist, and there are some measures that can be taken to solve the problems that do occasionally crop up.

First and foremost: Do not rely on the tenants to read the contract. Rental contracts are weighted to the advantage of the owner (as far as the law allows), but don't take too much comfort in that fact. Far too many landlords have relied upon their contracts, only to find them unenforceable or worthless. How can you sue someone for $5,000 who doesn't have $50 to his or her name?

Time for a quiz, to wake up those in the back row. Quick, now: How many contracts have you read from beginning to end? And how many of them have you understood completely? Add those two numbers and multiply it by your age. If the product is greater than zero, go to the head of the class. I'm not sure that even lawyers fully understand the meaning of every contract. I think there must be professional contract writers holed up in dark little attics, whose only pleasure in life is making up words like heretointhereinafterthereforeasabovementionedbelow. Never assume that tenants will read the contract, and never, ever assume that they will understand the contract.

Explain the terms of the contract, and have them agree verbally with you on every point. On the real biggies, such as remodeling and late charges, have them explain the terms in their own words so there is no misunderstanding. This whole process may seem like too much trouble, but think of the satisfaction you'll have when your tenants don't tear out a wall to install a 500-gallon fish tank.

The following are the rules of the game that are most often broken by tenants, and they should be guarded especially well:

1. **Tenant remodeling.** Called "creative interior decorating" by some of the most imaginative of tenants, this can range from simple epithets spray-painted on the walls to the super-sized fish tank cited above. Explain carefully and clearly before renting that any changes made in the apartment must be approved by you, in writing.

2. **Apartment maintenance.** You must establish minimum standards of upkeep, and you must expect those standards to be maintained at all times. Of course, your minimum standards should not be on the order of an operating room, but neither should small funguses be allowed to thrive in the living room carpet. Again, spell out the conditions clearly in advance, and make sure the tenants understand you right to enter and inspect the premises or show it to prospective buyers.

3. **Late rents and nonpayment of rents.** I have a hard time with this one, because I really am too softhearted. The only way to avoid this problem is to lay down the law and then enforce it. If your tenants are allowed to be "just a few days late, just this one time," I guarantee it won't be the last time it happens. They may not intentionally delay paying, but once you have shown them that you are willing to forgive and forget, somehow the rent doesn't have the same priority it used to.

    This is a business, and you are a businessperson. You must enforce late payment penalties.

    The second problem—nonpayment of rent—must be

190

dealt with swiftly and surely. Eviction proceedings usually take weeks, and you cannot afford to delay a necessary eviction. It's true: You are throwing people out of their only house and home, and it may be no fault of theirs that they can't pay the rent. But your only alternative is to subsidize them for who knows how long, so what choice do you have?

The best way to prevent this from becoming an even bigger problem, involving a lawsuit, is to ensure that you get a last month's rent and a hefty security deposit before renting an apartment or house. Then if the tenant can't afford to pay, at least you will not lose the last month's rent. Find out all of the laws regarding security deposits and eviction of tenants; they vary widely from state to state.

Nick Koon, a real estate investor and a good friend, always includes in the rental agreement a provision whereby he can charge the rent to his tenant's MasterCard or Visa in the case of default. As long as the account is good for that amount, he can use the account number to ensure payment.

4. **Bounced checks.** If you've never bounced a check, you're in a class of people as rare as honest politicians. Most bounced checks are the result of an honest mistake—a number transposed in the checkbook, or a deposited check bouncing. But here again, you must not allow a tenant's problems to become your own.

   Insist in the rental agreement—and discuss this verbally as well—that there be a charge of at least $30 on returned checks. That may be steep compared with the grocery store, but the store can afford to sustain a lot more bounced checks at $30 or $40 apiece. You cannot afford to have too many $400 or $500 checks returned; you need that money to run your business.

   Occasionally you may have a tenant move out, paying

the last month's rent with a bad check. The best way to prevent a problem there is to not release the last month's deposit (that you collected when the tenant moved in) until the rent check clears.

I recently heard of an ingenious solution to a prickly problem. A tenant paid his last month's rent with a bad check. By the time it was returned to the landlord, the tenant had skipped town. The investor was left holding a worthless $600 check, and the bank refused to clear it.

Going into the ex-tenant's bank, the landlord asked the teller to find out for him exactly how much the tenant would have to deposit to make the check good. It turned out that the account contained $575—just $25 short. So the investor made a deposit to the man's account of $26 cash and then cashed the $600 check. When the tenant found out he was enraged. He called the investor to chew him out, and he was politely informed that he could repay the $26 loan at his convenience.

5. **Utility payments.** If you haven't enjoyed a good ulcer for years, here's a recipe. Take two or three tenants and pour into rental units. Add utilities as needed, and make sure they are in your name. When bills are prepared and ready to be served, try to get tenants to pay. Watch them cook up excuses and complaints. Tempers will heat up quickly and juices should begin to flow. Toss in a few choice words and voilà! Guaranteed to get you burned every time.

If, on the other hand, you would like to avoid one of the worst problems in landlording, always have the utilities turned on in the name of the tenants only (except water and sewer services) and stay out of the picture entirely.

In addition to the above suggestions, I recommend that these general rules and conditions be added to your resident rental agreements. Each may save you everything from minor headaches to major lawsuits:

- No pets.
- No waterbeds.
- Children are not allowed to play in the common hallways of building.
- Tenants must park in their assigned parking spaces.
- Tenants will refrain from playing loud televisions, radios, stereos, or in any other way disturbing the peace of the other tenants between 10 P.M. and 8 A.M.
- All rent must be paid on or before the fifth of every month, to the landlord in person.

Getting the Tenants to Take Care of the Property

I am proud of this last section. It has taken years of experience for me to develop what I think is a foolproof system of managing rental properties. By implementing everything mentioned above, I have been able to avoid most of the hassles of managing, but there is still one bug in the system. Nobody likes to take care of the yard, or the trash, or the snow shoveling. That's the job for the landlord.

So I created a goose that has been laying golden eggs ever since. We decided years ago that whenever we run an ad in the "Apartments for Rent" section of the paper, we would include the phrase "discount rent for management responsibilities." To every caller (and the phone rings constantly), we explain that if the tenants pay before the fifth of every month, and if they don't call me unless the place is burning down, and if they maintain the property—yard, carpet and wall cleaning, minor repairs up to $25, and so on—then I will rebate a portion of the previous month's rent. The rebate is contingent upon an on-site inspection at least once a month (usually on the fifteenth). It is a check for up to $25 that is made out to the lady of the household (or to whichever tenant takes care of the house) and personally delivered to her on the mid-month inspection date. (Do you think she might make sure the rent gets in on time and the place stays clean? It sure works like dynamite.)

This concept of rewarding people for good behavior has never failed, and the small fraction of the total rent that I give up to have the tenant take care of the property more than pays for itself. When I reward people instead of punishing them, I find they react positively. Their rent is in on time, and the places are kept up. Also, by advertising "discount for management responsibilities," I am advertising to rent my properties to people who are willing to work. I have noticed that a large number of people today get ill when they see the word "responsibility." They wouldn't think of calling an ad that mentioned such profanity. And I probably wouldn't want to rent my property to them.

A Price You Have to Pay

I really despise this business of renting. Too many people have problems that I can't solve, and I feel like an ogre when I have to enforce a rental agreement to protect myself. Landlords have had a bad name since . . . well, since the first landlord evicted the first tenant (probably from a cave). But for a real estate investor, these difficulties are a fact of life. Management is a necessary evil and a price that you must be willing to pay for success.

The tax and appreciation benefits of owning real estate work and are worth having, as long as you can manage your properties without a lot of headaches. My system of management has fulfilled that need for me, and it will do the same for you if you put it to work.

If you have any specific questions about property management, send them directly to my wife, Paula Tripp-Garrison, at paula tripp-garrison@narei.com.

My only last bit of advice is to experience property management firsthand at least once if you really have to. After that—even for properties in your own back yard—have it done professionally.

Keep it real and don't let them scare you!

—Luke Waldo

Chapter 17

Selling Right

DON'T YOU HAVE A LOVE-HATE RELATIONSHIP with Baskin-Robbins? You love the ice cream, but you hate having to make up your mind; after all, thirty-one different flavors of the world's best ice cream is a little overwhelming.

I've given you ten tools for buying, hints for fixing up and renting, and now I'm going to inundate you with information on selling. Don't get overwhelmed! You only need to pick up one or two tools as we go along. Just make sure that the tools you choose fit your personality like a surgical glove, and you shouldn't need more than one or two for success.

Getting Ready to Sell

I love selling properties. I love it because that is where you make money. If you look around in the world, you'll soon realize that the people who make money are those who are involved in selling something.

Selling is a lot of fun too. I well remember paying for Scout trips with the proceeds of candy sales or Christmas card sales. I can't remember a time when I didn't enjoy the challenge of making a sale.

When you are ready to sell a property, the first choice is whether to sell it by yourself or enlist the help of a real estate agent. You may have guessed by now that I sell most of my properties by myself, but I'll try to be fair in showing you the pros and cons of each alternative.

Before we continue, let's set the stage. At this point, you've mastered the ten tools for finding good deals in real estate, and you've used one or more of them to locate an ideal property. You've made a careful analysis, including fix-up and selling cost estimates, and you've made an offer (with escape clauses) bound with a promissory note, which was accepted. You've bought the house, gotten title insurance, and now you have fixed it up and ready to sell. Or you may have it rented temporarily, and now you're ready to sell.

Terms and Rates

As a seller, you must decide a few things in advance. First there are the selling terms. How much do you want to sell for? Do you want the cash up front, or will you take your equity in payments? What interest rate should you charge if you decide to sell on contract? You must also take into account all selling costs, which we will discuss one by one. Failure to add up all of these miscellaneous costs will give you a nasty surprise at closing. Last—but certainly not least—you must decide whether to sell with the help of an agent or by yourself. We will take a close look at each method.

We can really get into a heavy, advanced course on calculating internal rates for return, or returns on investment, when we discuss the terms of a sale. But to be honest, there is nothing more complicated about structuring the terms of a sale than just simply making sure that you make money instead of lose it.

I love a simple, direct approach to investing, and when it comes time to sell, I love simple, direct terms that are easy to understand. It reminds me of the story of two M.B.A.'s who ran into each other two years after they graduated. One of them had graduated at the top of his class—he could perform complex analysis in his head—and was now working for a large accounting firm, counting widgets in factories forty hours a week. The other M.B.A. had barely made it through school, and he had never been noted for his academic abilities. Somehow though, he was now a multimillionaire, the owner of a large importing firm.

The brilliant widget-counter asked the other man what the secret of his success was. "In all honesty," he answered, "I have never figured it out. All I know is that I can buy something for $3.00 and sell it for $6.00. I never realized you could make so much money with just a 3-percent profit!"

All you have to know in real estate is that if you buy a house for $40,000 with 5 percent down on a thirty-year, 10-percent loan, and then sell it for $50,000 with 10 percent down, on a thirty-year, 12-percent loan, you will make money. Let's take a look at those figures.

Purchase price	$40,000
Down payment (5%)	−2,000
Amount to be financed	$38,000
Interest rate	10%
Length of loan	30 yrs.
Monthly payments	$333.48
Selling price	$50,000
Down payment (10%)	−5,000
Amount to be financed	$45,000
Interest rate	12%
Length of loan	30 yrs.
Monthly payments	$462.88
Monthly net income	$129.40

What else do you need to know about investing? You invested $2,000 plus some fix-up and closing costs, and you received $5,000 cash when you sold it. Estimating $1,000 for those extra costs, you made $2,000 on a $3,000 investment immediately and $129.40 every month for the next thirty years—a total of $46,584. Is that making money or not?

Of course a finance major would never settle for such a simple explanation, nor would an economist. After all, we do need to discount all of those future payments to come up with a real rate of return. But so what? While they are plugging numbers into their calculators, I am plugging profits into my bank account.

The simplistic—and admittedly ideal—situation described above is the perfect example of how a wrap-around mortgage works. This is one of two ways to sell real estate that I think are so superior to all others that I use them exclusively. There are almost an infinite variety of terms and techniques for selling, but after looking at most of them, I am perfectly happy with these two and they are the ones I teach.

The Wrap-Around Mortgage (AITD)

This is the best idea, and it is the one I use most. When I buy a house, I always try to assume the existing loans. The reason is simple. They usually have lower interest rates and therefore lower payments. The only alternative is to come up with new money, and that means going to the bank and paying not only the higher rate for the money to buy the home or income property, but also all of the origination fees and points that come with such new financing today.

Having assumed the existing loans, you can then pay the seller's equity on a contract. Here's how it works: When you buy the property, the closing officer prepares an all-inclusive trust deed or a land contract that legally binds you to pay the seller a monthly, annual, or a balloon payment in the future at the time that both you and the seller have agreed upon. Be careful when doing this; balloon financing can mean financial suicide if you are not in the position to refinance or pay off the balloon loan when it comes due.

Now comes the real trick to the program: when I sell the property, I do so on an all-inclusive trust deed (also called a wraparound mortgage). This is an all-new contract for the full selling price. The new owner does not assume the underlying loans; I keep them in my name and continue to make the payments.

Each month I collect a payment ($462.88 in the example), make a payment ($333.48), and put the difference in my bank account. Not only that, but I can get a local title trust company to do the collecting and paying for me. They will send me a check for the difference, less about $5.00 for their service.

With this system one of three things will happen:

1. The buyer will decide to pay off the contract early, in which case I will be forced to pay off the old loans and put the $5,000 or so cash difference into another property.
2. The buyer will continue making payments, and I will continue receiving that monthly cash flow without any management or ownership problems
3. The buyer will default on the payments, and I will have to take it back for free and resell it, making even more money.

It's a no-lose situation. If you can average $100 a month on every deal, and if you can buy and sell two houses every month for the next five years, that would build up a monthly income of $12,000. How much do you need to retire?

I really love those commercials for the Ginsu knives and other culinary tools that slice, chop, grate, cut, pare, shred, and do everything else imaginable to your vegetables. The real genius is the final tag line, after they give you the price. They always say, "But wait! There's more!"

Look at what I've given you above, for the price of a book.

You can go out and get a return on your money immediately and get a monthly income for thirty years. How much would you pay for information like that? But wait! There's more!

That's right. Not only do you get the immediate return and $129.40 every month, but with this offer you also get the entire $462.88 every month after the first twenty years or so. Why? Because the underlying loans that you assumed were probably in existence for five or ten years before you bought the property. That means that when they run out, you will continue to collect payments of $462.88, but you will not have to pay more payments on the old loans. Now that's retirement in style!

Again, don't let the numbers scare you off. If it still seems complicated, ask your title officer or another investor to help you with the details. Any competent title officer can help you through this process, and if your title officer doesn't understand AITDs, find a new one.

Understand me well: Buying and selling a house is no different from buying and selling a can of beans. If you can buy a can of beans wholesale for fifty-two cents and sell it retail for fifty-nine cents, you will make money. Don't let anyone convince you that it is a complicated business.

Taking a Second Mortgage

The second of my two favorite techniques is to accept a second mortgage for my equity. That means, simply, that I will let my buyer assume all of the underlying mortgages (instead of keeping them in my name, as in the wrap-around above), and I will accept a note—a second mortgage—for the balance.

Using the same figures as the example above, the buyer would take over the payments on the $38,000 loan that I assumed (making payments of $333.48), and I will take the remaining $7,000 owed me on a note for, say, ten years.

A note for $7,000 over a ten-year period, at 12 percent, will pay $100.43 per month. You can see the primary advantage of the wrap-around mortgage, which pays much more over the long run. The wrap-around has another advantage as well. Since you are holding the only trust deed, you will know the minute your buyer defaults. In the case of a second mortgage, you will have to file a "request for notice of default," and even then it may take two or three months after the buyer stops making payments before you hear about it.

Using second mortgages, however, offers its own advantages. First, such a mortgage is much easier to sell to another investor or a mortgage broker; second, it is easier to sell a property when you offer to let the buyer assume the low-interest loans with the lower monthly payments.

Of the two methods, I prefer selling on a wrap-around. However, both work very well and allow you to remain in control of the terms, rather than having to turn the reins over to a banker. It's just you and the buyer; only the two of you are calling the shots. The choice is similar to deciding whether you will use Phillips- or regular-head screws when you put up your for sale signs. Either one will get the job done and move you one step closer to retirement.

Closing Costs for the Seller

Whatever terms you arrange with the buyer for the sale, you will still have to face a few closing costs. Since you will be arranging your own terms, it is best to get the buyer to pay as many of those costs as possible. Let's quickly look at each of the typical sellers' costs.

First are abstract and title insurance. These expenses cover research into the past ownership of a property and insurance against the cost of any liens or ownership disputes that are not discovered before the closing. The seller is usually the one charged for these costs; however, there is no set rule. I always (yes, always) just write in the contract that the buyer is to pay for one-half—

I sometimes even try for all; they can only say no—of all closing costs, including title insurance. I have always been successful in getting the buyer to help me out with this cost.

Other typical seller's costs may include the following:

- New deed
- Termite inspection/bond
- Survey
- Agent's commission

- Loan points
- New mortgage fees
- Closing fees

Do not take unfair advantage of buyers who don't understand each of the costs mentioned above. But once they do understand, then you can negotiate for each point and come to an equitable agreement. I have never had a deal yet in which I felt either side had an advantage at the expense of the other side.

Sell It Yourself, or Through a Realtor?

You have one more decision to make before selling. You must weigh the advantages—and disadvantages—of selling by yourself or through a Realtor. I think you know which I prefer. If a Realtor receives the standard 6 percent cash commission on a sale, that's 6 percent that won't end up in my pocket. On the sale of a $50,000 home, I am giving up $3,000—enough for a weeklong trip to Hawaii for my wife and myself. On a $100,000 house, it's 6,000 big ones.

Nevertheless, there are some serious drawbacks to selling by owner, and I have to earn every penny of that commission when I sell the home myself. We'll take a close look at each.

Selling Through an Agent

I have a close friend who is a real estate agent. That means he has been licensed by the state to advertise and market real properties, find and qualify potential buyers, negotiate a sales contract, arrange financing, and arrange a closing. He complains occasionally about the misinformation that a lot of sellers have about real estate commissions. Too many people, he feels, think that the agent who sells their property collects the entire 6 percent commission. Actually, that agent is likely to collect only 1.5 percent—and sometimes even less.

The reason for this is that there are usually two agencies involved: the listing agency and the selling agency. An agent works for an agency, which is managed by a broker. When homeowners agree to allow an agent to sell their homes, they are actually (in most cases) allowing the agent's agency to advertise and list that home for sale.

If a second agent—from another agency—finds a buyer for the home, then the commission must be split between the listing agency and the selling agency (each receiving half, or 3 percent of the total sale price). Then the agent for the seller must split his or her commission with the broker of the agency. That leaves only one quarter of the total commission for the agent who did the actual selling. Using a $50,000 sale as an example, the total commission would be $3,000. One-quarter of that is only $750, and there are many struggling agents who count themselves lucky if they can sell even one house each month.

When you sell a property through an agent, keep in mind that many agents are willing to list your house and then sit back, waiting for another agent to make the sale through the Multiple Listing Service book.

Finding the rare agent who will work hard to both list and sell your property may be difficult. Ask other investors for recommendations. Your time is too precious to waste it waiting for a poor agent to get in gear.

If you sell through an agent, you will have to sign a listing contract, and there is more than one type of these. Each has advantages and disadvantages, and it is up to you, as the seller, to decide which kind of listing agreement to sign with your agent.

Exclusive Right-to-Sell Contract

This contract is exactly what its name implies: it is an agreement that gives the agent the exclusive right to sell the property. That means that if the property is sold during the period for the listing agreement (usually ninety days)—by anyone—the agent will receive the full commission.

This is great for the agent, obviously. It is also advantageous for the seller, because the agent will be highly motivated to sell the property. However, if Ima Buyer makes an offer to you personally, without any help from the agent whatsoever, you are still obligated to pay that agent the full commission.

Exclusive Right-to-Sell Multiple Listing Contract

The added feature of this contract is that the seller requires the agent to not only market the property through contacts but also through the local Multiple Listing Service. This Multiple Listing Service (MLS) is an organization that puts out weekly or monthly books to every agent in the area who is an MLS member. The idea is that the MLS will greatly increase the seller's chances of meeting the right buyer.

If an agent from another agency finds a buyer, the agencies will split the commission. However, it is the listing agent who represents the seller.

Net Listing Contract

A net listing means that the seller is able to stipulate a net amount that he or she requires from the sale. For example, in the $50,000 house we are using as our example in this chapter, the seller insists that he or she must receive at least $50,000—after the agent's commission. That means that the agent can try to sell the house for, say, $55,000, collecting $5,000 as a commission.

This is an interesting incentive program for the agent, because the lower the selling price, the lower the commission, and yet the higher the selling price, the less chance that the property will sell at all. It is up to the agent to hit upon a jolly fortune-teller . . . I mean, a happy medium. (Just checking to see if you're awake.)

This isn't a bad listing arrangement, if you have found an agent with a lot of initiative and drive.

Open Listing Contract

An open listing is practically no listing at all. It gives the agent the right to sell the property and collect the commission, but since the right is not exclusive, the seller is free to sign the same kind of listing with every agent in town. With that kind of first-come-first-served competition, there is little incentive for the agent to work hard for the sale.

This listing is really only good if the agent already has some interested buyers who fit the property exactly. Otherwise, it is just a waste of time and effort, and you might as well sell by owner.

Exclusive Agency Listing Contract

This listing is my favorite. It really combines the best of all the listing contracts. The agency is guaranteed that it is the only firm that has the listing on the property, but the owners, under this contract, have the right to sell the property on their own and pay no commission, unless the agency can prove that it was the source of the lead.

The agency has some incentive to work for you, since they are guaranteed the listing commission if they can find a buyer for you, but if you find one yourself they have no claim. The real advantage should be obvious: You are able to sell by agent and by owner at the same time.

When you are beginning your career as an investor, consider using the exclusive agency listing to sell all of your properties. That way you can get experience with both methods of selling.

Listing with an Agent

It's really easy to list a house with an agent. If you have asked around town (other investors, people who have recently bought or sold a home in the area), just call one of the agents who was recommended. Tell him or her that you would like to sell your property, and that you would like to do so on an exclusive agency listing. Everything after that point will be handled by the agent.

My hesitancy about selling through an agent was reinforced last week when I called on a house that was for sale by owner. The lady who answered was very discouraged. Her husband had been transferred 500 miles away, leaving her behind to sell the house. They had known about the transfer for nearly a year, but had trusted a real estate agent to sell their home. The agent had given his "expert" opinion that the house was worth $85,000—about $10,000 more than its actual market value—and had listed it at that price. The agent had nothing to lose. If another agent sold the house, he would get a commission; if the house didn't sell, he had only wasted a few hours' effort.

Needless to say, the house didn't sell, and the frustrated couple was now in the unenviable position of having to practically give away their home. If you want to sell through an agent, beware. Find a real go-getter who will do more than list it and wait for an easy commission.

Selling by Owner

If you decide to do the selling yourself, you must realize what this entails. You will have to figure out the financing terms and negotiate with the buyer; you will have to advertise well enough to attract buyers; you will have to qualify prospective buyers (if you don't have them go to the bank and get money to cash you out); you will have to show the home; and you will have to arrange for the closing.

Taking care of that many you's can be a time-consuming, frustrating experience if you don't know what you are getting into, so I'll go through each of these steps one by one.

Deciding on Terms

Your first step will be to decide on terms. You need to establish not only how the property is sold, as discussed earlier in this chapter, but for how much. You will have to balance the selling price with selling time. The higher the price, the longer it will usually take to sell.

Creating an Ad That Will Bring You Buyers

After deciding on price and terms, you must advertise. The key to effective advertising is to sell the benefits, not the features. Write ads that inform people of the facts they are looking for. Bedrooms and bathrooms are vital information, but what terms are you offering? How much are you expecting as a down payment? Are you willing to be flexible on the price or the interest rate? What kind of monthly payments are you asking for?

The secret to a successful ad is to stress a few of these key ingredients:

- Low monthly payments
- Low down payment
- Owner will finance, with no qualifying or credit checks
- Low-interest financing
- Nice, beautiful, clean, and so on

Here are a couple of ads; you decide which one would catch your eye if you were looking for a house to buy:

MUST SELL. Owner desperate, will sell for only $49,900, with only $3,000 down. Very flexible. Payments of only $475 for this beautiful 3 bdrm home in Rockville. No bank qualifying. 555-4899 or 555-3423.

FOR SALE by Owner. Nice 3 bdrm, 2 bath house in Rockville. Close to school and shopping center. Only $49,900. Call evenings 555-4899.

The first owner sounds willing to negotiate. Here is someone who is ready to sell; notice the two phone numbers, indicating that you can call anytime. Also, as buyers look through the classified ads, which one catches them where they really live—in their pocketbooks?

The first one is specific about the low down payment and the low monthly payments. The second one offers proximity to the schools and stores—so what? Those things may be important but they can be added to the sales pitch when the calls start coming in.

Which leads to the next point, answering the phone calls. If your ad is attractive to enough people, you will be flooded with curious callers. The best thing you can do is anticipate every call. You should know all of these things about the property:

- How close is it to the elementary school?
- Where is the closest park?
- What are the terms of sale? (How much will you need as a down payment?)
- What special features can you offer that you didn't mention in your ad?

In short, you must go through a whole list of questions you would ask as a prospective buyer, and you should have your answers prepared before the questions are asked. Many buyers will be turned off if you stumble around too much with a lot of unsure I-don't-knows. You should also leave an information sheet by each phone in your house. It really helps the other people who might answer the phone when you're not there to have something to tell the people who call on the ad.

Other Sources of Buyers

Don't rely on the effectiveness of your newspaper advertising. Utilize all of these sources of buyers as well:

1. **Neighbors.** Residents within a few blocks of your property may know of someone who is interested in moving into the area. A simple personal phone call or a talk with each might reveal the names of dozens of possible buyers.

   A flier distributed throughout the area is even easier, if somewhat less personal. The flier should announce to local residents that you will be selling the house at 810 Elm Street and that you would appreciate being recommended to anyone who they knew was interested in moving into the area. Offer a $50 finder's fee and everyone in town will be calling friends to find a buyer for you; most people will probably have a friend or two that they would love to have move into the neighborhood. (Check applicable state laws in your area to make sure this method is legal.)

2. **Your farm.** In real estate economics, there is a term called a metropolitan statistical area (MSA). This is defined as a market with over 1 million in population that economically rises and falls together; it also is known as a macro market. When we invest, though, we do not focus on the entire MSA or macro market. We focus instead on individual neighborhoods within the entire macro market; these individual markets are called micro markets, or farms.

If you had begun investing in 1986 in Tacoma, Washington, you would have learned by now that the properties in some of its neighborhoods are worth even less today than they were then. Why? Because those neighborhoods are full of crack houses and gangs. When we go into a new absorption market, we break the entire MSA or macro market down into individual neighborhoods (micro markets, or farms) that have the greatest potential for growth. We research about 178 things on each micro market or farm in an area. For example, the best way to find the neighborhoods within your target market that are going to appreciate is to go to each of your MSA's school district offices and find out which individual neighborhoods have the highest K–6 enrollment statistics. When we go into a market, we only go because we know the MSA or macro market is a gold mine. And within that gold mine, we have to find the very best areas to dig to find the veins of pure real estate gold.

A buying farm is a particular micro market you can buy properties from. Your can also develop a selling farm—that is, a group made up of those you can regularly sell properties to. Get to know investors, attorneys, and other professionals who would be interested in buying properties. Find out what their specifications are and sell accordingly.

I have a friend who has compiled quite an impressive farm of lawyers. Whenever he gets wind of a good deal that he knows he can sell to one of them, he buys it immediately, then he turns around and sells it with one telephone call. He may not sell it at a retail price, but he deals in a different market. He buys sub-wholesale and sells wholesale.

3. **Satisfied customers.** You might want to go back through your list of past sales and contact the buyers to see if they might be interested in buying another investment property themselves, or if they know of someone else who might be interested. You could even offer them a cash bonus for providing you with a lead, or let them miss a payment to you in exchange for a lead.

4. **Multiple Listing Service.** Try to get a copy of the Multiple Listing Service book in your area and look up what properties have sold recently. You might want to contact the sellers to see if they are interested in buying another property. A lot of people who have sold an investment property will need to get into another one as soon as they can to help their tax situations.

5. **New people in the area.** People who are new in an area are particularly good prospects for selling a home to, because many banks require at least one year of continuous employment for qualifying for a new loan, and if the new job is with a different company than the one left behind, newcomers may find themselves renting for a while. You are offering them an opportunity to buy a home that they would not otherwise have.

You don't know how to find out about these people? Join your neighborhood Welcome Wagon organization and volunteer to make them feel at home. Your local chamber of commerce can also help you meet your city's new residents.

Creative Advertising

A strange lesson I have learned is that if you really want to be successful, you sometimes have to do things backwards. I have developed a shotgun approach to finding buyers. The gist of the program is to advertise for buyers at the same time you advertise to buy properties yourself. I have developed an "I sell houses" flier that has given me a backlog of interested buyers. My investment program then turns into a matchmaking service where I find homes for sale to match people who are interested in buying. I tie up these homes with escape clauses and promissory notes (so I have no cash on the line) and then present them to my buyers. It works like a charm.

Consider putting out a few hundred of these "I sell houses" fliers every month in apartment complexes or trailer parks where young couples live. Before you know it, you will have a stack of qualified buyers waiting for you to find them a home.

WE SELL HOUSES

Tired of paying out rent? Tired of landlord hassles? If so, you might be in the market for a house—either now or in the future. We are not real estate agents, and we're not associated with any brokerage. We do, however, have houses for sale that, for the most part, require small down payments and no qualifying. If you would like to be put on our list for houses, please fill out the following questionnaire and mail it back. You'll hear from us soon!

Marc and Paula Garrison, (480) 813-6043,
4331 East Baseline Road, Suite B-105,
Gilbert, Arizona 85234-2961

Name _____

Address _____

City _____

Phone _____

I am looking for:

❏ 1 Bedroom ❏ 1 Bath ❏ Garage
❏ 2 Bedrooms ❏ 2 Baths ❏ Carport
❏ 3 Bedrooms ❏ Under 1,000 sq. ft.
❏ 4 Bedrooms ❏ 1,000 to 1,200 sq. ft.
❏ _____ ❏ 1,200 sq. ft. and over

I have for a down payment: *I can afford a monthly payment of:*

❏ $1,000 ❏ $4,000 ❏ $400 ❏ $700
❏ $2,000 ❏ $5,000 ❏ $500 ❏ $800
❏ $3,000 ❏ $_____ ❏ $600 ❏ $_____

Other things I could use for a down payment:

❏ Car ❏ Building Lot
❏ Mobile Home ❏ Trade _____
❏ Boat ❏ Airplane
❏ Camper ❏ _____

My gross monthly income is $ _____

I am employed at _____

Yes, I can qualify for new financing. ❏
No, I'd rather not or can't qualify for new financing. ❏

Preference for where I would like to live: _____

❏ Salt Lake ❏ South Salt Lake Valley ❏ Northern Utah County
❏ Orem ❏ Provo ❏ Springville
❏ Spanish Fork ❏ South Utah County ❏ _____

Each problem that I solved became a rule that served afterwards to solve other problems.

—René Descartes

Chapter 18

Negotiating the Sale

NEGOTIATING WITH A BUYER can be a tricky business, like a tightrope act. When you are selling, rather than buying, you must be careful to remember some points that are unique to this situation. First, be especially careful about establishing rapport. Buyers tend to be more wary than sellers.

On the one hand, if you sound as though you know everything there is to know about real estate and that you've been through this a hundred times, they will be scared off, afraid that you will take advantage of them. On the other hand, if you don't appear to be competent enough to handle every aspect of the sale, they are equally likely to be scared off by your apparent ineptitude and the deal will still be blown.

Tips for Negotiating a Deal

Walking that hair-thin rope is a skill that you will develop as you work with buyers and sellers, but I can give you a few tips that may help.

Tip #1: Establish Rapport

In selling a house, just as in buying, you must be standing on common ground before you can see eye to eye. The first step in establishing rapport is to understand the buyer's level of sophistication. The idea of an "all-inclusive trust deed" may be totally foreign and more than a little intimidating. And if you casually state that you want to sell the house on a wrap-around, they may think you intend to throw a roll of Saran Wrap into the deal.

You don't have to tell buyers that you are an investor unless they ask. Many buyers may feel that an investor is a con artist who will be trying to sell them oceanfront property in Kansas. Test the water a little before you jump in.

Find common ground at first, walking through the house and discussing the architecture or carpeting. Find out if they have ever owned a house before, and if so, what kind of financing was arranged on that sale. Broach the subject of creative financing gently, assuring the buyer that "We will be able to work everything out."

Don't profess to know more about real estate than you really do, and if a question comes up that you're not sure of, don't try to bluff your way through it. Smile and say, "I'm glad you asked that question. I have an excellent (attorney, title officer, and so on) who has offered to help us out if we have any questions, and I'm sure this won't be any problem."

My own approach is simple, direct honesty without volunteering any unnecessary information. It's like a game of Go Fish. You don't have to give away any cards unless the other player asks for them, and then you give only the cards asked for.

As you talk, try to find out exactly what the buyer needs. Don't go into a half-hour spiel bragging about how close the home is to every church in town, only to find out that your buyer is an atheist. Again, it's a matter of selling benefits, not features. Find out what the buyer wants and needs, and then show how this particular house will suit those needs perfectly.

Tip #2: Determine the Buyer's Motivation

As soon as possible, before you put a lot of time in with the buyers, determine whether they are serious. Do they really want to buy the home, or are they just looking around? Find out if they have been or will be transferred into the area. Do they own a home locally? Why are they thinking about buying a new home? These questions can be asked quite candidly once the ice has been broken, and if they are a "looky-loo" (not a serious buyer), you won't have to waste your time.

Tip #3: Obtain the Buyer's Confidence

As you talk with the buyers, tell them about other homes you have sold in the past and suggest that they make a call or pay a visit to people with whom you've done business. (Get permission first.) If you haven't sold other houses yet, tell them about yourself. If you just got out of Sing Sing you may want to avoid that fact. But you must find a way to get the buyer's confidence and loyalty.

Tip #4: Determine the Buyer's Financial Strength

After I had been involved in buying and selling properties for about two years, I sold a home to someone who owned a small business in town. He seemed prosperous, and I was sure he was good for his debts, so I took back a $12,000 second mortgage, which would net $3,000 annually for several years.

The first annual payment was on time, and I was delighted with my profitable deal . . . until the second payment came due. The buyer informed me that he couldn't meet his obligation. Further, he said, he was filing for bankruptcy, and he had not been paying his bills for some time.

What at terrible experience for a beginning investor! I was

forced to take the property back, and it made me feel somewhat like the bad guy in a melodrama, foreclosing on the mortgage and driving Penelope and her grandmother into the snow. (Actually, it was summer, and he owned a rental property that he could move into.) The fact that I knew I was doing nothing wrong eased the pain a little, but it was a nasty troublesome situation, and I felt as though I had been burned.

I was determined to continue investing, so I learned everything I could about prequalifying buyers. How would a banker, for example, have found out that my buyer was a poor risk? I learned a few keys that I think will help you avoid the same mistake.

First, never assume that the buyer is a good credit risk just because he or she is well dressed and drives a nice car. Appearance can always be deceiving. Here's the most important thing that you can do to protect your interests (now pay attention): Make your contract contingent upon your receiving from them—and your approving—a complete credit history. Insist on a personal balance sheet and a report from a credit bureau. The following points are the most important to consider:

- Source of down payment
- Monthly payment the buyer could carry
- Employment information for each wage earner
- Position
- Name and address of each employer
- Length of employment with previous employers
- Outlook for future employment
- If they are presently a two-income family, is that likely to continue, or will the wife quit work soon to have a baby?
- Monthly and annual income figures for the past several years (including any outside income)

If the buyers will be using the property as a personal residence, the total debt service (principal, interest, taxes, and insurance) should not be more than 30 percent of their monthly income.

If they are buying the property as an investment, they should have sufficient income to handle any balloon payments or negative cash flows from vacancies or unexpected emergency repairs. Lastly, the buyer's credit history should not have a record of delinquency or a default against a previous mortgage loan.

One of the difficulties that we all have as sellers is discussing the finances of the buyer. The subject seems rather personal, and it's one of the things that the bank usually takes care of. I've found that the simplest thing to do is bring up the subject when you are talking on the phone, before they ever come to see the property. Remind them that you are asking $3,000 cash and that the payments will be over $450 a month. Ask if that will be a problem. Most unqualified buyers will let themselves out of the deal at that point, since very few people will lie when they know the lie will be discovered later.

Tip #5: Explain the Benefits of Purchasing with Owner Financing

It is exciting to show buyers just how much money they can save by not going the traditional route of financing by a bank loan. Not only will they save the time and trouble of the bank's red tape, but they will save loan origination fees and the higher market rates. Few buyers need to be convinced that the seller can offer a better deal than the bank, and those few can be turned around with a little honest education.

Tip #6: Commit to the Buyer

This may sound strange, but I commit myself to the buyer's satisfaction before I commit myself to making the sale. I make no attempt to squeeze a buyer into the house if he or she doesn't naturally fit. With the hundreds of buyers out there, if a prospective buyer is an obvious mismatch, I offer to try to find him or her or them another house. Because I have made contacts with real estate agencies, banks, title offices, and with other investors, I can usually find a house that will fit the buyer, and I collect a finder's fee for my troubles.

If I don't know of a contact with just the perfect house, I will look for one that I can buy, fix up, and sell to this buyer. There is always a way to make people happy and make a dollar or two as well.

Get the Buyer to Say "Yes" Early and Often

The bottom line when negotiating with potential buyers is getting them to say yes. To do this, I use a type of question similar to the reflexive statements mentioned in the chapter on negotiation. The trick to these questions is to get the buyer to start saying yes. I will walk around the home and start pointing out important features of the home that I don't feel the buyer has noticed. I use statements similar to these:

- The closet space in here sure is roomy, isn't it?
- The living room is well decorated, isn't it?
- Hasn't the yard been well cared for?
- Doesn't the mechanical system look like it's in great shape?
- The kitchen sure is cheery, isn't it?

This isn't just a gimmick. Think about your experience the last time you bought something at a store because of a good salesman. Think about what he did that encouraged you to buy something and what he did that really bugged you. Then simply try to put into action the good things you have noticed in other sales situations, and avoid doing the things that really bug you. That is exactly what I have done to make the selling of my investment properties the fun experience it has been.

Well, are you excited about selling? I remember the very first time I tried to sell a home; I called up an agent (at the time I thought that was what I was supposed to do) and listed the property. I don't want to go into much detail, but the whole experience was one big disappointment. I was really upset; after all, wasn't the agent supposed to sell the property?

I took the property off the listing, started to study everything I could about the selling process, and I made several visits to title companies to ask about making up an offer. A few days later I had my buyer, and before I knew what had happened we had closed. Afterward, I felt like I had just gotten off one of those roller coasters in an amusement park. My head was spinning, not because of the hassle of setting everything up, but because it was so easy.

When the dust had settled on that first deal, and somebody else owned the property, I went back and did a little calculation. I had cleared $3,660 with just under twenty-two hours' work. Breaking that down with a calculator, I realized that I had made over $166 an hour—not bad for a few hours' work.

I don't think you will really enjoy the process of investing until you close your first sale. It won't be until you have that cash in hand and a steady income stream for years that you will get really enthused. The first deal is the hardest, but if you can make it all the way through to that first sale, your investing career will take off like a rocket.

PART VI

Level Two Investing: Domestic Absorption Markets

Wealth does not guarantee happiness.

—Spencer W. Kimball

Chapter 19

The School for Self-Made Millionaires

AFTER BECOMING A SELF-MADE real estate millionaire, I decided to reward myself by making one of my dreams come true. Ever since I was a small child, I had always wanted to learn how to fly a plane. As a youth, I would ride my bicycle to a local small airport and just stare at the planes taking off and landing. I even went so far as to ask the owners of the private planes if they would let me sit in the pilot's seat for a minute in exchange for my washing their planes. That was a lot of fun, and it brings back some incredible memories, but my dream became reality about four years after I started investing in real estate. I no longer had a nine-to-five job where I had to punch in a time clock.

I was then attending college full-time during the day and investing in real estate from one to three hours in the evening Monday through Friday nights. Saturday became my day for learning how to fly.

For a month I attended a private ground school, which taught me to learn by just the way you are learning right now—by studying the basics out of a book. After I had mastered the basics of flight, I hired an instructor to sit in an actual plane with me and to teach me how to fly.

Can you imagine my fate if I had decided to bypass that flight instructor? What do you think would have happened to me if, by the grace of God, I actually had been able to figure out how to fly that plane off of the ground? Who would have shown me what it was like to avoid a stall? Who would have taught me how to avoid a spin? Who would have taught me how to trim out the plane? And who would have taught me how to communicate, navigate, and, finally, how to land that plane safely back on the runway? The answer to who I needed to teach me these things is very obvious: my flight instructor.

Think for a second about the horrible possibility that you found out that you had heart problems. Think about visiting with your family physician and being told that you should go see a specialist who could fully repair your damaged heart. Would you trust a surgeon to operate on you if he had only read about "how to do a heart surgery" in a book? The answer is no, absolutely not.

The Power of Knowledge

Successful real estate investing is not brain surgery, but it also isn't like picking dollar bills off of a money tree. Real estate investing success today boils down to just a few things:

1. You need to understand the economic relationship of "supply and demand" that directly affects the value of all residential non-owner-occupied income properties.
2. You must then apply that basic economic relationship and take a clear-eyed look in your own back yard. The question to ask is, "Is the area where I live in expansion, or equilibrium, or decline, or absorption?"
3. Once you have made that judgment, you must apply the insights that we have taught you so far. If you live in an

expansion market, do your research and find out where the developers in your area are building new apartments. Find out when those apartments will be finished. Understand how much time you have before the new inventory hits the rental markets and destroys the value of older existing residential rental properties. You need to form a definition of value for the type of real estate that you plan on investing in. Then, focus your time on properties that you can buy/rehab/upgrade, and fill every unit. The reality of real estate investing in the twenty-first century is that in every single economic cycle stage—expansion, equilibrium, or a decline market—the only way that you are going to make money today is either by luck or by being willing to commit yourself to work at nothing but deeply ugly rehab projects. Every once in a while you will find a good deal based on your forming a definition of value for your area—there will always be imperfections—but to make any real money you are going to need to buy properties with defects that you can inexpensively fix and cosmetically improve so that you can resell that property at or just below market value.

4. You need to learn to recognize and identify absorption markets. We focus our research every year into every single metropolitan statistical area (MSA) that has a population base of over 1 million. In those markets we look for new companies moving in and new professional job growth. We look at the vacancy rate for income properties in that town, and we look at what the average apartment unit is selling for today, compared to what it would cost today to replace.

Since 1986, we have become relentless with our research. The biggest up-front cost of being able to be with us on a BuyingTour is spent on research. We track companies that are relocating. We track companies that are expanding their facilities. We look at their unemployment statistics. We look at every single thing that is for sale. We then leave the quantitative logical part of choosing a target market, and we fly into that town firsthand to see what is going on. If things look good at that point, we start building a real estate investing team in that market that can help us find the very best deals there.

Doing It Yourself

This research is nothing that you can't do yourself.

One of the most important Web sites that we use today is *www.ecodevdirectory.com*. This site is worth its weight in gold. It gives links essentially to every single economic development agency in the world. Go there. Study the site, and follow the links. Then print out that city/county/state/country's "contact us" page. And then pick up the phone and fire away with your questions. The mandate for every single economic development agency in the world is to attract new business into that area, such as the serious real estate investors—and that includes you and me—who will come into that town and start investing when everybody thinks that we are crazy.

Joining a Tour

Last summer we had a magical week with a group of twelve investors from all around the United States and Canada. They flew into Phoenix and spent about twelve hours a day learning everything that I and several of our best students could teach them about how to make money in real estate investing today. Half of that course was spent in the classroom. The other half was spent out in a bus doing case studies. Over the years, we have developed that program to help prepare people for investing either by themselves or with us on a BuyingTour.

The feedback from that class, and now from the twenty-one—videotape course that we had professionally taped at that event, has been incredible. In that video course, you can spend seven days learning from an entire group of documented self-made millionaires what it takes to make money today. But what is really great about the course is that it shows exactly what happens through investing in an area that completes the economic cycle and ends up back in a decline.

When we first brought students into Phoenix back in 1991, thousands of companies were relocating here. We did our research and confirmed that data. I remember driving out with a BuyingTour group and pointing out into the desert on the south side of Phoenix's East Valley where Intel was going to build its brand-new production facilities. We showed our students where Boeing was going to come in. We also showed where Motorola was going to be building.

We had the data. We knew the growth. We built an incredible real estate investing team, and on several BuyingTours, we bought as individuals millions upon millions of residential income properties. This past summer, as a group, we boarded a bus and drove out to what was once desert and now saw Intel plant after Intel plant, campus after campus. We saw what Motorola had done and how Boeing had built up. Phoenix is an incredible example of an MSA that has been brought back to life through the perks Arizona's economic development offices have offered to companies that moved in. New companies moved in, creating new complexes, new manufacturing plants, and new office buildings. During this time, Phoenix's unemployment went down hand-in-hand with the way in which any and every single rental income property was filled up. I remember a ten-unit building that one of our students bought back in 1991 on a BuyingTour. They paid under $60,000 for that building. About four years later, they sold that building for over $400,000.

Remember the basic concept of "supply and demand."

We tell our students where and when to buy. And then we tell them when to sell. One of the highlights at the end of this seven-day training was to tour one of the seemingly endless supplies of new apartment developments. Out in front of this new apartment complex were balloons and signs offering three months' free rent. As we toured this 800-unit apartment complex, we saw beautiful lakes, playgrounds, swimming pools, Jacuzzis, and a gym. The thing that was wildest about it was that the amount of rent that they were offering their units for per month was absolutely identical to what we had been getting on our "older" no-amenity apartment units four years earlier when we sold out of Phoenix and moved on.

We got into Phoenix right before absorption started. As usual, at that point everybody thought that we were crazy to be buying in Arizona. And, by the time that we sold . . . real estate prices had gone crazy, and everybody wanted to get in. As always, there was no communication between developers, and soon the market was flooded with new apartments with beautiful pools and gym clubs. At that point the new units cut their rents, tacked on incentives like free rent, and battled between themselves for all the tenants who now want to move out of the older units.

Timing is everything in real estate today. You buy before absorption hits the streets. You sell right when the rents are raised high enough to justify new construction.

I like to go and look around in some of our "old markets." Salt Lake City is a real estate bloodbath now. The newly built units are half empty; the older units are half empty. The price of housing did skyrocket, but now that the prices have gotten so high, many companies are being forced to relocate to other markets that are more affordable to work in. All over Salt Lake City you will see brand-new apartment complexes that have been built with signs offering free rent, a free trip for two to Cabo San Lucas, a free microwave. The same thing with Dallas, Las Vegas, Boise, Denver, and now Phoenix.

You buy right.

You sell right.

Success is a journey, not a destination.

—Ben Sweetland

Chapter 20

Learning to Be Successful

WHERE DO YOU GO WHEN YOU WANT to be alone to think? I love to jump in my car and drive down one of those long and lonesome roads the West is famous for. I was on such a road yesterday, thinking about the last forty-two years. It was forty-two years ago, give or take a month, when my mother bundled a little boy up in a big coat and sent him off to school for the first time. I've spent twenty-four of those forty-two years attending some type of formal education. Imagine that.

Now looking back over the thousands of hours that were spent in hundreds of classes, I am unable to remember one lesson on achieving personal success. I memorized centuries of history and juggled jillions of numbers, but I was never taught how to set a goal and see it through.

Amazing.

All of these thoughts swarmed in my brain as I chewed up a hundred mountain miles. I asked the same questions that have puzzled successful people for years. What is wrong with our system of education, that we could turn out generations of graduates capable of building skyscrapers and saving lives but who were unable to save enough money to retire in comfort? I know that the American dream is not dead. People can do anything they want with their lives, but so many don't. Why? What is wrong with such people?

Success: The Missing Part of Your Education

The real question is, what is missing in our system of education and training? And the answer is this: There is no course in school that teaches individual responsibility, that teaches entrepreneurial skills. There is no Success 101.

Let's look at the idea a little further. Why is success not taught? Is it because of a lack of knowledge, a lack of teachers, or a lack of interest? The answer, I think, is none of the above. We know what is necessary for success. It is quantifiable and teachable. A course could certainly be offered that would allow students to identify their needs, establish their own definition of success, and set goals accordingly.

Maybe it is a lack of qualified teachers. After all, if you want to teach piano, you must know how to play. If you want to teach ballet, you must know how to dance. An instructor can't just teach students these skills by reading them out of a book. It stands to reason that if you want to teach success, you must be successful. And few teachers are truly successful as entrepreneurs. Few of them can do what they want to do, when they want to do it. They have docked their boats in the safe harbor of educating, which frees them from the risk-taking demands of carving their own financial freedom in the "real world."

Well, where are the people who could teach others this missing course, Success 101? They probably are so busy making money for themselves that they don't have time to help others, right?

I think I can lay that argument to rest. Of the many successful people I know or have read about, I cannot think of one who would not love to teach such a course. I'm sure Robert Allen would teach it. I would love to teach it myself. Robert Kiyosaki would be great at it as well. And so would any of the 700-plus documented self-made real estate millionaires whom I have taught, mentored, coached, kicked in the butt, and helped create on my BuyingTours since 1986. If the establishment of public education would elevate success to its rightful place—at the top of the curriculum—I don't think that there would be any shortage of teachers.

Why don't our schools teach our children how to take control of their lives and shape their own destinies? Why isn't Success 101 being taught in schools? I'll hazard a guess. It would destroy our establishment. It would literally destroy hundreds of years of so-called progress if suddenly everybody learned—and was able to apply—the keys to success.

Where would the factories find assembly-line workers? People would all insist on working for themselves. If grade school children were taught how to budget their pennies instead of just how to make change for a dollar, they would have enough in high school to start their own enterprises. And then who would serve you your Double Whopper?

If every college freshman had to set specific, success-oriented goals, and then had to achieve those goals before the end of the semester to pass the class, what would the result be when he or she graduated? Everybody would insist on setting goals and then working toward achieving those goals. Nobody would be satisfied with a weekly hand-to-mouth existence.

Chaos would reign. There would be no human robots left to perform the menial tasks that need to be done. We would finally be confronted by true capitalism at its best.

So I suppose we should be grateful that success isn't taught. But still, it's kind of a shame that millions of Americans go to bed every night feeling frustrated and worthless. Maybe that's the price for progress. Just think what would happen if everybody knew how to buy houses at wholesale prices. Both the wholesale and the retail markets would adjust, and we, as investors, would be confronted with competition from every citizen.

Of course, I am being facetious. I would rather that everybody would learn the keys to success. The alternatives for any person are virtually limitless, once they learn how to apply their energy toward achieving a goal. Armed with that knowledge and confidence, they could achieve success in anything they chose, be it real estate investing or starting up a company for making coat hangers.

What's Keeping You from Achieving Your Dreams?

So far, a book like this is the only type of success course offered for investing, other than some seminars and workshops . . . oh yes, and life itself. Unfortunately, life waits about seventy or eighty years before giving the final, and when you finally realize why you've failed, it's usually too late to retake the course.

This book is meant to be a success book, and it has a very clear-cut message about how to reach the degree of success you desire. I firmly believe that, through study and experience, you can find in real estate the monetary base you will need for true wealth—wealth that cannot be measured in dollars and cents.

I believe strongly that if you will apply every one of the tools to your life, every day, you cannot help but succeed. To me it is as obvious as saying that if you jump onto a speeding train, it will carry you away. It's true. Once you jump onto the train of success, there is no escape unless you jump off again. And why would you want to? It's not just a principle of success; it's a law.

What I have shared with you is a proven plan for achieving financial freedom through real estate investing. I know that real estate investing is the surest, safest road to financial freedom. But you could take real estate out of my plan. Use any other vehicle for your success. If you work with educated persistence toward a clear goal, the result will eventually be the same. If you need to choose something other than real estate, then great. I simply believe that real estate investing will get you there faster.

What I have tried to do is teach you that class you didn't get in school. If you take this class seriously, I don't think you will be willing to climb someone else's ladder. Instead, you will build and climb a ladder of your own.

America is the land of opportunity. In no other country can people take their lives in their own hands and determine their future as they can in America. It's the reason why so many people look to this country as a beacon of hope, a chance to succeed. Hundreds of thousands of people have come to this country with no more than a pocket full of dreams and a suitcase full of hopes and have reached their financial goals. These people weren't conditioned to believe that "it can't be done . . . the economy is depressed . . . the country is falling apart."

I hope that I have helped strip away the years of negative conditioning that have stopped you from achieving your dreams. The economy is on track, the opportunities of yesterday live on. Today is a time when anyone willing to put forth effort can achieve any dream they have.

*I am a great believer in luck,
and I find the harder I work the
more I have of it.*

—Stephen Leacock

Chapter 21

Investing Profitably in Your Spare Time

WHILE THE CHAPTER TITLE SUGGESTS SOMETHING akin to "licking stamps in your spare time for fun and profit," the truth is that you can invest—successfully—in real estate while using no more than five to ten hours a week. For the person who is content with his or her job, who has no desire to retire early and escape from working-class drudgery, this is the easy way to invest.

There is no reason that an investor must do everything himself. Friends, relatives, college students, part-time help, Realtors, bankers, and countless other real estate professionals who become part of your target market investing team are all available as assistants. By borrowing money from other people and paying them back later, you are leveraging your money; by using other people's time and efforts and paying them back in the form of real estate commissions or increased business, you are leveraging your time.

Real Estate's Five Keys to Success

Five items have proved to be necessary keys to success in real estate investing today. Those keys are the following:

- Working in the right target markets
- Educated persistence
- The ability to recognize good deals
- Being computer literate
- Having access to the Internet

This book has been written to serve you as a source of education, motivation, and reference, and to help you develop that educated persistence. Learning this lesson is essential preparation for your journey to financial freedom.

No matter how well this or other books have been written, they cannot and will not ever change your financial life unless they turn your dreams and desires into a concrete plan of action. With that plan you must then dare to succeed, conscientiously working to turn your goals into reality. How does that happen? There is no other way than through your own hard, smart work and guts.

Another necessary key is the ability to find good deals. You might know how to be the perfect manager, how to structure a hundred-and-one creative contracts, but if you can't consistently find and recognize good deals in real estate, you will never make a dime. You will be like a painter without paints—lots of talent but no product. To find good deals, people often spend countless hours driving around looking at homes for sale by owner or listed through a realty agent. They begin to realize through the frustration of these wasted hours that there must be a better way. Many people stop investing at this point because they feel confused. They know of the potential in real estate investing, but they can't seem to make it work in their lives. So they give up.

Those who don't give up force success on themselves by putting more and more time into real estate investing. They spend even more hours looking for deals, as if they were building a home without power tools. After I had been investing for a while, I found myself spending countless hours a week trying to find those good deals. I was on my road to success, but my wife, children, and mental health were in jeopardy. I was making money but losing or missing out on the things that I really consider to be important.

Necessity is the mother of invention, and this necessity drove me to find another way that would fit the life of someone who wanted to be human, enjoy his family, and still make it in real estate. What I started with was a piece of paper that I called my property analysis system. On the front side of the page I had a series of questions that I would ask any and all sellers before I made the decision to visit that property. On the back side of that sheet was a step-by-step checklist for the onsite inspection of that property. I used this system for years. But recently the need to do all of that research on my own was replaced by the Multiple Listing Service (MLS) of the National Association of Realtors, which you now can access directly via the Internet.

Finding Deals

When I started to think about putting together a system for finding good deals in real estate, I realized that the normal methods of finding them are analogous to hammering in a nail with a teaspoon. It can be done, but it takes about three months of full-time work. I knew there must be a better way—a hammer, so to speak, that could pound the nail in with seconds of work, not weeks. There must, I thought, be a better system for finding good deals.

I went through every problem I had faced—lack of organization, wasting time visiting properties I didn't want to buy, and so on—and developed one of the greatest investing tools in existence at that time.

Let's look a minute at "normal investing." Most investors find that about two out of one hundred people they contact are what they can really call motivated sellers. Of those two people who want practically to give away their homes, only about three out of ten cases really have something to offer that is worth buying. In the other seven cases, something makes the deal unprofitable, such as the property's financing or state of disrepair, and the investor wouldn't want to touch it. The danger here is that some investors may not recognize that many of the deals that look good on the outside contain a hidden flaw. How can they get to the point where they can recognize these hidden flaws? Have patience, we'll get to that.

In other words, most investors have to kiss about 166 toads to find a good deal using the conventional newspaper ad/waste-your-gasoline/drive-yourself-around-town-and-drive-yourself-nuts method. From my very start as a real estate investor I have been driven to find ways to find good deals without having to ever work our real estate investing as a full-time job.

But this is the twenty-first century, and the whole world has changed since I started investing in real estate in 1977. When I started investing, by law every single real estate agent/broker in the United States and Canada always represented the seller. If you worked with a professional real estate agent, their fiduciary legal code of ethics demanded that they do every single thing possible to make you, the buyer, give the seller not only the highest sales price, but also the very best terms. When I figured this out, I ran away from Realtors and concentrated exclusively on for-sale-by-owner properties, bank owned properties (REOs), preforeclosures, and government foreclosures (FHA and VA). But, based on a landmark judgment in Hawaii, real estate agents now can actually represent the buyer. What a gift! Imagine that in each of your target markets you have a professional real estate agent who represents you as the buyer and will do his or her very best to find you the very best properties in that area at the very best price to you and at the very best terms. As I've mentioned before, this type of professional real estate representation is called a "buyer's broker." Their job is to understand who you are, where you are financially and in terms of consumer credit, and what type of properties that you are looking for.

To find a buyer's broker for your target market just open up the phone directory and start calling real estate offices in your target area. Over time, I have found out that 99 percent of all real estate agents only represent homeowners who are buying and selling. It is a rare eagle of a real estate professional that specializes today in residential income properties. As we get ready to open up a new area, that is one of our biggest challenges.

The Most Valuable Site in Real Estate

Fortunately, it is now getting easier and easier to find residential income properties. Let me explain.

Right now, I would like you to get to a computer that has an Internet connection. Real estate agents are joined together in a national organization called the National Association of Realtors (NAR). This association is broken down into local county boards of Realtors. In the past, these local county associations put all of their current real estate listings into a printed Multiple Listing Service book (MLS). That book was considered gold and was never shared openly with anybody but a state-licensed Realtor in that county.

But all that has changed. Turn your computer on. Then access the Internet. Now type into the address line *www.realtor.com.* When you get to the home page of this Web site sponsored by the National Association of Realtors, look it over and try to fathom the fact that you now essentially have direct access to the over 2 million properties that are listed for sale in every zip code, every city, every county, and every state in the United States of America.

Start by typing in the name of your target city in the space provided, then type in your target state, and/or the zip code range that you are looking to find good deals in. On this page you can also specify a price range, the number of bedrooms, and the number of baths.

I truly believe that every single real estate investor needs to start researching his or her own back yard before going out of state into a domestic absorption market. When you have your data and constraints typed in, click search "go." Within seconds, every single multiple listing property in that area is going to be right in front of your eyes, with the most inexpensive listed first. From that list you can click to find out even more details on the property. You also have a picture of the property and a complete summary of its features. You also have a diamond in the rough—you have the name and phone number of the agent who has the listing and all the details of that property.

This really is a real estate investor's dream come true.

Tools to Research Markets and Agents

As a pilot, I have come to love checklists. They essentially remove most all of the risk in flying. Think back to what we told you already, about how you should always start your real estate investing research in your back yard. Remember how we referred you to the *www.ecodevdirectory.com* Web site. Remember how we told you to look up your state, county, and city economic development agencies. Remember how we told you to determine which economic cycle stage your local market existed in. Now, based on that knowledge, you have a free picture of every single property in your back yard that is listed for sale by a Realtor on the MLS.

You could and should spend hours here researching. You might also remember that each macro market (the entire area) is divided into micro markets (individual neighborhoods). Now remember what we told you about checking the local elementary school statistics to find out where young families are moving— where there is the very best opportunity to make money and to appreciate with. Now just find out what zip code ranges that area exists in, and narrow down your online research into just those areas.

I don't think I need to tell you how easy this makes investing in real estate today. Since 1986 we have invested almost exclusively outside of our back yard. With the advent of the Internet and sites like *www.realtor.com* and *www.ecodevdirectory.com,* in the comfort of our own home we can be investing all around the United States, without even having to get in the car and drive across town to check out a deal.

But the big bonus here is that you have direct access to all of the hard-working agents in your target market who are out there working deals. Again, what a gift. If you give me a fast Internet connection and thirty minutes and a telephone, I can tell you exactly who the very best real estate agents are in any target market. And through those contacts, I can find out who specializes in residential non-owner-occupied income properties. I also can get referrals to the very best real estate professionals in that town. At the same time, I can begin to narrow my focus and define my market, and I can enlist the help of multiple real estate agents in a given market who will now start sending me the very freshest deals, complete with pictures, right to my e-mail address.

It really does not get any better than this.

Your First Steps

If you have never done any real estate investing at all in the past, now is the time to start right in your back yard. Do the research that we have taught you how to do. Find out who the players are. Form a definition of value. Screen properties via the Internet and from e-mails from the buyer's brokers whom you have chosen to work with in that area. I remember to this day the first time that I flew a plane solo. My wife and my mother were there. I was scared, but breathlessly excited. When I started that plane's engine, I was ready. And all during that flight, I had a radio to speak with my instructor should any problem arise.

In real estate investing, I have come to believe that a mentor is one of the biggest things that you can have. Through the National Association of Real Estate Investors, I have direct access to hundreds of self-made real estate millionaires. Many of these financially independent real estate investors donate time to help beginners just like you. If you are that serious about investing and you want a mentor, then please let me know. E-mail me at marcstephan garrison@narei.com.

Your First Property Analysis

Your real estate solo flight will be the first time that you meet a real estate agent at a property that is listed for sale. If you are a beginner, be friendly but honest; if you are an absolute beginner, let them know. Have that real estate professional teach you how to inspect a potential income property. The most important thing that you can do is to look at that property through the eyes of your potential tenant. Some things you should do include the following:

- Actually flush the toilets.
- Check the ceilings (a discolored spot may indicate a leak in the roof).
- Look for out-of-season problems. It may be sunny and hot outside, and the air conditioning may work beautifully, but what about the heater? Six months from now, you may find yourself wishing you had tried the heater in the middle of summer.
- Write down exactly what type of appliances are included in the sale. I have felt too many times the disastrous effects of writing down "fridge" instead of "17 cu. ft. Amana almond refrigerator." It's amazing how a seventeen-cubic-foot, brand-new refrigerator can shrink to a nine-cubic-foot clunker by the closing date.

With a careful property analysis, you will be able to investigate only the few properties that really are good deals. If, as I'm visiting the property, I find that I like everything, I will immediately tie the property up with an earnest money agreement. Using what? you may ask. That's right, a promissory note as consideration to bind the agreement, with at least several good escape clauses. If I am not quite sure, I thank the sellers for their time and tell them that I will think about it for a while. Regardless of which step I take, I always do a careful property analysis.

The Financial Analysis

The next step: Do a financial analysis. Let me tell you the key points of any financial analysis.

1. Determine the market value of the property.

Find at least three houses or income properties in the area that are similar to the property that you are considering buying. Try to find properties that are as identical as possible in size, general condition, and amenities. (You can find these comparable properties through your buyer's broker, or by looking up some recent sales of similar homes with the help of your local title company.) Find out the selling price, and then adjust the price by estimating the value of the differences between these properties and the one you are analyzing.

If a seller is asking $72,000 for a house, how do you know whether or not that is a fair price? You look at comparable sales. With this system, you have done your homework and you know that the market value for the house is $65,000. Obviously the owner is way off base, and you shouldn't consider offering any more than $60,000, and hopefully a lot less. You have to buy equity.

Add the adjusted sales prices together, and divide by the number of comparable homes you found. That amount is the adjusted sales price for the property you are considering. If the property is to be fixed up, find at least three houses in the area that are similar to what the house will be like when you are through with your repairs. Do exactly the same as you did with the current condition estimate, and you will have a good idea what the market will bear when you are finished working on the property.

Comparative Analysis Grid

Item	Subject Property	Comparable #1	Adjustment	Comparable #2	Adjustment	Comparable #3	Adjustment
Price	?	$63,500		$67,000		$62,300	
Lot size	100' x 200'	100' x 250'	-500	100' x 200'	0	100' x 200'	0
Landscape	good	poor	+500	good	0	poor	+500
Sq. feet	1200	1100	+1,000	1150	+500	1200	0
Age	5 yrs.	10 yrs.	+1,000	2 yrs.	-2,000	10 yrs.	+1,000
Ext. features	patio	patio	0	no patio	+500	patio	0
Ext. features	sprinklers	none	+500	yes	0	none	+500
Location	good	poor	-1,000	poor	-1,000	good	0
Time of sale	current	3 months	+500	3 weeks	0	last month	0
Financing	11.5% assum.	12.5% assum.	+1,000	9.5% assum.	-2,000	non-assum.	+2,000
Extras	appliances	none	-1,000	mower/stove	+1,000	none	-1,000
Total adjustments		+2,000		-3,000		+3,000	
Adjusted sales price		$65,500		$64,000		$65,300	

Average Sales Price = $65,500
64,000
65,300
$194,800 ÷ 3 = $64,933 Adjusted
Averaged Sales Price

If this is a rental property, find other rental properties that are similar, and get comparable rents—for both the present condition and the proposed condition.

2. Estimate the proposed costs of purchase.

Find out how much the closing and other costs will be. Don't just assume these. For free estimates of those costs, call an expert. Find out from a title company what closing costs would be.

3. Estimate the costs of repairs.

If repairs are needed, you may want to call in a contractor to give you estimates. Most contractors will not charge a dime for this estimate. You could also first have the city inspector come in and point out any major repairs that are needed, then call up a contractor and get a quick verbal bid on these anticipated fix-up expenses. As you get more experienced, you will find that you will be able to give your own ballpark estimates of the fix-up expenses.

4. Estimate your total out-of-pocket.

Your out-of-pocket expenses will include the down payment (unless you are going to borrow that or bring in a partner); the fix-up costs; the closing costs; the monthly payments that you will have to make before you sell the property; the advertising costs when the time comes to sell; any attorney fees for closing or handling the legalities; and the closing costs that you will have to pay when you sell the property to someone else.

If you cannot estimate these costs, call an expert to help you. I recommend that you compile a list of local experts, including the following: an attorney who understands real estate; a title officer who is willing and able to help you; other investors who are willing to offer advice; a professional appraiser; and electricians, carpenters, and other contractors who will give you bids on work that needs to be done.

5. Make your decision.

Write down the estimated resale price (using the adjusted sales price as the actual market value). Subtract the total estimated buying costs, including all financing and closing costs. That will give you an estimate for your gross profit. Next, write the down payment that you think you will receive when you sell. Remember, your property will move quickly if you are willing to accept a small down payment—maybe just enough to cover your out-of-pocket expenses with a little left over for the next deal.

Then subtract the estimated down payment to be received from the estimated selling price. That will give you an idea as to how much equity you will have after selling. You may be tempted to ask for all of that equity in cash, but if you are willing to take it on an interest-bearing note, you will have a monthly income for many years, and you will find the property easy to sell.

6. Flip it or hold it.

To make this decision follow these simple steps. First, estimate the money cash flow on the property if it were rented. This is done by subtracting your monthly payments from the estimated amounts of net operating income you are generating. If you are in a high tax bracket, you might also want to grab a tax schedule and throw in the proposed tax benefits. I then suggest that you estimate the amount of money you have available for reinvesting if you choose to hold the property as a rental.

If this property totally drains your investment fund, I suggest that you consider immediately reselling the property. This would instantly give you a 100 percent return on your investment capital, but it also hopefully creates some instant cash profit besides the equity you may have taken back in an AITD or a second trust deed.

Making the Offer

If the financial analysis indicates that the deal is profitable, you should be ready to make a written offer. This is the point where many would-be investors drop out of the pack. If you have inspected the property and estimated your profits, nothing should hold you back at this point. You can obtain an earnest money and purchase offer form at any local office supply store. Only use a purchase offer form made for your state. You should customize the forms with some of the clauses we have talked about, such as escape clauses. If you need help writing up the offer, call a professional—a title officer, real estate attorney, or real estate agent. You will find that a good real estate professional will be happy to help you for free if you indicate that you will conduct the closing at his or her office, or do some business with him or her in the future.

When making an offer, keep in mind that your original offer may only be a springboard for negotiations. Allow yourself some room. A rule of thumb is to make your initial offer at least 15 percent below market value and negotiate from there. If you think the property is worth $56,000, and you know that you might be able to buy it for $53,000 but you would love to get it for $50,000, offer $48,000. You are $8,000 away from the actual value of the property, but that is a good place to start, and you will be amazed at how many times your offer is immediately accepted.

Take the offer to the owner. What else do you need to do?

Buy It, Save It, or Give It Away

If your offer is accepted, you own a new property. If the owner is willing to negotiate, all you have to do is iron out your differences, and you own a new property. If the owner rejects your offer and won't negotiate, file the offer away in an organizer, in a section entitled either "properties to refer to others" or "properties to check on later." If you know someone who is looking for the same type of property, why not turn it over to him or her? You can establish a reputation as a professional investor, and people whose backs you have scratched will usually be happy to return the favor.

If you feel that the deal is a good one, and the seller is close to negotiating, file it away to be checked on later. Three weeks can do a lot for a seller's motivation, and two months can positively work miracles.

This is what I do. I date-stamp each refused offer and call back two weeks later. I ask the seller if he or she is still serious about selling. If he says he is, I then identify myself and say that I would like to make him the same offer again to purchase his property. As crazy as this may seem, at least 25 percent of the people say yes to my offers the second time through. Why? I think it's because they haven't received any better offers, and they are now more aware of the true market value of their property. They are tired of keeping it in the paper. But most important, when you say that you are calling back two weeks after they refused your offer to make the same offer again, they are impressed with your organization and persistence. They recognize you as a competent person. In fact, you are someone who they probably now believe would make payments on time. They want to sell to you.

By keeping the entire system up to date, you can literally have an entire computer of good deals at your fingertips. So many people have said, "I've looked, but I haven't been able to find any good deals." But when they are asked, "How many ads did you call on, how many houses did you look at, how many offers did you make?" The answer is invariably the same: "Well, I . . ." If you call on several properties each night, it won't be long till you have found several properties to look at each Saturday.

Soon you'll be writing one or two offers a week. Soon you'll be getting one to two accepted per month. Soon you'll have enough money to do what you want, when you want. I think you can see how successful you can be if you put just one or two hours a day into this. You'll be getting bites on all your fishing lines and only spending time on the ones that are worth it.

This system works, but only if you do.

Do It Again

Here is the real key to success. It really needs no further explanation, does it?

You can invest in real estate in your spare time, but you will have to spare at least ten hours a week, every week. (That's just two hours a day, five days a week.) If you can commit that much time, there really is no way you can fail. Once you have educated yourself thoroughly and made good use of the many experts in your area, it's just a matter of time before that good deal comes along. The good deals are out there waiting for you. What are you waiting for?

I am reminded of one of our students, John Stuart from New York City. John is currently working single-family homes in one of our markets. To date, he has never paid more than $15,000 total for a single-family residence. That's not the down payment. That is the total purchase price. John just does one deal at a time. But each night he goes to *www.realtor.com* to see any and all of the properties that are currently listed in his target area. John buys a home. Then John does the cosmetic repairs needed to give that property curb appeal. Then John uses a government program titled Section 8 to find long-term tenants. Once that tenant moves in, John has a professional appraisal. John then either finances the property or does a "crank." (A crank is when you buy a property all in cash and you then get a new first mortgage after the property has been cleaned up, with a tenant in place, and a new appraisal.) On many deals like this, John cranks $30,000 to $40,000 out of the property as he finances it up to a near neutral cash flow. You need to realize that the money John pulls out of each property is tax-free since it is borrowed funds.

Another technique that we have taught John is to buy with a minimal down payment and to finance all of the repairs. Then place a tenant in the property and get a new appraisal. Based on that appraisal, John flips—a flip is when you buy and quickly sell—his property to an investor who is looking for a turnkey piece of real estate.

The bottom line is that John is doing one deal every two or three months and is pulling out $30,000 to $40,000 dollars per deal. All of this he does totally outside of his back yard in New York City. You also need to understand that John was not born with a silver spoon in his mouth. John is a hard-working young man who, through cash advances on his credit cards, pulled out enough money to pay for his first BuyingTour and to finance his first two deals. John Stuart is an inspiration to us all. His only problem is that he needs to slow down so that he can spend some time to find a wife and get married.

PART VII

Three Realistic Plans for Financial Freedom

You can't turn back the clock.
But you can wind it up again.

—*Bonnie Prudden*

Chapter 22

Plan Now,
Before It's Too Late

THERE ARE ONLY A FEW COMMON GOALS that link people together. Every individual has a unique place in life, a past, present, and future that compels that person to march to his or her own drummer. However, everybody desires security and comfort, freedom from worry, and the ability to choose.

Seeking to satisfy those needs, we embark on careers, making the transition into the mainstream of society as smoothly as possible. A few of us are lucky. We are satisfied with the lots we have cast, thoroughly enjoying our careers. The majority, however, find their dreams shattered by reality and their futures shaped by circumstance.

Even for those who are satisfied—or happy—with the choices they have made, the future is far from certain. The statistics quoted earlier about the harsh financial realities of retirement are horrifying, if we are willing to even consider them. A full 20 percent of Americans have no net worth by the age of sixty-five. That magical age sixty-five is when we all hope to be enjoying a leisurely retirement. But think about it: Only 15 percent of us will have more than

$250 cash at that point! And that means you and me, not just the guy next door. The vast majority will be dependent on the government or their families for even a meager living.

Somehow, retirement poverty is like cancer. Nobody wants to even think about it, let alone talk about it. It's something that happens to someone else, not us—until we wake up in a cramped and dirty one-bedroom apartment, hobbling from the bedroom to the living room to waste another day, and realizing that it's far too late for anything but despair.

The alternatives are clear. We can accept things as they are, find a new career, or find a plan to save and invest for the future (and the present). I have shown you a basic plan for investing in real estate. It sounds easy, right? But I'm worried. In spite of my best efforts, and in spite of the fact that most readers will be convinced, only a small fraction of them will actually do anything. It's a common reaction when investment experts try to teach, stimulate, motivate, and generally goad the public into action. Most people say, "That was a great book (or lecture), and it should work . . . but I still don't feel like I know what to do Monday morning to get this thing off the ground." For lack of a concrete plan of action, they fail to take even the first step.

Planning on Failure

I read the following article in a southern California newspaper.

> A bank robbery suspect in Oxnard was arrested Monday after police found him desperately searching for a bill small enough to make change for a pay toilet at a laundry.
>
> A Security Pacific National bank branch was robbed Monday by a man who handed the teller a note claiming he had a gun and demanding money.
>
> The man escaped with $13,492 in cash and checks. No change, no small bills.

A bank employee followed the man to the nearby laundry and pointed him out to the officer.

A witness inside the laundry said he saw the man pull a large wad of bills from under his shirt and flip through them in search of a denomination small enough to operate an automated change-maker.

The officer arrested the man and described him as "very excited" after the robbery and in need of the bathroom. The suspect was booked on suspicion of bank robbery at Ventura County Jail after being allowed to use the restroom.

As reported in the *Orange County Register*

What does that have to do with investing? Well, it's about the best example I've ever heard of someone who failed for lack of planning. You must plan now for your future. When I first read this article, I doubled over with laughter at how ridiculous this story was. Think, a man had gone into the bank to commit a robbery, had gotten over $13,000 in cash—that is almost as good as Amway—and had lost it because of a simple lack of planning.

It is sad that millions of Americans are on a downhill slide, and yet, even though they must be aware of its final destination, they refuse to get off. We're no longer satisfied with trying to keep up with the Joneses; we want to be the Joneses. We all live within our means, even if we have to borrow to do it.

Set Financial Goals . . . and Achieve Them

In 1986, when I started investing out of my own back yard, I felt like a kid in a candy store. I had essentially no competition and found an almost unlimited supply of good deals. Soon a lot of my friends who were members of the National Association of Real Estate Investors figured out what I was doing and wanted me to bring them out and introduce them to investing out-of-state in domestic absorption markets.

As time has gone by, I have quietly watched more than 2,500 students come out with us on our BuyingTour in small groups of fifteen. During that time I have totally changed my goals for my students. Instead of focusing on their becoming a self-made millionaire, I start with a few very simple goals.

1. To pay off all their consumer debt.
2. To own their residence free and clear and to put it into a legal entity that would ensure no one ever could take it away from them.
3. To develop a $10,000-per-month inflation-adjusted positive cash flow by the time that they plan on retiring.
4. Then, and only after then, do they start investing so that their personal dreams come true.

To pay off debt and to generate cash, you are going to have to do what John Stuart is doing today. You are going to need to buy and sell. You are going to need to focus on single-family homes and small rental properties (but preferably single-family homes). You are going to have to add up all consumer debt that you have and then work to pay it off, $30,000 to $40,000 at a time per deal. In the five markets that we are currently working, you could be doing two or three of those a year.

After your consumer debt is paid off, celebrate—go on a cruise, have a blast, get pumped. And then, come home and get right back into it. Add up what you have already done, and then focus on how many more deals that you have to flip or crank to pay your home off free and clear. And then do it.

After your home is paid off, you need to find a local attorney who specializes in asset protection. To find one, contact your county bar association and ask them for a referral to an asset-protection attorney in your area. Then, make an appointment with that attorney and simply ask him or her to put your home into the right trust or legal entity that guarantees that no court, not even the IRS, could ever take it away from you. If you can't find that attorney,

I have several referrals that I could give you to attorneys who specialize in this kind of work. They can help you find a local attorney in your state who, with their help, could build you your own financial fortress.

At the point at which your home is paid off, our next goal for you is to aggressively find ten single-family homes with a slight positive or a neutral immediate cash flow. I want you to buy each of these homes in the name of the trust or limited liability corporation (LLC) that you already have set up. I want you to pick a day, a month, and the year when you want to retire. I then want you to work these ten single-family homes and have them paid off in full by the date you have chosen to retire.

After you have locked down these ten homes—dream a little. Add up their positive cash flow today, and then ask yourself: "If these homes were paid for free and clear, could I live off of the sum total of those ten rental homes." In most cases today, that would equal about $10,000 per month before expenses.

To make that picture even sweeter, plug in the fact that for years now, the gross monthly rent on single-family homes has far outpaced inflation. That means that your ten single-family homes are going to give you for the rest of your life an income that is adjusted above the costs of living.

This is not a pie-in-the-sky dream. It's reality. And this is why 97 out of 100 self-made millionaires make their money in real estate. Essentially, real estate is the only type of investment in which you can use leverage. In other words, if you buy ten ounces of gold, you have to come up with all the cash. If you are buying a $100,000 single-family home, your down payment is going to be well under 10 percent in most cases.

Once you have paid off all of your debt, paid off your home free and clear, and bought ten single-family homes that will become your retirement vehicle, what then? Now it's finally time to work on your dreams.

At this point, you may want to get into larger units. I would suggest, though, that you always stay under fifty units per apartment building. I do not want you to start competing with all-cash New York Stock Exchange–traded real estate investment trusts (REITs) that focus exclusively on larger rental properties. The real key here is to focus on what motivates you and on the things that you would consider worth working your butt off for. Maybe it's a classic 1957 Chevrolet. Maybe it's a summer in France. Maybe it's a trip to Sweden. Whatever it is, define it.

If it's a summer in France, go to the bookstore and buy all the books about France. Talk with a travel agent. Find out what the best things to do there are. Find out exactly how much that extended trip would cost. And then earn it. You have to promise yourself that from this day on, for the rest of your life, that you will never buy anything that you cannot pay for with cash—with the one and only exception being real estate.

There is always room at the top.

—*Daniel Webster*

Chapter 23

Plan #1: Investing for Cash Flow

ONE THING THAT I HAVE LEARNED is that you can lead a horse to water, but that you cannot make it drink. If you are somebody who is rather intimidated by investing, let me give you three other plans that I myself lived from 1977 to 1986. These three plans—one in this chapter, and the next two in the chapters that follow—are really only for those of you who want to limit yourself to investing only within your back yard. In any case, choose the plan that fits you best and get started now.

The first plan, designed to take only a few hours a week, will give you the extra cash to afford a trip to Mazatlán in Mexico for sport-fishing every spring, or just to pay the bills. This plan will give you the extra cash to allow you to live comfortably and escape the problems of being stuck in a job you like but that may not pay enough.

Investing for Cash Flow

Objective: Extra income

Strategy: Moderately invest in single-family, bread-and-butter homes in your back yard. Focus in on rundown properties—the ugliest homes in an area. But make sure that you have formed a concrete definition of real value for the type of real estate that you would like to purchase.

Step 1 Master classified ads, empty properties, working with a real estate agent, and advertising for sellers. You should develop at least one good real estate farm. In essence, you will have four fishing lines in the water, all trying to catch good deals in real estate. You should set aside one to two hours each weekday to look for real estate bargains.

Step 2 Develop a real estate investing team. Seek out and work with a good real estate agent, mortgage officer, building contractor, and title officer. Have these people available to help you write up your offers and close your properties. Have them help you understand what you need to do. Tell them how they can help you.

Step 3 Establish a firm goal to purchase one property every six months.

Step 4 Achieve that goal by following a weekly investing program that includes further education (books, seminars, work-shops, and so on), telephoning, and visiting sellers in person only if the deal as presented (as defined by your research) would give you a positive cash flow from day one.

Weekly schedule:

Monday	Call on each possibility that you pulled out of the Sunday paper or got on your answering machine while you were at work.
Tuesday	Drive through your real estate farm and note

	any "for sale by owner" ads in the windows or on the lawns. Knock on the doors, or call the sellers immediately when you get home. Call on any messages you received on your answering machine.
Wednesday	Follow up on any leads you got Monday or Tuesday. Bring some earnest money agreements and promissory notes with you when you inspect the properties.
Thursday	Review your local paper for any motivated sellers. Call on these ads, and decide if they are worth investing time in.
Friday	Visit any properties you are interested in buying. Place ads at the stores in your farm area to let the public know you are interested in buying and selling real estate.
Saturday and Sunday	Do something fun with your family. If you absolutely must, spend some time Saturday looking at some properties or fixing up something you have bought.

Every month:

- Pass out ads in your farm.
- Check with your local postal workers and newspaper carriers who deliver to your farm and see if they know of any empty homes or rentals.
- Read at least one new book on investing each month. If possible, attend one real estate seminar or convention.

Buying strategies:

- Assume existing FHA/VA and pre-1978 conventional loans that don't have due-on-sale clauses.
- Only buy positive cash-flow properties. Always structure low payments.

- Determine the maximum amount that you could receive for a down payment if you were selling the property. Then subtract from that down payment figure your estimated repairs plus what profit you would like. Then offer that amount as your maximum down payment. For example, if you were to estimate that the maximum down payment you could get when you resold a property was $5,000, you would subtract your estimated fix-up costs of, say, $500, leaving you with $4,500. You would then subtract your required instant profit of $2,000—and be left with $2,500 as the maximum down payment you can offer the seller. Offer $500, and leave yourself a lot of negotiating room.

Selling strategies:

- Use, on a limited basis, the "I sell houses" flier technique.
- Let your buyers assume your mortgages, and offer to take back a second trust deed on your equity with a monthly, an annual, or a large balloon payment.
- Maintain control over your loans by using the wrap-around or all-inclusive trust deed technique.
- If you have trouble selling your properties, cut your required down payment and send out fliers with a picture of your property to local rental units.

Profit points:

- Immediate profit from selling your properties.
- Immediate profit from selling your notes at a discount to private investors or loan institutions. (If you take back a second mortgage on the sale of a property, you can sell this "paper" at a reduced percentage of its face value to an investor.)
- Long-term profit from AITDs (wraps) or seconds.

Five-year potential:

One home every six months
Year 1: 2 homes bought and sold

Year 2: 2 homes bought and sold
Year 3: 2 homes bought and sold
Year 4: 2 homes bought and sold
Year 5: 2 homes bought and sold

Five-year summary:

- Ten homes bought and sold
- Conservative five-year projection: $100,000 total profit ($10,000 profit per transaction).

This kind of profit (an extra $20,000 a year) sure beats working overtime at the old job. It also buys a lot of time to do what you really want to do.

Learn to live on less than you earn consistently!

—Becky L. Carter

Chapter 24

Plan #2: Affording Today and Tomorrow

THIS SECOND PLAN IS DESIGNED to give you not only cash today but also to provide the equity buildup to help you have the kind of retirement you deserve. This is the plan that I would like you to use in your back yard until you get itchy for making more money by coming out with us on a BuyingTour.

Affording Today and Tomorrow

Objective: Immediate cash and long-term income
Strategy: The basic steps of this investing plan are the same as those of Plan 1, but with important additions.

Addition 1 Increase your number of fishing lines by four. Find a good real estate agent, and develop a close working relationship. Actively promote yourself as a real estate investor to friends and relatives. Call the "for rent" ads each Tuesday and Thursday, and investigate foreclosure properties after the auction—from the bank, the FHA, and the VA.

Addition 2   Increase your investing to a solid two hours each day. Also set aside at least four hours a day each Saturday to check on your rentals and tie up any loose ends you need to check on.

Addition 3   Start your career as a real estate investment owner by keeping the best properties (in terms of cash flow, future appreciation, and low maintenance) you find instead of reselling them immediately.

Addition 4   Get a telephone answering machine and designate part of your home as your office for tax and mental health purposes. Get a file cabinet, a business phone, and develop a filing system to keep track of your real estate.

Addition 5   Buy at least one property every two months.

Addition 6   Involve your spouse (if you are married) in your investing. You will need the full support of your marital partner, or your marriage will feel the strain of your new part-time career.

Addition 7   Keep at least one property a year as a rental property. Keep the very best one in terms of condition, cash flow, lowest vacancy potential, and so on. You should take care to establish from the first a professional attitude toward property management: Have all of your properties managed by the best property management company in your area. Don't become an uncle or aunt to your tenants.

Addition 8   Develop a second, third, and fourth investment farm.

Addition 9   Have some nice-looking stationery and business cards made up for your investments.

Weekly schedule:

The weekly schedule is the same as in the first plan, only you must increase your time by two hours a day as need demands. You will also be working at least four hours on Saturdays, following up on leads that you got during the week.

Every month:

- Get involved in your local real estate investment groups. The National Association of Real Estate Investors helps sponsor small investment groups throughout the nation. For information on your local investment group, go to *www.narei.com*.
- Visit several real estate offices and leave your cards with the agents you see there. Tell them to call you if they ever come across any good deals.
- Visit several REO (real estate owned) officers at local banks. Leave your business card with them. Ask them to call you if they ever have something they want to sell fast.

Buying strategies:

- Write to your local government repossession agencies and get on FHA/HUD or VA mailing lists, or contact your real estate agent and have him supply you with a copy of the list.
- Advertise for partners. Don't let your lack of funds keep you out of good deals. It's better to get a piece of the pie than no pie at all.
- Develop a signature line of credit at a local bank.

Selling strategies:

- Become a matchmaker: use, on a regular basis, the "I sell houses" flier technique.
- Develop a list of professionals (doctors, lawyers, and dentists) who might be interested in investing in real estate. Present your properties to them before you buy.

Profit points:

- Immediate profit from selling your properties (flipping).
- Profit from buying properties and renting them out with a positive

cash flow. We have never, since 1986, paid more than $50,000 for a single-family home. Today we are consistently buying single-family homes in one of our target absorption markets for well under $20,000 (full sales price) and we are renting them out through Section 8 housing from anywhere between $825 and $1,525 a month. It's insane. But the demand is there, and the supply is limited.

- Depreciation and tax savings. When you become a real estate investor, you become self-employed. Being self-employed is the greatest tax haven and savings program that exists. Using today's federal tax laws, you can start taking pretax income dollars and divert a ton of your "normal living expenses and travel" and use them as write-offs. One of our students just flew to Paris with his wife and partner to check out investing in real estate there. He documented the appointments that he had with real estate professionals in France during his stay. Their airfares, hotels, rental car, and most meals are 100 percent tax-deductible from their real estate investing profits. (Be sure to check with your CPA or accountant regarding your own situation.)

- Profit from selling (assigning) your contracts to other investors before you close. You can make a profit merely by selling your right to purchase a property to someone else. (Include a clause in each contract that states, "Title to be vested in the name of (your name) and/or assigns.") Consult a local attorney concerning the laws in your state.

Five-year potential: One home every two months

Year 1:   6 homes purchased
                5 sold at a fair profit
                1 kept as a rental
Year 2:   6 homes purchased
                5 sold at a fair profit
                1 kept as a rental

Year 3:   6 homes purchased
                5 sold at a fair profit
                1 kept as a rental

Year 4:   6 homes purchased
                5 sold at a fair profit
                1 kept as a rental

Year 5:   6 homes purchased
                5 sold at a fair profit
                1 kept as a rental

Five-year summary:
        30 homes purchased
        25 sold at a profit
        5   homes kept as rental units

Conservative five-year net profit from buying and selling: $250,000 ($10,000 profit per real estate transaction).

Not bad, huh? But what about the five rentals you now own? Don't worry, I didn't forget about them. They are actually the best part. If each unit was purchased for $85,000, at the end of the year you would be looking at $63,812.82 increase in values with a mild, 7-percent inflation rate. The total value of your properties at the end of the fifth year would be $488,812.82.

This doesn't take into account the fact that these loans have been paying off (and you have built up a couple more thousand dollars' worth of equity as a result), or that you might have been enjoying some nice positive cash flow, or, even better yet, by your fifth year well over $10,000 a year in tax write-offs.

You now are making as much money by going to sleep at night and having your property appreciate as you would if you had a moonlighting job. (Your property during the sixth year would have appreciated $34,216.90 in value to $523,029.72.) And you are sleeping better, aren't you?

Nothing great was ever achieved without enthusiasm.

—*Ralph Waldo Emerson*

Chapter 25

Plan #3: Full-Time Real Estate Investing

THE LAST STEP-BY-STEP PLAN IS DESIGNED to accomplish not only cash flow and equity buildup but a net worth in excess of 1 million dollars in as little as three years. Here's one word of warning: this last plan is for those who are willing to live, sleep, and breathe investing. It is not for the weak-kneed.

Real Estate Investing Full-Time

We each have had dreams of untold riches, of being one of those people who can afford the yachts, trips, and all the little fun toys like Lear jets that most people can't afford. I hope you now realize that there is a realistic approach to investing that every living American can achieve, no matter what level of involvement he or she might choose, whether it is Level One investing in your back yard or Level Two investing in out-of-state domestic absorption markets.

If you want to supplement your regular income, so you can enjoy the summer in Europe instead of the back yard, use Plan #1 (described in Chapter 23). If you want to build up some equity for the future, and have enough for more than one nice trip each year and a new car when you need one—Plan #2 (in Chapter 24). Either plan is excellent for anyone who wants to keep the current job and invest. And all they require is five to fifteen hours each week.

Now for Plan #3: a cool million in five to ten years. It can be done in five years—as many investors, including myself, can attest—but you will have to commit yourself literally full-time at night and on weekends to reach your goals. If you want to make it a little easier, allowing yourself ten years might be more realistic. However long you end up taking, ask yourself this: Where will you be ten years from now if you don't do anything? You will have to organize your time, money, and effort, making the most of leverage. But the rewards are somewhere between phenomenal and staggering.

Objective: $1,000,000 in five to ten years
Strategy: Begin with Plans #1 and #2, and slowly work yourself up to four to eight properties during your first year of investing. If things look good, and if you enjoy investing, then move into Plan #3 and come out with us on a BuyingTour.

Million-Dollar Principle #1

Do whatever it takes to put together at least $50,000 to invest. This money could come from what you have earned from investing in your back yard. It could be an equity line of credit on your home or even cash advances on several credit cards.

Million-Dollar Principle #2

Come on a BuyingTour and gain our trust. Since 1986, we have never seen one of our students lock down a good deal and then not be able to find the money to fund the deal. I love the story of Sid Lester. Sid's wife died of cancer after he had spent every dime of his equity and savings taking her all around the world seeking alternative therapies to prevent her death. After his wife's death, he was dealt with another blow. He was laid off from his teaching position at a local university. His back was entirely up against a wall. I have zero idea how he came up with the money, but Sid came with us into Phoenix on a BuyingTour. As a result of that BuyingTour, Sid found an incredible deal—a complex of five four-plexes, all with pitched roofs and individual metering. The area his property was in had the highest amount of K–6 enrollment in the state. Sid locked down that deal with a promissory note and was now faced with a big problem: Where was he going to get the $50,000 required as his down payment to buy the property? The answer was that we taught Sid how to package that property, and we helped him find an investor who put up every single dime of the down payment in exchange for 50 percent of the profit. Within days, Sid sold his home in San Jose, California, and moved into one of his apartment units and started working to improve the property. During this time, I visited Sid several times and suggested that he contact the local school district to see if they were interested in buying that property as a site for a new elementary school. Guess what? They did want it. But the best part is that within months Sid and his partner were faced with the problem of splitting $500,000 in pure profit.

I also think of Howard Sklar. Howard came to us unemployed. He scraped together every single dime he could and bought a small rental property in Denver. Howard couldn't afford moving his entire family, so he also moved into one of his rental units and started to work. I have already told you this story, but I am constantly blown away with the common threads that our InnerCircle of documented self-made real estate millionaire students have:

- Sacrifice
- Value-based goals

- A future dream that is in Technicolor
- Hard work
- No excuses
- A willingness to kick butt
- Humility

If you don't have any cash, equity, or available credit, then find a partner with investment capital. To find such a partner, make a list not just of professionals, but of every relative, businessperson, or investor you know who might have access to cash. Go visit them all, share with them this book, buy our new video course and let them watch it, access our InnerCircle and have them e-mail you copies of their deals. Show your potential partners pictures of these deals. Help them to understand the new paradigms and the new strategies, tools, and tactics for investing in real estate today.

Tell potential partners that on occasion you are able to purchase properties for as little as 50 cents on the dollar. Offer them a 50 percent position in the property and all the tax benefits if they put up the money. (The property can be owned in their name with your interest being secured by an option to purchase a 50 percent position for $1.) You might go through a dozen people before you find your investor. But if you never give up, you will find a way.

Million-Dollar Principle #3

Use the most advanced real estate investing tools, such as foreclosures before the auction and at the auction. Use your investing partner's cash to purchase properties at a substantial discount in these forced-sale situations. You can buy a $60,000 property for as little as $30,000, and then refinance the property with an 80 percent, non-owner-occupied loan.

This loan would give you $8,000 cash. The $30,000 would be returned to your investor partner, plus 50 percent of the $18,000 profit. You could then rent out the property or sell it. In the meantime, both you and your partner would be enjoying approximately $9,000 tax-free cash. (You don't have to pay taxes on money you borrow against property you own.) As word spreads, you will soon have investors calling you up, offering you access to their cash. Always be aboveboard and honest with your investors.

Million-Dollar Principle #4

Don't go out and hire a full-time staff to maintain or fix up your properties. The overhead and headaches will kill you. Subcontract out every job on a competitive bid basis. Use only professionals. Avoid hiring relatives or local college students. Get a list of experienced painters, carpenters, and so on, who are willing to work part-time on a bid basis from your local buyer's broker.

Million-Dollar Principle #5

Buy at least two properties a month. That may seem like a lot. But you could easily do this if you simply put in the time. I was once there myself. I worked a day job full-time, and then I invested after work and at nights. I just kept telling myself that if I was willing to work for three years like other people will not, I could live the rest of my life like other people cannot.

To make this happen you need to be organized. I would highly suggest that you use the Franklin Covey time management system. To request a catalog, call (800) 819-1812. I have used that system for over two decades and would credit that system for a great majority of our financial success.

To make it you need to treat your investing career like a regular job with set hours, and don't deviate from your schedule. Actually keep a written record of how much time you spent every day on real estate and what you did during each hour.

Million-Dollar Principle #6

Keep at least one property for every six you buy and resell. This will allow you to zero out every year on your income taxes. I have never met anyone who was against that!

Million-Dollar Principle #7

Get a separate outside phone line for your real estate investments and your fax machine. Never use your personal home line for investing. You will need to have the peace that a separate phone line and answering machine or service provides. You also need a fax and an Internet connection at the highest possible speed that you can afford.

Million-Dollar Principle #8

Contact your target market's local county and city housing authorities. Find out which federal programs are available in your area. Today I called both agencies and found out more details on a government program that my tenants can sign up for to get new storm doors, windows, insulation in the ceilings and walls, and weather stripping installed free. I also found out about a federal low-income rehab program that will loan me money to rehab (fix up) units in an area that we are working. That program will loan me one-half of any rehab costs at 8 percent interest on a ten-year, interest-only note, provided I follow three of their rules:

- I must not convert to condos.
- I must not discriminate in renting.
- I must advertise any rentals according to a plan worked out with the housing agency.

If I follow these three rules, I won't ever have to pay back the principal on the loan. At the end of paying interest-only on the note, the principal amount will be waived.

Use these government programs. Be aware, these programs are constantly changing. To keep up on them, stay in contact with the local housing authorities that administer them. And please— never forget about Section 8 housing. Section 8 is a government-assisted rent program for families or single parents with children. In one of our target markets right now, Section 8 housing is giving out vouchers for up to $1,525 per month as rent in return for your letting a Section 8 tenant live in one of your rental homes. I have seen dozens of Section 8 properties in that town where the owner has less than $20,000 total into the property and through Section 8 they are getting up to $1,000 a month in rent. Run the numbers—those properties are free and clear in fewer than two years.

What's fun is to have a new student become a member of the National Association of Real Estate Investors. What typically follows next is that they buy a copy of our twenty-one–video "Challenge" real estate investing training course. Then, once they have completed that course, we schedule students to have direct access to me. What I do with them is to try to know exactly where they are financially right now—and then I explore where they want to be in five years. If I feel good about that person, I then line them up with one of our InnerCircle members for free mentoring. At that time, I also will give the student who has completed our new video course my direct private work number. I have done this now for almost seventeen years, and never once have I been taken advantage of or have I felt that I was wasting my time. A lot of people helped us on our road to financial freedom, and I feel an obligation to return what was once given to me. My only requirement is that a student has to care enough to purchase and study all twenty-one videos of our new course before we talk. That way we are both singing from the same hymnal.

Buying strategies:

Use every technique we have talked about so far. In addition:

- Use options to tie up properties. An option is the right to buy or sell something such as a piece of real estate during a specified period at a specified price.
- Buy discounted paper (notes on real estate) and resell it at a profit. We mentioned in Plan #1 how you could take your "paper" (financing that you are carrying on properties you have sold) and sell it at a discount to investors. This discount may be as much as 50 percent of face value. Consider investing yourself in discounted paper. You can resell this paper at a profit or trade it for full face value on a property you are buying.
- Negotiate deferred-payment notes (owner financing in which the payments won't start for a year).
- Negotiate the right to extend any balloon payments you might assume.
- Run an ad in the "Real Estate Wanted" section of your local paper. A sample ad would say something like: "Family man seeks to buy home with assumable loan or seller financing. Call Marc 222-8888."

Selling strategies:

- Sell half interest in a property to a partner to cover any negative cash flow.
- Put out some "I sell houses" fliers every week. Make sure that every laundry in town has one.
- Run an ad in your local paper under "Homes for Rent." A sample ad would say something like, "Are you sick and tired of throwing away your money in rent each month? I have some homes for sale. No qualifying and low down payments. Call Marc 222-8888."
- Exercise your escape clauses before you close if it looks like you're going to have trouble selling or renting a property.

- If you have purchased something with the intention of flipping it (buying and selling immediately), but are having trouble selling it, cut your losses immediately. Rent it out as soon as possible, and then try to sell it as an occupied rental.

Profit points:

- From buying and selling contracts (and/or assigns).
- From optioning a property and subleasing it to someone else or exercising your option and buying it for rental or resale.
- From buying and selling properties (flipping).
- From buying and selling discounted paper.
- From trading discounted paper for full value when you buy a property (for example, trading a $10,000 note you purchased for $5,000 and a full $10,000 equity in a property).
- From the positive cash flow on rentals.
- From refinancing properties.
- From getting low-interest government loans and rental subsidies.
- From bringing in partners.
- From appreciation.
- From good property management (increasing the rents and lowering expenses).
- From changing a property's use. (A friend of mine just bought an older home with some attached land. He's now putting up an office building on the vacant land.)
- From developing part of a property purchase into a building lot that can be sold separately.

Five-year profit potential: Two homes every month

Year 1: 8 homes purchased (starting phase)
6 sold at a fair profit
2 kept as rentals

Year 2: 24 homes purchased
20 sold at a fair profit
4 kept as rentals

Year 3:   24 homes purchased
               20 sold at a fair profit
               4 kept as rentals
Year 4:   24 homes purchased
               20 sold at a fair profit
               4 kept as rentals
Year 5:   24 homes purchased
               20 sold at a fair profit
               4 kept as rentals

Five-year summary:
               104 homes purchased
               86 sold at a profit
               18 homes kept as rental units

Conservative five-year net profit: $860,000 ($10,000 profit per real estate transaction).

So where is the million dollars? Remember the rentals? With just a 7 percent inflation rate, the appreciation on your rental units has pulled your five-year profit over the $1,000,000 mark. If you had purchased each unit for $85,000, you would have earned in excess of $202,000 in appreciation on your units during those five years. The next year's appreciation alone on the units would be over $300,000. (Are you getting a feeling for how this snowballs?) This again doesn't take into account one dime of increased cash flow from the tax advantages of your properties' depreciation or your ability to write off a great part of your new income as a business expense. You may also have carried back your excess tax benefits to previous tax years and recaptured a great portion of the tax you paid in the past three years. It's legal, if you have a net operating loss. (If your tax write-offs exceed your income, you can recapture—get a refund on—the tax you paid during the past several years or apply the amount to future taxes.) If you do that, please don't invest it. You deserve to blow it on yourself. You have earned it.

What I love is that fact that if you do what I just told you in any market—regardless of whether it is in expansion, equilibrium, decline, or absorption—with some hard work anybody could do this.

But consider what John Stuart is doing in one of our absorption markets—$30,000 to $40,000 tax-free on each deal. How about Sid Lester with his half of $500,000? Or how about Pok Ward, with her $1.8 million that began as only $7,000, or how about Howard Sklar, who now has earned a net of $3.47 million since he first started with us? Remember Howard? He had to leave his family behind and move into one of his own rental units. He had never once in his life used a hammer before we got him started in real estate investing with us.

Do you feel a little bit scared? Is this a bit overwhelming? If you didn't feel apprehensive, I would worry about you. But don't worry, the following section will give the do's and don'ts you'll need to steer clear of any pitfalls on your road to success.

PART VIII

Ten Keys to Success: The Do's and Don'ts

Failure is the opportunity to begin again more intelligently.

—*Henry Ford*

Chapter 26

Welcome to Success

SEVERAL YEARS AGO, I BECAME a certified scuba diver. I spent hours in a dry, often boring class, learning the basics of successful diving before the instructor ever allowed me to jump into the water.

I know what your motivation was when you cracked the cover of this book. You wanted to be given specific tools for buying and selling houses. You wanted me to hand over the equipment that you will need to dive in and get started. And that's all you wanted.

Well, I've given you those tools, but I don't want to turn you loose just yet. Instead, I am going to ask you to sit in class for a few more chapters and learn the basics of true success in real estate investing. You need to learn the keys to success before I turn you loose on the investing world. Otherwise, your chances for success are very slim. It takes more than the right tools to do the job; you have to know how to use them properly.

If you don't want to "waste" your time learning how to avoid the dangers that catch most investors, and if you want to jump in, go ahead and do so—at your own risk.

If I had taken a tank and a wetsuit and simply dived headfirst into the waves without first learning how to dive safely, I would have surely lost my life or been seriously injured and afraid to ever go out again. The same thing happens all the time to new investors who fail to prepare thoroughly.

The Winning Edge

Before you begin investing, you have a few choices to make. How many hours will you work each week? Is this going to be a full-time venture, or one that just occupies a few minutes a day? Do you have the drive and determination to succeed that will see you through the tough spots? Should you give up your job tomorrow?

The remainder of this book will give you what you need to separate yourself from the pack. I want to give you the winning edge. At least nine out of every ten would-be investors never reach their goals, and I believe strongly that they fail because they are unaware of the basic principles of success.

The next two chapters include my ten keys to success. I've reviewed them carefully, and I can't find one of them that is really a lot of fun. They all require time and concentrated effort. But it's effort that every successful person has applied in his or her life, and if you want the same thing in your life, there is no shortcut.

Realistically, I think you should start out slowly. Keep your job until you are financially free because of your real estate. To start with, for the first few months, you should spend only ten hours a week or so. Start in your back yard. Call on ad after ad; visit seller after seller. When you find the perfect deal, buy it. When you've fixed it up, sell it. Take your time, and do it right. Please, learn to walk before you run. I have been teaching the principles of real estate investing around the country, and it has been very gratifying to hear of my students' successes. However, I recently received a letter from a hopeful investor who had quit his job to begin investing in real estate. It was a frightening revelation for me that someone had taken part of what I was teaching—how to find good deals and invest profitably—without heeding my advice to start slowly. The student was now faced with a lack of cash flow and was very concerned. My response was to strongly urge him to go back to work and build his investing career carefully, not blindly. I worked full-time and invested full-time for a couple of years before I became a self-made millionaire and quit my job. If you want to start reaching a point where you can quit working for the boss and start working for yourself, that's great. Set a goal, make plans, and reach that point! But please don't put down this book and pick up the phone right now to let the boss know what he can do with that job!

Take as much time as you need, especially with the first deal. Be fussy. And then, when you have finished your first real estate deal, sit down with a blank piece of paper and a pen and review. Draw a line down the middle of the page. On the left side of the line, write everything that went right. What were you especially pleased with? On the other side of the line, explain to yourself exactly why those things went so well. Commit yourself to the same success on every deal.

Now turn the page over, and do the same things except this time write down what went wrong and why. Analyze your mistakes, and figure out how you can improve. How can you keep from making those mistakes again? The first few times you fill out these analysis sheets, you may have a couple of pages of mistakes and only half a page of good points, but that will change after two or three successful investments.

Dealing with Your First Taste of Success

After you've tasted success, and you can afford to quit, will you give up your job and become a full-time investor? It's up to you, of course, but here are a few guidelines.

1. Do you like your job? A lot of Americans love their jobs. The problem is they can't seem to make enough money. If

you fall into this group, then you should continue to invest, but only as a way of supporting the work you love. If you don't like your job, then perhaps your investments could support you through an educational program so that you can eventually do what you really want. (Makes sense, right?) Real estate investing should be the means by which you are able to do what you want, when you want, wherever you want it, and with whom you want.

2. Are you a self-starter? Are you driven? I think few people have the drive to stick to a concentrated program of investing long enough to make the millions that are possible in real estate. I've noticed that most people make a little money and immediately reward themselves by spending their profits. They just don't have the self-control necessary to reinvest.

Those who succeed in real estate seem to listen to a different drummer. They reinvest most of their profits, keeping the ball rolling and growing. They balance their lives so that they make money and still have time left over to be with families and friends. They associate with other investors. An old saying is that if you want to be an alcoholic, you should hang around in a bar or a local Alcoholics Anonymous chapter. I would say that if you are thinking about being an investor, you should start hanging around with investors. You should find people with interests that are similar to yours and associate with them. Your investor associates will keep you motivated and on the road to success.

Successful full-time investors realize that there are no time clocks to punch, and therefore they must find other incentives for sticking to investing full-time. Many investors seek areas of real estate investing that they thoroughly enjoy. Some concentrate on single-family dwellings, smaller rental units, or large projects. Others enjoy investing in foreclosures, calling newspaper ads, or advertising for sellers. They find their real estate investing niche. Paula and I have found that we like investing out of our back yards in absorption markets. We like owning properties that are professionally managed. We like doing the research, building a real estate investing team in that market, and then sharing that entire package with people just like you on our BuyingTours.

3. Are you making as much money with your investments as you were working? This isn't a hard-and-fast rule, but few people can step down on the economic ladder comfortably. When your investment profits are outpacing your paychecks consistently, then you should consider investing full-time.

I love investing full-time, mostly because I have mastered the ten keys to success and now have the freedom to enjoy my time, my family, and my future.

He who hesitates is interrupted.

—*Franklin P. Jones*

Chapter 27

Five Rules to Follow

THERE IS A LAND THAT YOU'VE DREAMED OF, and it's not somewhere over the rainbow; in fact, it's right around the corner. You probably know a few people who live there. When you look through the bars that separate you from this land, you wonder how anyone could get inside. The people look happy. In fact, they are obviously enjoying their lifestyle.

What you don't realize is that the bars are not there to keep you from getting in. Instead, those are the bars on your own cell, keeping you from getting out. There are several doors in your cell that would let you out. Most of the doors have thousands of bars and chains that are almost impenetrable. But one of them, marked "real estate," has only ten keyholes. If someone were to give you those ten keys, you would be able to escape into the land of success.

Well, I have those ten keys dangling on a keychain that I carry with me wherever I go. And I've made copies of those keys, which I've embedded into the pages of this chapter and the next. Take the keys and insert them into the locks, and I guarantee you freedom. Beware! The keys are good, but the locks won't turn easily. Each key will require work—lots of it. But the alternative is to continue to look through your bars.

The first five keys are the do's of real estate, and the second five are the don'ts. Once you have mastered all ten, you will be ready to break free. Got your key chain ready? Okay, here's key number one:

Key #1: Do Set Aside Time Each Day for Success

Mis-spending a man's time is a kind of self-homicide.

—*George Saville, Marquis of Halifax*

"It was the best of times; it was the worst of times." These words, from Dickens's *A Tale of Two Cities,* seem to sum up a common feeling in today's real estate market. For some, it is the worst of times. When interest rates are high, money is tight, and inflation is running away with housing prices, they are afraid of the market. When the opposite is true, they are afraid of competition and stagnant prices. Their financial growth comes to virtual halt, and they sit on the bank watching the tides of fortune and wondering when to jump in.

For others, it is the best of times. They recognize that now is the time to act. They don't wait to see what will happen; they make it happen. Successful real estate investors know the benefits of investing now, and they regularly set aside time to accomplish their financial dreams.

The time is never right for someone who is unwilling to seize opportunities, and it is always right for the rest of us. I have to laugh every time someone tells me that all the money in real estate was made in the 1970s. Nothing could be further from the truth. But it takes the right attitude and a willingness to set aside time if you want to succeed. You must learn to set aside time every day to study, research, and invest in real estate.

You may be wondering how you should be spending that time right now. The answer is easy. Spend your time on education before anything else. That's the only way to approach any new situation. I'm reminded of the city cousin who went to visit his country cousins out on the farm. He was so eager to be a real farmer that he insisted on taking the bucket down to the milking shed and taking care of that chore himself.

He dragged the poor cow into the shed, took the milking stool off the hook, carefully placed the pail under her udder, and waited. And waited. And waited…

He's probably still waiting for Bossie to do her stuff. The fact is, too many novice investors trudge out to the milking shed with an empty bucket and a hazy knowledge of how the process works, and they then find themselves waiting and wondering when they will reap the tremendous rewards they have heard about. That really is the magic with our video course—it took us over sixteen years to put it together. In this professionally filmed course, you have seven days of training, with half the training in the classroom and the other half of the day in the field. The people who attended that training paid for their own airfare plus just under $6,000. You yourself can personally view that presentation for pennies on the dollar. One of our recent students commented that when they watched our new video course it was just like being there in person. I loved hearing that. Another viewer said that being able to view the testimonial after testimonial that some of our past students gave during that seven-day training blew her away, because she could feel how we were just like a family and that we actually cared about our students. My favorite thing about the video course is being able to rewind and go over a sticky point over and over again until you are caught up to speed.

The second question is, how much time and effort do you need? Start with two hours a day. Don't tell me you don't have the time—make the time. Set your alarm a little earlier, give up *I Love Lucy* reruns for a month, or abandon the wasted extra hours of beauty rest. Which would you rather be, wealthy or beautiful?

Valuable Seconds, Minutes, and Hours

How would you like to have an account opened for you at the local bank, with an opening balance of $864? There is one catch to this particular account: at the end of the day, your account is cleared—reset to zero—and you start the next day with another $864. You may withdraw any or all of your money and invest it; but if you fail to withdraw any of the money, you lose it. What would you do?

The answer is almost too obvious to write. You would withdraw every penny, every day. And I'm sure you would invest your money wisely, so you could be wealthy in no time at all. Well, the bank is open and your account is active. It's the First National Bank of Time, and every second is worth one penny. You start with 86,400 of those little hummers at the stroke of midnight, and twenty-four hours later every one of them is gone. How many did you invest, and how many did you squander on meaningless trivialities?

Why do you lock your doors at night? Because you fear being robbed. And yet we rob ourselves of treasures infinitely more valuable than Grandma's silver service for eight. We take away the opportunities for accomplishment and success.

Enough sermonizing. I hope I have convinced you that setting aside time for success is a crucial part of the process, and I trust that you are ready to put aside at least two hours a day—every day—for success.

If you can set aside at least two hours a day, five days a week (less than half the time most serious investors spend learning and earning), in a year you will have spent 520 hours working toward the goals you have set. You will also have spent 2,000 hours at work, earning enough to get by from one day to the next. Which hours will pay the biggest dividends? You figure it out.

Those two hours are sacrosanct. They are the hard labor that will be required if you don't want to serve a life sentence in a padded cell. If something does come up, and you absolutely have to give up that time, make it up on Saturday or Sunday, but don't allow one week to go by without spending at least ten hours investing in your future.

Actually scheduling your time will be an extremely difficult task if you're used to living by the credo "I'll get to it someday." I suggest getting used to the idea of budgeting your time, and I further suggest that you use a daily planner, like the Franklin Covey time management system that I use. It allows you the freedom of a flexible schedule and yet acts as a constant time organizer and work planner.

Expect the Unexpected

What can you do about unexpected delays and emergencies? Plan for them, and reschedule when necessary. After a while, a whole lost weekend will barely cause you to break your stride. It may at first seem like too much work, but the rewards for organizing your time are unbelievable, and the alternative is to continue wasting your life, wondering how the hours escape you so easily.

As I write this, it is a cold and rainy Wednesday night. The last thing I will do before giving in to the temptation of a warm bed is to consult my planner and prepare for tomorrow. After filling in the "must do" hours—tomorrow there's school and an afternoon appointment—I am free to arrange my priorities and schedule accordingly. I prioritize the assignments I have given myself, so that if I need to reschedule my plans everything that has to be done still gets done.

No, I'm not a robot; I'm just organized. How much difference does that make? Well, think about it. If you sleep eight hours a night, work eight hours a day (and add another two hours for driving and getting ready for work), and eat for one hour, that only uses up nineteen hours out of twenty-four. I'll even take off another hour for the minutes between this and that—the going-to and coming-from time. You still have four hours to account for—and that's on weekdays. You may have plans for the weekend; you may even think that weekends really were made for Michelob. But the only ones ever to achieve wealth with that guideline are the people who sell Michelob.

I'm feeling generous, so I'll allow you one wasted, who-knows-what-happened-to-the-time hour, and one solid hour for your family. That still leaves you with two hours!

"But I need my fun time too, don't I?" you say. Sure you do; we all need to have fun. All work and no play not only make Jack and Jill dull kids, but it warps their spirit and destroys their emotional health. But concentrate your energies on what you are doing. When it's time to play, play hard. When it's time to work, buckle down and work hard. Too many people lead bland, colorless, marshmallow lives, like an old black-and-white movie with no plot. They just live day to day in a miasma, never enjoying life's peaks.

Don't let anyone or anything keep you from success. You are the master of your own destiny, and you are the only person standing between your current situations and getting everything you want.

Do set aside time for success. That's the first key. And the second is this.

Key #2: Do Learn Before You Leap

The greatest artist was once a beginner.

—*Farmer's Digest*

Your first key still shines like the day it was made. Perhaps you've even tried putting it in the lock. Maybe you actually set aside the two hours and committed yourself to reaching your goals. The second key is to use that time to learn how to invest. You should read everything about real estate investing that you can get your hands on, and you should talk to the experts.

Forget real estate for a minute. Instead, set your sights on becoming a produce manager. You really want to excel; you want to be the produce manager that all the other produce managers are talking about. What would be your first step?

You might attend a produce managers' class. Don't laugh—there really is such a thing. You would want to know everything there was to know about fruits and vegetables. You would need to know market values. How much is a good watermelon worth in the middle of September, as opposed to the first of July? What is the resale value of avocados after they have been on the shelf three days?

If you don't know all of this and much, much more, you won't last two days on the job. The key to success in the produce manager's world is a good education in fruits and vegetables.

You want to buy and sell houses instead of bananas? Fine, but the same rules for success are valid. If the investor does not gain the necessary knowledge of real estate principles, the economic realities of supply and demand, and market values, he or she will have one of the shortest careers on record.

This does not mean that you have to know everything about real estate to buy a property. But you must at least know the basics, and you must have developed the ability to accurately estimate market values so you can buy wholesale and sell retail. How do you acquire this knowledge?

Books and Seminars

When I first became interested in real estate investing, I was stunned by the gibberish that fell trippingly off the tongues of other investors. Every other word was incomprehensible. When I tried to look up definitions, I found that there was no reliable investor's encyclopedia, so I wrote one myself. It took a couple of years to get all the information together, but I think what you will find on our Web site, *www.narei.com,* is the most authoritative encyclopedia and reference guide to real estate.

Talking to Experts

There is no better way to obtain a free education than by talking to the right people. Is there an investors' group in your area? If so, attend the meetings. Count that as your two hours for that day. Take a successful investor out to lunch, and while the cook is grilling your hamburger, you can be grilling the investor.

In this book we introduced several experts who can help you. The amazing thing is that the education they can give you is often free, if you know how to ask the right questions.

Talking to Sellers

As you continue to learn, start cutting out "for sale by owner" ads in the classifieds and calling the owners. We've already discussed this as a method for finding good deals, but how do you organize your time?

A simple schedule for following for-sale-by-owners is to read the paper and clip ads as soon as you get home from work, and then call the owners in the evening, right after dinner. If any of them has a house that sounds interesting, make an appointment to see the owner and talk to him or her.

You can spend a whole day at the mall without buying anything, can't you? Why not spend a whole Saturday looking at houses without any intention of buying? Leave your wallet and earnest money agreements at home. (What do you mean, you don't have any earnest money agreements? Get over to the office supply store and buy a dozen.) Talk to owners and walk through houses; what have you got to lose?

The MLS Book

Another source of homes for sale is the Multiple Listing Service at *www.realtor.com*. In the past, before *www.realtor.com*, real estate agents were not allowed to let you have a copy of that book.

I know of a lot of real estate investors who used to check the garbage behind the local real estate office to find a used copy. The Internet has changed the world. This morning I checked *www.realtor.com* to see the lowest priced single-family homes that they had listed in all five of our current absorption "out-of-state markets." I saw single-family homes in each of the five markets for sale for less than $1,000. The most inexpensive was under $400. I hope that you are beginning to understand why since 1986 I have almost exclusively worked absorption markets in towns that for years had been in a deathly market with almost zero demand. We do not buy anything that will not give us an immediate cash flow after rehab and cosmetic repairs. We buy only in the path of progress. We research and target regions of opportunity (absorption markets) and avoid at all cost regions of obsolescence (equilibrium and decline markets.) The Web site *www.realtor.com* can be an incredibly rich source of real estate knowledge. When a property is included on the site, there typically is a picture of the property and a link that brings you to a complete description of the property and gives the contact information for the real estate professional who is listing this property for sale. On this Web site, you will get tons more information than you ever could get by simply driving by and looking. Again, *www.realtor.com* will have a picture of the property, the asking price, the down payment, the loan information, as well as a complete physical description (bedrooms, baths, and amenities). Take a couple of days this month and do nothing but surf around all the properties that are listed for sale in your own back yard. Call the agents who are listing the properties that you like. Then get into your car, and meet the agents at their properties. Always remember that at this stage you are comparing features, neighborhoods, prices, and trying to find the very best real estate agent to help you start making money in your back yard. After just a few weeks of driving around, talking to owners and comparing prices, you should begin to get a good feel for prices in your area.

A Lifetime of Learning

What's the difference between my wife and me, on one hand, and you on the other? It boils down to knowledge and experience, nothing more. You can gain both, if you are willing to apply yourself.

We have already done the necessary studying. We know how to recognize a good deal; we know how to buy and sell a property quickly; we know what we need to know to succeed as an investor. That's the only real difference. Everything else follows from education. It's what allows a surgeon to charge an arm and a leg (to use an expression). And if we were hard pressed for an answer as to why over 2,500 students have come with us on our BuyingTours since 1986, the answer is that we know how to make money today in real estate. If you were to go with us on a BuyingTour, you would need to first complete our seven-day video course. You would need to be using a good time management system like the Franklin Covey. You also would need to know how to work a Hewlett-Packard 12-C financial calculator. A lot of people know how you could have made money back in the 1970s, but they don't know what it takes to succeed today. The reason that we do so well is that we have never quit studying. We have adapted to today's markets. Investing outside of our back yards is rather like slicing open a cold watermelon and eating only the heart of it. Just the very best part—no seeds, mushy parts, or bruises. We just go where it is good. I think by now you have come to realize that all residential income properties are in a cycle—expansion, equilibrium, decline, and absorption. And, I think that you have come to understand that the heart of the watermelon—or the very best economic cycle stage to invest in—is a domestic absorption market that is just getting out of a decline. End of story.

My wife and I haven't stopped learning. We study every day, learning new words, and new financing devices and making new contacts. In time, we may reach the forefront of real estate knowledge in one narrow segment of the business, but we will never know everything there is to know about real estate. We do, however, know everything there is to know about watching television, so why should I spend any more time studying the fine art? Why should you?

Here, take this key. It's called education, and it will be the largest key on your chain. When it is inserted into its lock, along with the time management key, all the other locks should turn more easily. Learn before you leap. Start working your back yard. Attend ground school.

Key #3: Do Organize Your Personal Finances

The taller the building, the deeper
The foundation must be.

—John Tripp

I had a dream. From the time I was a little kid, running and playing on the dusty sidewalks of Long Beach, California, I wanted to get away—in an airplane. I suppose all kids want to fly a plane when they are little, but I wanted it so bad. I thought I would die if I couldn't be a pilot. I remember time after time taking an aerobatic plane up and trying a series of accelerated stalls, spins, hammerhead stalls, inverted flight, and barrel rolls. I love flying; it's everything I dreamed it would be, and more.

The dream has become a reality, and I have real estate investments to thank for that. Coupled with real estate knowledge and experience, the third key allowed me to afford the fulfillment of a dream. If you have dreams that you haven't experienced because they cost money, you need the third key. And you need it even if you never buy a stick of property; you need it to fulfill any financial dreams.

This key is an old, rusty skeleton key. It's so old that your grandparents may have passed it down to you from their grandparents. It's such an ugly old key that you are inclined to ignore it completely, eager to get to the good stuff. And ignoring it, you will live like many investors I know who have a million in real estate and have trouble scraping together ten bucks in cash.

Ready? Okay, the third key is personal financial planning. I know, I know: "Oh brother, not budgeting!"

Let me tell you a little more about flying. During the months of study and preparation for getting my pilot's license, I was continually impressed with the importance of checking my plane thoroughly before each flight.

I would literally check each nut and bolt on the plane to make sure it was tight, intact, and ready for the rigors of flying. I would crawl under the plane and check the tires to make sure they would support the loading caused by the stress of takeoff and landing. The engine, gas, and oil reserves, the prop, radios, antenna, carburetor heat, and magnetos would all be thoroughly and methodically checked. Why all the worry?

Because I didn't want to crash!

Your financial foundation must be established now, not after you are wealthy. Now. It's time to begin budgeting your money and putting a little aside—not for a rainy day, but for a bright future. It's time—today—to establish a spotless credit record.

One of the best and worst things about real estate is that money is not a prerequisite for success. You can find excellent nothing-down deals everywhere. But you can't eat equity; you need money to live on while you're achieving your goals.

I know an investor who was doing very well—on paper. He had amassed enviable real estate holdings, and he justified his lack of cash by saying that all he needed was enough to get by on while he built up his equity. His sophism finally fell apart one day when he was on his way to buy a house.

There he was, clipping along the highway, contemplating the great deal ahead, when suddenly, whap-whap-whap-whap-whap—a flat tire. Not just any flat tire; it was the spare, which he had used to replace another flat only one week before.

Well, he bought the needed tires and watched someone else

buy the house and make $18,000 on the resale because he didn't have enough money to close on the deal. He ruined the deal because he had to buy two tires, so that works out be about $9,000 a tire. (And they were only retreads!) Had he developed his ability to plan for his own finances first, he could have bought the tires and the house, and maybe a nice dinner to celebrate. Instead, he is still broke, chasing the few deals that he can afford and passing those that he can't afford to me. Who do you think is getting the better deals, and building a higher building?

Little Savings Add Up Big

Who do you pay first when you receive that paycheck? The bank for the credit charges, or the rent, or a little gas and groceries to get you through until next payday? And who do you pay last, if at all? Yourself. That's what happens whenever you fail to drop a few dollars in the savings account: You are cheating yourself out of a share of your income. Everyone makes money from your labors, and you fall into another week of the same routine.

You may be tempted to say, "But, Marc, I'm just barely getting by as it is! I can't possibly save any more." Have you ever tracked your expenditures? You might be surprised how the pennies and nickels slip through the cracks. Try it for a week or two. Record every expenditure of cash, check, or charge, noting whether it was an absolutely necessary expense. Don't forget to write down every nickel, dime, and quarter; that's where much of our wasted money goes.

When you have tracked your total spending for two weeks, add up all the unnecessary expenditures and multiply by twenty-six. That will give you a rough idea of how much you could be saving every year. The more accurate you want the system to be, the longer you will have to track your expenses.

You may be surprised to find you could be saving literally thousands of dollars every year. That makes for a pretty poor foundation, doesn't it?

As practicing members of a Christian church, we believe in the law of tithing; that is, we pay 10 percent of our taxable income to the church. That money comes right off the top; I pay the Lord the first tenth of my income, and myself the second tenth. That leaves me with 80 percent for the butcher, the baker, and the candlestick maker. I believe that anyone can survive on 80 percent of his income if he absolutely has to.

Let me put it to you differently. The next time you arrive at work, you find out that you will have to take a 10 percent cut in pay. What will you do? I'll venture a guess. You'll manage somehow. It won't be easy; it may even seem impossible, but you'll make it.

If you have climbed on the credit card carousel—spending all of your time trying to catch up with the bills while creditors spend their time trying to catch you—then you should seek professional counseling. Get your financial affairs in order before investing a dime in real estate. If you can't control your current income, it will be impossible to control a $10,000 cash profit from the sale of a property.

Planning a Budget

Setting up a budget isn't very hard. It's like setting up a diet schedule. It's after you've set up your budget that things get difficult. Bad habits can be killed, but they fight every step of the way, so you'll have to arm yourself with determination. That means complete agreement with your spouse and at least a two-year commitment. But, as we already have said:

> *If you live for three years like most people won't,*
> *you can do for the rest of your life what most people can't.*

Planning a budget is a three-step process. Step one is projecting your income and expenses; step two is designing a budget;

and step three—the killer—is sticking to that budget like these letters are stuck to the page.

A budget can be as complex as a full accounting system, involving ledgers and a daily journal entry, or it can be as simple as a record of expenses and a loosely defined limit for each expense account. Hopefully, your budget will be as complete as possible without being so complex that you lose interest and give up after only a month.

If you own a personal computer, consider getting one of the dozens of home budget programs available, which will make budgeting an almost painless process.

If I were to attempt to explain a working budget in detail, this chapter might well turn into a small book by itself, so I'll go through the basic steps and leave you to figure out a budget system that will work for you. For a more involved explanation, I recommend either Sylvia Porter's *Money Book* or Jerome Rosenberg's *Managing Your Own Money*.

Plan out your expenses for an entire year. Remember to keep controllable expenses, such as entertainment and groceries, to a minimum. Use old bills for reference to get an idea of average monthly costs. Don't forget to count gifts and annual expenses, such as insurance premiums.

Break down all expenses into a monthly average, and compare that with your estimated income. (Break down occasional income, such as an annual bonus or a tax rebate, into monthly averages also.) If your income exceeds your expenses, there is no reason you shouldn't be putting aside a little every month. If your expenses exceed income, you'd better cut down on all variable expenses, such as entertainment, groceries, and clothes.

After estimating expenses and planning a budget to control spending, you must keep track of your expenses and compare your actual spending habits to your budget. You can pick up a ledger book at the nearest stationery and office supply store and track them in separate accounts, or you can sit down once a week with your spouse (or with yourself if you're single) and see how close you are to your budget. If you find yourself overspending, determine which needs to be adjusted—the budget amounts or your self-control.

Rewards Make It Worthwhile

If the thought of living for two years as a financial monk, locked up in a monetary monastery while all of your friends are living it up, is simply more than you can bear, take heart. I have no intention of advising you to give up entertainment and recreation. Instead, consider working toward a goal: a real vacation, instead of allowing your "fun money" to be frittered away ten or twenty dollars at a time.

I work best under a reward system, so I set one up for myself and my family. We established a budgetary goal—so much saved, so much spent—and agreed that if we could achieve that goal, we would reward ourselves. And the rewards can be great.

The first goal I set was to live within the budget and save $5,000 from my day job within an eight-month period (remember that we never touched a dime of our investing profit—all of that was reinvested.) My wife and I agreed that if we could achieve that goal, we would treat ourselves to a trip. We would fly to the tropical resort of Mazatlán, Mexico, for eight fun-filled days in the sun, just like winning the Grand Prize on *The Price Is Right.*

We did it. We lived below our income level, we reached our goal, and we took our trip. We lived like royalty: we parasailed, swam, burned ourselves to a crisp, and ate shrimp the size of your fist. It was a perfect second honeymoon. There was a new light in my wife's eyes when we returned home. She could hardly wait to start saving for the next trip, because she knew from experience that the reward was well worth the sacrifice.

We had so much fun, in fact, that the next summer we found ourselves once again in Mazatlán. It was even better than the first time, and when we returned we redoubled our efforts to save. Now it was fun seeing how much we could save and invest. And we planned for something exceptional: a trip to Europe.

We never imagined that we would be touring Europe so early in our lives, but there we were, traveling through fabled countries and cities only seen in magazines and dreamed about. Soon we spent weeks and months with our children in Sweden. Soon we bought a fixer-upper manor home in Sweden that was originally built in 1872. Now we have a farm in northern Michigan. What's next? Australia? Last night we talked with my wife's father about a cruise to Alaska. After that, who knows?

These trips are free, in a sense. It costs us the same to live at the top of our income level as anybody else. The only difference is that instead of eating Big Macs and wishing we could go to Europe, instead we eat a few sack lunches, mow our own lawn, and clean our own home. A great book to read about developing financial independence is the classic book *The Richest Man in Babylon*. This book was written in the 1920s, but its story is even truer today. If you are to become a real estate investor, you are going to need to develop some financial self-control, and actually go to Europe with the entire trip being paid for by money earned and saved by you as an individual, or you as a couple, or you as a parent of children, all earned from your day job while every dime of your real estate investing profit is being used to pay off all consumer debt, to own your home free and clear, and to develop a portfolio of ten single-family homes that will be paid for free and clear by the date you have chosen to retire.

The truth for us has been that the cost of the trips is only a fraction of the money saved, so we still have most of that money available for investing. Is it worth the sacrifice? You bet it is.

A Key Not Just to Investing Success

If you put this book down right now and never buy one piece of property, but turn this one key, your life will be changed permanently. You will experience an increase in marital happiness.

You will feel better about yourself. You will be able to establish financial security, and when retirement time rolls around, it will be a time to treasure, not fear.

Well the key is yours now. It might not look like much of a key, but it will open the strongest lock between you and success. Put it in the keyhole, and let's move on.

Key #4: Do Set Realistic Goals

Goals without plans are just dreams.

—*Megan Elisabeth Garrison*

As a southern California city-bred Boy Scout, I especially loved the hikes—getting away into the mountains, where there were live animals and no parents. One trip, a fifty-miler, stands out more than any other because it is where I earned my fourth key. I may have earned a merit badge or two as well, but it's the key I really value. It's the same fourth key as the one you're looking for here.

I must have been twelve or thirteen that year. My pack still weighed more than I did, and I still hadn't accepted girls as full-fledged humans. We would be in the mountains for a week—pure fun for twelve-year-old boys, pure hell for a fifty-year-old scoutmaster. After we finally arrived in the mountains and hiked up to our base camp, a friend and I decided that we were going to go hiking up to a lake that we had heard about.

We started down a trail and had hiked for about a half hour when we came to a fork in the trail. Each of us turned to the other at the same time and asked, almost in unison, "Which way do we go?" Neither of us knew where we were going. Each of us had assumed that the other had brought a map. We knew we were on the right trail, but after getting started we were stopped because we had no way of knowing which way to turn. We had no way to reach our goals, so we turned and hiked back down the mountain, bitterly disappointed.

I've seen too many real estate investors stumbling back down the mountain for lack of a clearly laid-out path. They may have set a nebulous, long-range goal, "To get to the top," but they got to a fork in the road and had to give up in defeat. They may have stuffed their packs with knowledge and a sound budget, but they left their maps at home.

Your map will be a carefully laid-out plan of action. The most successful people are those who are capable of setting realistic goals and planning intermediate goals as stepping-stones to get them from the present to the future.

You want to retire to a thatched hut in the tropics in two years? That's fine. It's an achievable, if pretty unorthodox, goal. But that goal without a plan is nothing more than a desire. Between now and then, you will have to set and accomplish many intermediate and short-range goals. Let's take a few minutes here and analyze your goals.

What's Realistic for You?

I can't begin to estimate what might be realistic goals for you. Only you can do that, based on your own personal situation. I can, however, give you some basic guidelines that you can use to determine goals for yourself. For me, an unrealistic goal would be to buy two houses a month while I was still in graduate school. I would do poorly in both my schoolwork and my investing career. Your goals might be unattainable for me, and vice versa. So the first step is recognizing that your goals must be custom-tailored for you, by you.

We have a friend who is an excellent runner. He can run like a gazelle in his size-nine Adidas. I wear thirteens, and I can still run a fair race myself. But if we switch shoes, he flops all over the track like a drunken penguin and I can only lace his shoes to my feet if I'm willing to lose a couple of toes in the process.

But that person is neither Paula Tripp-Garrison nor Marc

Stephan Garrison, and we aren't anything like him. In fact, we are not Robert Allen, or Ronald Reagan, or Buck Rogers. You can only please yourself. We can't set goals that will be things you really want, nor can you set goals that will please me. If you want to spend your life on a tropical island, that's fine. You have to realize before you set any goals that we are motivated by different desires. We may be traveling the same pathway and going in the same direction, but our ultimate goals are different. Don't let anyone set your goals for you.

The Time to Set Goals Is Right Now

I'm expecting you to do more than read here. I want you to do some serious thinking and planning. This is meant to be an active course, not a passive one, so if you are not willing to set some major goals right now, then put the book down and turn on the television.

You're still reading. Okay, here's the next step. Commit yourself to your goal, on paper. I'll even supply the paper. Run and get a pen, I'll wait right here.

If this is your own book, write at least one major goal in the spaces provided below. It should be something you want to do, such as taking a two-week tour of Europe or just quitting your job—unlocking the handcuffs. Include an objective and a completion date. Example: "I will quit my job—inserting widgets into wangles on the assembly line—no later than May 1, 20__:

If this is not your own book, ask to borrow it for a couple of years, or better yet, go buy your own copy so that you can write in it. You could even use a makeshift facsimile of the spaces below. (Drawing four lines on a piece of paper will work.) The key is to do it now. One characteristic of successful people is an ability to act and live in the present. If you've been meaning to join a procrastinators' club, but just haven't gotten around to it yet, then you probably didn't get a pen when I suggested it, and you are going to leave the spaces below blank and fill them in later. Good luck.

_____

_____

_____

_____

So far so good, but don't put away the pen yet. Now set a dollar goal for your retirement income—a monthly cash flow that will allow you to leave your job in comfort. Nothing extravagant, but you should plan on a little more than they are paying you. No sense in giving up your current standard of living and slipping a few notches just so you can be an investor. Kind of defeats the purpose, doesn't it? Knowing what we know about the 2,500 students who have been with us on BuyingTours in the past, I have no problem telling you that through real estate you could easily build, by investing in ten single-family homes, a minimum of a $10,000 inflation-adjusted monthly income by the time you retire. I really don't care who you are, but I seriously believe that anybody today could quite easily live off of a $10,000 positive monthly cash flow.

Goal: to have a monthly investment income of _____ .

There. You've set two goals—major goals—on paper, and it wasn't hard, was it?

Now you must plan a timeframe. Knowing you want to get to the top of the mountain won't help much without some idea of the distance involved. You need to know exactly how far away the pinnacle is from your present position. You need to take time into consideration and set intermediate goals. Furthermore, you will have to take inflation into account.

Your age at present: _____
Your age when you want to achieve the financial goal you
  have already set: _____
How many years do you have to achieve that goal? _____

Your goal will allow you to retire at that level of comfort—if you retire today. However, if you are planning to retire at a future date, you will have to prepare for inflation. I don't have to repeat the first part of the book here, so we don't need to discuss the need to plan for inflation. To adjust your monetary goals, you will need to use your financial calculator.

To stay on the safe side, base your inflation projections on current trends. An average inflation rate of 8 percent is not out of line, as the rate is likely to fluctuate between 5 and 10 percent. With an 8 percent inflation rate, the value of your money will be cut in half approximately every twelve years. Now apply that factor to your goals, taking time and inflation into account. Update your goal below:

I will need $ _____ in _____ years to reach my goal.

Now you have set definite, worthwhile goals, adjusted for projected inflation—a financial goal for a monthly income that will allow you to enjoy doing whatever you enjoy doing.

Steps Along the Way

For every great goal, there must be a series of carefully planned intermediate goals, each of which are attainable. Just about anybody can get excited about setting the big goals, such as quitting a job and becoming a millionaire, but the daily grind of taking small steps to get there is about as exciting as a blood transfusion. Here again you will face the challenge of daily persistence.

I read *The Greek Treasure,* an excellent book by Irving Stone. I almost passed right by the best part of the entire book, a small obscure quote buried in the text. Fortunately, my mind did a double take and forced my eyes back to the line that sums up my idea of success:

If you add only a little to a little and do this often enough, soon that little will become great!

A good way to look at this is to imagine the next few years as a hard climb up a very long ladder. One step at a time, very sure and safe, you will progress toward your big goal. Some of the steps may require you to stretch a little, but it will be worth the effort. You will be moving up. If you get bogged down, or reach an apparent impasse, you should get help from others who have been successful in that particular step. Be willing to share your problems with them so they can help you make the climb to the top.

Don't allow yourself to get so caught up in your financial success that you lose everything that is precious. The foundation for a happy life is not reaching a goal of $5,000 or $10,000 or even $100,000 a month. It is striving to reach a goal, keeping your priorities in order and well balanced as you work toward that goal. The joy is in running a good race and knowing that you deserve the rewards, not what awaits you at the finish line.

Goal setting is the fourth key, and it might be the most important for your long-range goals without key number five.

Key #5: Do Establish a Reputation for Honesty

Honesty is simple—the truth is what really happened.

—Paula Tripp-Garrison

We spend every waking minute in a world where taking advantage is the norm. Lying and cheating are accepted business customs. But as investors, we must set a higher standard for success. If you choose to "skin" a few buyers or sellers now and again, you may make a quick buck; you may even make a quick 100,000 bucks. But you will develop a reputation.

I recently got a phone call from a person living two houses down from a house that I had bought and resold within a week. That person knew how hard I had worked to improve that house. She knew how straightforward I had been in both buying and selling the home. She called to tell me that another house in the neighborhood was empty. She mentioned that the owners had tried to sell the home, couldn't, and had left it empty to move to where they had been transferred. The neighbor that called wanted to let me know that it was available. In fact, she even provided me with the forwarding address and phone number for the owners.

Thanks to her help I was able to get a good deal for myself, help out the people who had been forced to move, and help out the neighborhood as well. Before the deal was closed, I had the home rented out and had arranged to have the overgrown lawn and messy yard cleaned up.

Problems do come up on occasion. There is nothing you can do about it. If you have a track record of honest dealings with people, you can avoid a lot of heartache and problems. Your reputation is branded on you and follows you throughout your investing career.

Word Gets Around

Two or three years ago, I heard about an interesting concept in salesmanship, discovered by Joe Girard, who has earned the title "The World's Greatest Salesman." The essence of his success is what he calls the "250 Rule."

His father was an undertaker, and as a boy it was Joe's job to arrange for the printing and passing out of the funeral service cards to the mourners. After doing this for several years, he noticed a remarkable statistic. He realized that the average number of people to attend a funeral was about 250. There seemed to be no discernible reason for this number, but it was consistent. When Joe Average died, it was time to order 250 more cards. Some time later, Girard shared this statistical oddity with a friend who catered weddings. The friend told him that the same number of people was usually in attendance at weddings also.

Girard was a thinker, and now he had a riddle to solve. He spent some time thinking about it while he was in college, studying selling. Then he came to a startling—and obvious—conclusion. Everyone has a circle of about 250 friends—friends close enough to attend a wedding or funeral. Now, some of us know more people and some fewer, but as a ballpark figure it will do. That means that when you buy or sell a home, you are establishing your reputation with about 250 people. One year from now, when it comes time to purchase another investment property, don't assume that you and the seller are total strangers. He or she may know someone with whom you have dealt, and your reputation will either make or break the deal.

Don't sell your scruples. You will sell them cheaply and pay dearly for them later—if it isn't too late. Honesty isn't just the best policy, it's the only policy for success.

If you develop a reputation as a good landlord or a fair dealer, the day may come when you can literally sit at home and have people call you to offer you excellent deals. Then you will be harvesting a crop that you planted at the beginning of your career—today.

Those are the first five keys to success in real estate investing—everything you should do. If you can master this much, your success is almost guaranteed. But I have five more keys to offer in Chapter 28—the don'ts of investing. Read them carefully, and avoid the stumbling blocks that trip most beginning investors.

> *I believe that most people considered a genius are individuals who have the capacity for taking life by the scruff of the neck repeatedly!*
>
> —*Jasen Waldo*

Chapter 28

Five Pitfalls to Avoid

KNOWING WHAT TO DO IS WONDERFUL, of course, but knowing what not to do is just as important. Here are five more invaluable keys.

Key #6: Don't Believe Everything You Hear

> *Trust, but verify.*
>
> —*Russian proverb*

What a name for a key! And with the pride we take in having a positive attitude, what kind of keys are we offering here? Well, if there is one lesson that is usually learned the hard way, it's how not to trust. After living through several treacherous deals, I am almost inclined to say, "Don't believe anything you hear." I have found that things are rarely as they seem, and many people, eager to buy or sell, are willing to say or do whatever it takes to get a good deal.

There are sellers who will misrepresent both the monthly payment and the interest rate on a loan just to make a sale. They must know that their lies will be discovered in due course, but many buyers after having made a commitment to such a seller, are inclined to hold on to the myth that this is a hot deal—when, in fact, it is nothing more than a hot potato that should be dropped. Maybe a seller isn't lying; maybe he's just made a mistake. But if you don't double-check his figures, you could find yourself tangled up in a nasty situation.

Check Out the Whole Story

I was recently in the process of closing on a home that the owner presented as having no liens against it other than the VA loan, which I was to assume. In my earlier days as an investor, I would have taken the seller at his word, but experience has taught me to check—just in case.

Unfortunately, this was just such a case. One way of avoiding costly entanglements is to be sure that you handle every closing through a competent real estate attorney or a professional title company, with a complete title search and the issuance of title insurance. In this case, the title company with whom I dealt made a preliminary title search and found that there was a $2,000 thorn hiding among the roses. I almost kissed my title officer when she told me they had uncovered a tax lien against the property.

A tax lien is attached to the property itself, not the owner. Buying that property as is would have been like buying a car with a flat spare. Guess who would get stuck with the cost? Right. Yours truly, the new owner.

We managed to work out a deal. Or rather, I managed to work out a deal. The owner, who had somehow managed to forget all about the tax lien, agreed to pay the $2,000 to the IRS prior to closing.

We don't want to scare you away from investing, nor do we

want to suggest that you should lose faith in humanity. Just take the time to check out the whole story. We've been told a few malicious lies motivated by greed. We've been told lies as innocent as a baby's breath, and I've heard hundreds of misrepresentations that live in the shadowy world of half-truths. Rarely have we been told the whole truth by anyone in the real estate profession other than our buyer's broker in that area who represents "us" and not the seller. A good buyer's broker wants to represent you to the day you die. They want your referrals. They want your business not just on this deal, but also the 200 more deals that you will do down the road.

Truth itself is subjective, and our interpretation of it is likely not to agree with yours. When the seller insists that his house is perfect, and you can see it will take a week to make it habitable, he may simply have a new and unique definition for the word "perfect."

Trust in another human being is a noble trait. And occasionally, it is a fatal flaw. John F. Kennedy trusted his advisers (or vice versa, as some historians say) and precipitated the Bay of Pigs fiasco in Cuba. Little old ladies allow con artists to bilk them out of every penny in their meager bank accounts, and an entire nation once put its faith in a madman named Adolf.

There is another—possibly worse—type of trust. It's the trust in a friend who in innocence destroys your future. There has never been one successful person who was not told at least once—by a dear friend or relative—that he or she couldn't succeed. Wives tear down their husbands' ambitions (or husbands tear down their wives'); parents destroy their children's dreams; and best friends, perhaps sensing a permanent separation, deride lofty goals.

The reason this trust is especially insidious is that all the bad advice is based on truth—a narrow, uneducated truth. A few hundred years ago, you would have been horrified to find out that your best friend was planning on taking a bath. Everyone knew that bathing induced all manner of sickness—even death. You would do whatever was necessary to prevent your friend from making a fatal mistake.

"Truth" may be false.

Key #7: Don't Trust Instinct Alone; Use Experts If Necessary

1 + 1 = 3 (definition of synergy)

—Ryan Waldo

Leverage. A truly remarkable force. I remember my amazement when I first found out about the principle of leverage in real estate investing. I could control $50,000—even $100,000—with only a $2,000 investment. And we can use that incredible power every day as investors.

Then we learned another, possibly more important, use for leverage as an investor: people leverage. We could use the help of experts to multiply the effectiveness of our efforts. We could leverage my knowledge by relying on the experts around me.

We recently heard a sad tale, related by the victim. He had bought a property without securing title insurance. Right off the bat he had failed to use Key #6, "Don't believe everything you hear." It turned out that the title was as cloudy as a tropical rain forest. There were enough liens on the property to collapse it entirely. But he had taken the seller at his word, and now he was stuck with a much-encumbered property.

If he had used the leverage that a title officer could have offered, he would have been able to avoid the heartache. The value of such help is worth many, many times the cost. Often the price of excellent advice is nothing more than a sincere thank-you or a nice lunch. Let me tell you about some of the most important real estate experts you will need to have on your team.

The Buyer's Broker

A buyer's broker is a real estate agent licensed by the state to enter into a contractual relationship with a client to buy and sell your real estate. To sell the real estate, agents advertise the properties and show them to prospective buyers.

If you want to get some free education and develop good working relationships, try this. Call any Realtor in your Yellow Pages and ask to talk with an agent who is a "buyer's broker." Tell the agent that you are interested in buying a rental home in the area. Describe what kind of property you are looking for and how much you can afford to spend. That agent will take you to as many houses as you would like to see and give you a free seminar in home values and real estate principles. Continue going with different Realtors. You will see how much difference there is among them, and you may find one who is not afraid to go out of his or her way to help you.

A couple of the characteristics that make a good Realtor are personal investing experience and a willingness to work with creative financing techniques. If a Realtor tells me that the only way to buy a house is to put a large down payment on the property and to get financing from the bank, I tell that Realtor goodbye. My wife and I need someone who understands investors and who is willing to help us with our real estate investing program.

Once you get to know an agent well enough to feel confident that he or she will work with you, begin asking any and every question that you need answered. They have taken special classes and have probably learned more about real estate than you are likely to learn in a year on your own, and that's real knowledge leverage.

The State Real Estate Commission

This commission is charged with the regulation of real estate laws. Every state has one. Having the telephone number of your commission is essentially the same as having a staff of legal experts waiting on call. Imagine having a battery of lawyers who charge no fee, waiting for your calls. As a real estate investor, you have the next best thing—your state real estate commission.

I learned the value of this source early in my investing career. I was involved in the purchase of a really nice duplex, which was being sold by two old-time real estate agents. The price and terms were almost too good to be true, which should have been my first clue that everything wasn't rosy.

The problem slowly surfaced, and as the closing date approached, we became aware that the agents had made several misrepresentations. In fact, it was soon apparent that the misrepresentations could not have been unintentional. These people were out to skin me alive. When we confronted them with the facts we had unearthed, they warned me that if we attempted to withdraw from the contract, I would lose all of my earnest money. (I hadn't yet learned to give earnest money in the form of a promissory note.)

Desperate, I called the real estate commission, as a friend had suggested. I was informed not only that I could recover my earnest money in full, but that the agents could lose their real estate licenses for willfully misrepresenting the property. When I called them the next day and informed them that I had been in touch with the commission, the agents quite suddenly experienced a change of heart. They were happy to give me a full refund, with a (sincere?) apology, and I got the distinct impression that they would have been happy to double that refund if I had asked.

The Appraiser

An appraiser is a highly skilled professional who, based on years of schooling and experience, is qualified to render an opinion as to a property's value. When you are considering the purchase of a small two-bedroom house, how can you tell what its market price is? You can't look it up in *Consumer Reports,* can you? An appraiser, for $250 or more, will take a look at the house and render his or her opinion.

I prefer to appraise properties myself, based on my experience as an electrician and the property analysis system that I have developed. However, I have found a rather inexpensive way to leverage the expertise of an appraiser. Call an appraiser, and offer to buy a nice steak lunch in exchange for letting you follow him or her around for a day. You can act as a secretary or helper all day, asking questions as you go along. That one day may pay greater dividends than a whole day of reading about investing.

The Title Company

A title company prepares an "abstract of title" for a property and provides title insurance. Despite its impressive name, an abstract of title is nothing more than the up-to-date history of a property. But they can't very well call it an "up-to-date history" and still charge $100, so why not call it an abstract of title?

When the title company searches the title (the rights to a property), they will find all easements, liens, and encumbrances that might be attached to the property. For example, if state property taxes are owed on a property, the state has a right to a portion of that property's value. You might not find out about that lien until six months after the sale, when a letter from the state tax board appears in your mailbox. The title company would have discovered the problem and alerted you long before the closing date.

After the title company has prepared the abstract, they will offer insurance guaranteeing that according to all known information the property is being sold with only the liens and encumbrances listed in the abstract.

Now for the leverage. You have an expert waiting at a desk for your calls. This expert is a title officer, and he or she can save you hundreds of hours and dollars.

We have found ourselves at the desk of my title officer at least a hundred times, asking her whether the earnest money offer we are presenting says what we want it to say. With that woman we have actually had her write out complete earnest money forms for us. The boxes of chocolates and the flowers we have given her are nothing compared to the money she has saved us.

Recently we were closing on a property and needed some help in writing a special clause I wanted to include as protection. I called and talked to her for a few minutes, but she couldn't help me with it. Ten minutes passed and the phone rang. There she was, calling to tell me that she had called several other title officers until she got the right answer. We wouldn't trade her for all the Porsches in Hollywood.

If you want to find a good title officer, pick up your Yellow Pages and start calling title companies. Explain that you are an investor, and ask the title officer what services he or she can offer. They are looking for loyal customers, so let them make a sales pitch to you. After all, investors are likely to buy more than one house in twenty years; active investors may buy four or five houses a month. When you find a good title officer, one who will go out of his or her way to help you, then start calling and asking questions. Or stop by the office and have your officer help you write an earnest money contract. Then drop a thank-you note in the mail, or (you guessed it) take your title officer out to lunch.

The Real Estate Attorney

A real estate attorney is just what the name implies, an attorney who specializes in real estate law. Such an attorney is often capable of handling all of the legal aspects of a real estate transaction, right through to completing the closing right in his or her office. Nurturing a relationship with a real estate lawyer will not necessarily give you access to free legal advice, but it will help tremendously as a source of bargain properties.

The reason is that real estate attorneys often handle foreclosure proceedings. People who are facing foreclosure will often call such a lawyer, looking for alternatives, and if they want to sell their house quickly, the lawyer can say, "I do know an investor in the area who can buy your house quickly and who will give you a good price."

The Property Manager

This valuable member of your team is a professional who manages rentals. At least five out of every six people think that managing rental properties is a piece of cake, and all five of them are nuts.

Property management is a specialized skill that must be developed through years of training. It seems to require a certain personality type, and I'm too much of a softie to ever be a good manager. I always succumb to the first-of-the-month emergency stories, such as the tenant who had to spend the rent money on her cat, who desperately needed open-claw surgery. My wife Paula is just the opposite; she is not only fair but very firm. In our home, Paula and I both have very distinctive roles that fit our personality types.

I do the research. I do the acquisition of a property based on her physical inspection. Paula then orchestrates the rehab or cosmetic work that needs to be done to either rent the property out to a tenant or to prepare it for a flip. She doesn't do the actual work itself, but, rather, she leverages her time and orchestrates and inspects the work that has to be done. Month by month Paula baby-sits our property managers, whom we have contracted with to manage and to maintain our properties. Almost 100 percent of this communication is via e-mail with attached pictures of the properties. I then get the job of continuing to research that market so that I can time the sale based on its price peaking right and rents skyrocketing to a point where a lender will approve a developer's loan. At that point I step in and get the fun of selling the property. For me and Paula, this is a perfect marriage. Together, Paula and I are like missing puzzle pieces in each other's lives. We have made real estate work. She balances the books, and she pays the bills. She takes care of the properties, while I get to pour myself into researching the best areas for not only our family but also to our students who will be coming out with us on a BuyingTour.

Hiring someone who you know is competent (based on their

track record with their other clients) to handle the special pressures that the job entails will greatly leverage your time and money. But if you insist on managing the property yourself, you can still use the skills of a professional manager. When you write an offer to purchase the property, include the phrase "Offer is subject to the inspection of all rental records and the satisfactory acceptance of their performance." With those records in hand, visit a professional property manager and ask him or her to render an opinion. You may need to raise the rents. Find out what the going rate is for units such as the ones you are planning to buy.

This is one area of investing that I leave to Paula and other experts. Actually, I have been forced by circumstance to become something of an expert in this field, but I thoroughly detest the job. So why not spend a little money to increase my free time for what I love to do—buy and sell properties?

The Real Estate Consultant

This paid professional can help you establish and carry out investing goals. Usually, a paid consultant is an investor with extensive experience. He or she will charge a fee, with an initial retainer paid up front and then an hourly charge for services rendered.

In 1986, I began teaching other people just like you the paradigms of real estate investing in the twenty-first century. I love to mentor new investors. But I refuse to help anyone who hasn't made a sincere commitment to themselves. Over time we have developed a seven-day training called "The Challenge" program. That is a Ph.D. course in real estate investing today. It answers thousands of questions and allows you to actually meet and hear the testimonials and stories of some of our very best students who went out and practiced that which we preach. I really do not have time for anybody who hasn't been through that course. Nobody in the universe does what we do. Over sixteen years we have not only pioneered this program but also perfected it. To get a copy of this course, contact my wife, Paula, at paulatripp-garrison@narei.com.

Both Paula and I have enjoyed helping new investors get started. It is something like a series of climbers working their way up the face of a mountain, each turning to help the next reach a new level. We are perhaps three-quarters of the way up the face of the mountain, and it is with real pleasure that we turn and give a hand to people below us who are struggling.

There are two major advantages to having a mentor/consultant help you get started. First, as an experienced investor, a financially independent mentor can take a step back, away from the emotional engagement of a first-time investor, and clinically evaluate the pros and cons of an investment. Second, most would-be investors stay at the would-be stage all of their lives, too overwhelmed by the seeming complexity of the process to ever make a written offer. An experienced investor can take the novice by the hand and lead him or her through the process for the first lime. Admit it. Once you've been walked through a sale, you wouldn't have any trouble investing on your own, would you?

A good mentor will often uncover defects in your best-laid plans and by doing so may save you many times the cost.

The Loan Officer

A loan officer represents a lending institution in processing a loan. As such, he or she wields more power than you might at first think. The position has grown in stride with the newly competitive nature of banking, as deregulation has thrown all lending institutions into the same ring to fight for customers. Today's loan officer is more than an order taker; the position requires a full customer-service manager.

Many investors have an aversion to banks, rightly preferring to deal with the homeowners themselves when it comes to arranging financing. But through my contacts at local banks, I have been able to put together some fantastic deals simply because I could secure financing with one phone call.

The Professional Property Inspector

These inspectors can evaluate the structural soundness of a property. One of the most common questions asked by the beginning investor is, "How can I check a property for structural damage without having to pay for a full inspection?" Well, you could learn about construction as I did, installing electrical systems for eight years. But if that doesn't seem feasible, try doing what a group of investors I met in California did. While I was working as an apprentice, my boss would be called in by this group to inspect a property before they would make an offer on it. They wouldn't pay for the inspection, but there was an agreement that if they bought the house and it needed electrical work, my boss would be the one to do it.

You can do the same thing with every home you are going to buy. If the work needs to be done anyway, you might as well pay a professional to do it right. And if that professional will give you a free structural inspection, what better way could you work together?

Don't be intimidated by the expertise of someone who can help you. In school, were you afraid to ask your math teachers about math, just because they knew about a million times more than you? Of course not; that's why they were teachers. We often have the misconception that we will be imposing on someone else when we ask for help or advice. Usually nothing could be further from the truth.

Imagine for a moment that you are a Tinker Toy sculptor. A young man approaches and meekly asks you for a few words of wisdom. In fact, he will treat you to lunch at a fancy restaurant, such as Chef McDonald's, if you will explain how to balance the little round blocks with the long green dowels. How would you respond? Chances are you would be very flattered, and you would be glad for the opportunity to expound on the virtues of Tinker Toy sculpting. (In the back of your mind, you also recall the old adage, "The teacher always learns more than the student.")

328

Why should a title officer feel any differently? They are bored out of their minds. They process these abstracts all day long, and nobody appreciates the knowledge they have spent years accumulating. Now they have the opportunity to get a nice lunch, and what does it cost them? Nothing, except sharing information they know as well as their own names.

Their Knowledge, Your Determination

It would be a good idea to start a special phone book, filled with the names and phone numbers of these contacts. It's like having a book of levers and pulleys that you can use to greatly increase your investing power. With this book by your phone, you can have almost any question answered in seconds. That's leverage.

Synergy occurs whenever the whole is greater than the sum of the parts. Combining an expert's knowledge with your own determination and hard work is synergy at its best.

If I were to describe this key, I would imagine that it is a very long key, capable of tearing the lock right out of the door. This key is an absolute must. The alternative is to open the lock without the help of a key, and that's never the best way to open a door.

Key #8: Don't Wait for Success; Make It Happen

The secret of walking on water is
knowing where the stones are.

—*Marc Waldo*

If you want to succeed at drilling oil, you have to drill where the oil is. That advice may seem as helpful as "Buy low, sell high," but it is another overlooked fact of success. We often receive calls from beginning investors who can't wait to tell me about their "great deals." They may have found an $80,000 house that is selling for $2,000 under market value, on which they only have to put down $10,000 as a down payment. For some reason, they seen surprised when I am not impressed. Don't jump into the first property that looks good at first glance. It takes more than a glance to assess any property, and you may find yourself drilling where there is no oil.

You may have to investigate five or even ten houses before finding one that will be truly profitable, but persistence pays off. When it comes to making success happen, knowledge is useless without persistent effort, and all the work in the world is useless without knowledge.

We have reserved a name for the person who combines education with persistence until he or she achieves a goal. We call that person an entrepreneur. Webster's may have a slightly different definition, but mine really sums up the meaning of the word.

From Ogg Ooog, inventor of the wheel, to Thomas Edison, inventive genius extraordinaire, the true entrepreneur has been the person with creativity, intelligence, and the ability to see something through from beginning to end. The other 99.9 percent of the world's population may have the intelligence, but only one in maybe a thousand is willing to push beyond the threshold of despair.

Do you want success—as an investor, or as a parent, or just as a human being? Then you will have to do more than set goals and educate yourself. And you will have to do more than organize your time and your finances. You will have to commit yourself to success right up until the day of your first failure, and then one more day, and then another. You cannot quit if you want to succeed.

In 1858, Irving Spalding decided to create the ultimate soft drink. He combined soda water and natural fruit juices and called his concoction 1-Up. It failed miserably in taste tests across the nation. Back to the laboratory went Irving and down the drain went 1-Up. Undaunted, Irving tried a new combination and called it 2-Up. It bombed miserably. Soon 3-Up followed, and then 4-Up and 5-Up. Each in turn followed 1-Up down the drain.

At the end of his patience—and money—Irving tried one last time, combining soda water, lime juice, and banana puree to make 6-Up. But it was a failure as well, so he gave up in despair. He died three months later of a broken heart, never knowing how close he had come to success.

When you start (if you haven't started already) spending most of your "free" time investing, you will quickly find yourself discouraged. Your friends and family, if they aren't ridiculing you, are at least enjoying themselves while you are out there killing yourself. And overnight success is as rare as snow in Los Angeles. To maintain the necessary drive, take a moment to look at the rewards and the alternatives.

The rewards are a wealth of time and money, and of the two a wealth of time is by far more valuable. The alternatives are grim to say the least. I've thrown enough retirement statistics at you already, and you should have a pretty good idea of what lies ahead. This is it—now. You must make success happen.

A man from Florida whom I worked with about his personal investments was just about to give up. He had been trying to find investment properties that he could afford, but with no luck at all. Discouraged, he called me one last time to say goodbye. I told him that he had passed my test. I remember him saying "What?" Before we let anyone come out with us on a BuyingTour, we require that they not only complete our seven-day video "Challenge Course," but we also require two more things.

The first is that they have consistently worked the tools of investing that we have taught them in their back yard. We refuse to work with people who haven't found out the reality of "normal investing" in their back yard. We want students who have made several dry runs. We want people who will not embarrass us.

As part of each and every BuyingTour, we introduce you to our entire real estate investing team in that area. At that same time we teach you the "etiquette" required today for working with a buyer's broker. One of the things that you will first realize on a BuyingTour is that we deal exclusively with residential non-owner-occupied income properties. The majority of the properties that you will ever see with us on a BuyingTour have no "for sale" signs. Why? "For Sale" signs scare tenants. The tenants freak out and can't sleep because to them, a "For Sale" sign means that a new owner is going to come in and raise their rent. On a BuyingTour, we spend several days out in a bus, driving to and stopping at literally hundreds of properties. And, as often as we can, we stop and get out and physically inspect the property with the owner, one of our property managers, or one of our property inspectors. Our buyer's broker is on the bus with us. One time we stopped and got off the bus and quietly toured the property. During that time one of our students knocked on one of the doors and asked the woman who came to the door how much she was paying in rent. The woman asked why he wanted to know. He told the woman that his reason was that the property was for sale and that he was interested in buying it. The tenant went ballistic and instantly called the property manager (who knew nothing about a possible sale). Then the property manager called the owner and demanded to know if she was going to get fired by a new owner.

The second thing we require of all those on our BuyingTours is that I want you to be able to tell me in rich colorful detail what you are going to spend the money on that you make in real estate. I am not kidding. I want a really well-thought-out answer. As I already told you, students who have monetary goals based in deep personal values will make it. Those who focus on getting rich quick and on owning the biggest house in their town and the nicest new BMW will never make it.

Persistence Is the Key

You can be a financial success. Not because you are lucky, but because you have persisted. You will not quit after 6-Up fails. You will keep on trying, and the answer to your dreams was waiting just around the bend.

Try this tonight, just as an experiment. Stay home and watch television, or lie down for a while and read *People* magazine. But keep a pen and a notebook handy. Now, every time someone calls you tonight and offers to sell his or her house to you—below market value, with little or no money down—be sure to make a note of it. Count all the calls you receive and send me the total. I'm really interested in seeing just how many people get more than one such call in their lifetime.

If you don't receive any calls, don't you think you ought to do something about it?

This key is solid cast-iron. It is unbreakable. No matter how hard the lock seems to be, if you are willing to push as hard as you need to, for as long as you need to, the lock will eventually give way. There's no surer guarantee of success than this key, because it is virtually indestructible. The only way it will fail is if you give up.

Key #9: Don't Eat All Your Profits

Save for a time of need.

—Spencer W. Kimball

There is an old fable about a man named Wong Li, who lived long ago in China. He was a very wise man who helped the emperor out of a tough situation. To thank Wong, the emperor insisted that he name his own reward. Nothing was too much to ask.

"O great Chung Fou," said Wong, bowing low. "I have only one humble request. I would like to have only one grain of rice today, which shall be put into a storehouse. Every day for two full moons, whatever rice remains in the storehouse must be matched by an equal number of grains. If I leave my rice in the storehouse tonight, then there will be one added to it; if I leave those two again, then there will be two more grains on the next day. If I could only have this one wish granted, then I would be the happiest man in China."

The emperor, of course, thought he was getting a good deal, so he gladly granted the man's wish. By the tenth day, the emperor had to pay Wong only 512 grains of rice, hardly enough to fill a bowl. But by the end of the first month, he began to realize the full price of his agreement, so he called Wong into his castle.

"Wong," said the emperor, "you are very smart, but not very wise." And so saying, he called in his guards and had Wong Li put to death.

Just how many grains of rice would the emperor have had to pay on the last day of the second month? Well, if there were sixty-one days in the two months, he would have received a king's ransom in rice: 2,305,843,000,000,000,000 grains—almost two and a half quintillion grains. Literally more than all the rice in China. And that would be for the sixty-first day alone.

That is an example of the power of multiplying the outcome of every equation, or what mathematicians call a geometric progression. Now that we have such an amazing outcome, let's play with the figures a little and see what happens. First, what would have happened if Wong Li had eaten the first grain of rice on the first day? That one is easy. If you add zero to zero, you still get zero, and the emperor would have paid the full contract price.

Now what if Wong Li had waited until the second day to take a grain of rice, leaving one grain for the second night? That one is not too much more difficult: he would have shortened the entire contract period by one day, shortening the sixty-one days to sixty. He would then have lost his 2.3 quintillion grains for the sixty-first day.

Now for the real heart of my discussion. What would the result have been if he had always left one grain in the storehouse and always taken one to eat? The answer should be obvious: Wong would have been paid exactly sixty-one grains of rice.

As a real estate investor, you will share with other investors a unique opportunity, the chance to make 100 percent annual profit (and sometimes more) on your investments. Quite a few first-time investors will eat every grain of rice as they receive it. They will eat the first grain on the first day, taking the profit and the original investment to buy a new stereo system and a DVD player to go with it. They have just cleared out the storehouse, and they have thrown away unimaginable wealth.

But most people make just as serious a mistake. When they recover the original investment plus some profit, they immediately spend the profit and reinvest their original capital. And they think that they are investors, because they have a new DVD and it didn't cost them anything. It was "investment profit."

They may double their money again and again, taking the profit and buying another gizmo each time, but they will never create any wealth. They are taking away one grain every day and leaving one grain in the storehouse.

Success requires a willingness to forgo spending your profits. You must have the ability to delay the day of celebrating your wealth just as long as possible. The longer you wait, in fact, the more you will be able to afford to celebrate when you finally do. Obviously, had Wong Li waited until at least the end of the first month, he would have been able to take home a ton of rice without seriously affecting his wealth. He could have taken home the thirtieth day's pay—slightly over 1 trillion grains of rice—without sending himself to the poorhouse.

In Chapter 27, we stressed the necessity of paying yourself first and of rewarding yourself. We have also suggested living below your income level for most of the year and then blowing a portion of your savings on an extravagant vacation. Now I am telling you not to spend your profits. "C'mon, Marc and Paula, which is it?"

I consider those vacations an investment. They are a reward that feeds the flame of success. But they are only a fraction of your savings. I'm suggesting that you eat a handful of rice on about the tenth day, when there are 1,024 grains in the storehouse. Then eat a bowlful on the twentieth day, and put off the day of real celebration—the trip around the world—until the end of the first month.

Translating that into more realistic terms, I would suggest that you build up equity and cash flow. Sit tight in a small house for several years; put off changing your style of living until you have amassed your second million in real estate and have developed a monthly income of over $10,000. Don't take a trip to Europe the first year: try something a little closer to home, something that will cost about one-fifth of your real estate profits. And don't waste one penny of profit until at least your third successful investment.

A few years ago, I opened my mailbox and found a $23,000 check—a very nice real estate profit. It would have been easy to spend all of it as a down payment on a nice car. Instead, I took my wife out to a nice prime rib dinner. It's hard to track that $23,000, but I would have to estimate that that profit is worth at least $90,000 today. Now I can buy that $23,000 toy and have $67,000 left to reinvest.

This is an interesting key, because you will find that after you have finally opened the door to success, the landscape may surprise you. It is not a flat plane. There are hundreds of levels of success, and you can exist at any level you desire. But it is always an uphill climb, and you will face a new locked door at every level. This key opens every door. As long as you are willing to reinvest your profits and spend only a small fraction at each level, you will be able to unlock the door that opens onto the next level.

That's all but one key. Each one by itself is valuable, whether you invest in real estate or not. The last key is made especially for the real estate investor:

Key #10: Don't Buy Without a Good Property Analysis

If only foresight were twenty-twenty,
we'd have no need for hindsight.

—*Candice Small*

It's interesting watching the high jumpers in the Olympics as they prepare for their jump. By following the movements of their head and eyes, you can actually watch them go through every step of the jump in their minds before they take as much as one step.

You can do exactly the same thing when you prepare to make an offer on a house. It's possible, with a property analysis system, to plan every step of the process from the initial offer to the final sale. A failure to do so can often prove very costly. I have heard of many investors who, in their excitement at finding a nothing-down deal, have learned that the exit is every bit as important as the entrance. They don't realize until it is too late that the seller was simply unloading an alligator onto them, and the fact that there was no down payment does not mean it was a good deal.

One difficulty encountered in real estate investing is the mathematics of finance, which is complex. For me, figuring out the payments on a thirty-year fully amortized loan wasn't just a headache, it was an impossibility—until I learned how to use a financial calculator, a marvelous tool produced by the same computer technology that has given us everything from Pac-Man to space shuttles.

My very strong suggestion is that you invest in a good financial calculator, such as the HP-12C, made by Hewlett-Packard. I've had my 12C (for short) for a few years now, and it has paid for itself a thousand times over. I have compared it to all of the other financial calculators, and as an M.B.A., I can attest to the fact that it out-adds, out-divides, and generally out-everything's any other financial calculator on the market.

Unfortunately, when I first popped open the friendly Owner's Handbook and Problem Guide, I was sure it was written in Greek. I even had trouble figuring out how to add one and one.

It wasn't until I asked a fellow student in graduate school that I finally figured out how to use the HP-12C, and then it really took off. The experience was comparable to taking flying lessons in a Lear jet. I knew I had a powerful tool, but I had no idea what it could really do until I learned how to use it.

This isn't meant to be an advertisement for Hewlett-Packard's calculator, but if you are serious about investing, the HP-12C comes highly recommended by me. It has saved countless hours and has increased the profitability of my investments. If you own an HP-l2C, or if you plan on buying one, you may be interested that we maintain a free link on the Internet just for my students to learn how to work their 12C. Send me an e-mail, and I will give you the link. I also have a great friend—one of our students—named Dale Maxwell who does personal live coaching on the telephone where both of you have your HP 12-C financial calculators and he guides you through the keystrokes until you completely understand real estate math. Dale charges by the hour for private coaching on the HP 12-C to our students. After being instructed by Dale, you will never lose a dime; he is simply one of the very best. To get a hold of our free Web site and/or Dale's phone number, just e-mail me at marcstephangarrison@narei.com.

I think that the combination of a good calculator and a good system is essential, and I will not make a buying decision without first performing an analysis. It has allowed me to consistently pick a winner.

Here's a word of caution. In every real estate transaction, there are far too many factors involved to be plugged into any simple form. There is only one computer that can take that much information into account and come up with an answer: the human brain. The financial analysis will crunch through the numbers that would take a person a year to figure, but there is a point where instinct takes over. Well, if you have managed to stay with me through all ten keys, and if you are willing to apply every one of those keys, there is no way you can fail. I defy you to fail.

That's the end of your basic training. You're ready to be certified as prepared for success. It's time to take your learning and put it to use.

If you are really ready for success, move ahead and put everything you've learned to work. Take your keys, open the door, and follow me. There is nothing holding you back from a bright future but your own insecurities. Conquer them, and achieve the success you deserve.

PART IX

Ultimate Wealth

■————————————————————————■

CHAPTER 29
People Can Change the World

CHAPTER 30
A Checklist for Success

The fragrance always stays on the hand that gives the rose.

—*Dalton Small*

Chapter 29

People Can Change the World

A COMMON COMPLAINT ABOUT THE WEALTHY is that they only care about their money. The real problem is that a few selfish millionaires get all the attention because they flaunt their wealth. Who cares how much money Julie Andrews spends helping starving children around the world? We'd rather see Princess Caroline carousing on a royal yacht.

What do you think would happen if *People* magazine decided to concentrate on only the philanthropists, while *Us* continued to show off the playthings and pleasures of the idle rich? Which magazine would go out of business within two months?

Giving Something Back

I'd like you to meet a few people who have enjoyed tremendous financial rewards and tell you a little about how they chose to spend their fortunes.

On a Mission for Others

Locked away in the history books is the fascinating story of Sir Moses Montefiore. Raised in seventeenth-century England, this man rose to wealth through hard work. After spending time as a stock-broker and as a lender, this man quit at the age of forty to devote the rest of his life to his dream: alleviating the pitiable condition of the Jewish people both in Europe and overseas, particularly in the Holy Land.

Montefiore could easily have spent the next sixty years of his life indulging in every pleasure imaginable, but instead he chose to devote himself entirely to his cause. His mission on behalf of the Jewish people generated universal concern for their cause and helped to free them of the discrimination that had been prevalent in Europe for centuries.

Would you like to do something along the same lines as the incredible accomplishments of Sir Moses Montefiore? Would you like to be able to actually change the world? Your friends will prob-ably say that you would be crazy to even entertain such an idea. After all, they can hardly keep up with their bills and who won the last football game on television. Its just too much effort—in their eyes—to do anything more than fend for themselves.

A Passion for Education

Robert H. Dedman began life with a natural desire for educa-tion. Within four years of leaving high school, he had finished three college degrees: one in law, one in economics, and one in engi-neering. He did all this while working full-time. That is impressive, but even more impressive is the full story of this man who has changed the world.

Mr. Dedman went on to become a successful lawyer. Noticing an investment opportunity, he began investing in building his own chain of country clubs.

His gamble paid off. But today he is not just living a life of carefree ease. This man, with his love for education, has granted $25 million to Southern Methodist University's undergraduate liberal arts and sciences college. He has also endowed the college with $1 million to establish a center for lifetime sports.

The attitude that he lives with is one that is almost common among the self-made millionaires of the world. He has worked hard for his success, but after providing for his family and his personal needs, he wants to share his wealth with those less fortunate.

This attitude may seem incredible to those who cannot fulfill their smallest dreams. But once you have a house to live in and enough money to cover all of your expenses, what else is there? All of the toys lose their luster when you can afford as many as you want, and you really can't take it with you. Have you ever seen a hearse with a luggage rack?

"Our Lives Can Mean Something"

When Harry Chapin lost his life to that all-American death, the car accident, he was a young, successful singer. His songs were popular for their haunting melodies and clear insights. He could have chosen the party life that has attracted so many pop singers, but instead he spent his entire career raising money for charities. It is estimated that before his death, Harry Chapin had raised over $6 million in contributions for the humanities and the arts. Of the more than 200 concerts he performed annually, half were benefit concerts.

Besides the benefit concerts, Harry served as founding trustee of World Hunger Year, and he served on the boards of many performing arts foundations. He once said, "Given this short opportunity we call life, it seems to me that the only sensible way—even if you have pessimistic thoughts about the 99 percent possibility that things are going wrong—is to operate on the 1 percent that our lives can mean something."

People Who Inspire Others

Life is fantastic, life is fun. These people did something more than just satisfy their physical desires. They went one step beyond and left a mark on the world. They weren't content to leave an estate for the inheritors and Uncle Sam to fight over.

I am inspired by these stories and the story of Paul Mellon, the great philanthropist whose contribution to the arts constitutes a gift to mankind that can never be tarnished. I also think of John Jacob Astor, founder of the Astor fortune, whose personal contribution of his book collection formed the cornerstone of the New York Public Library. Today, the great Astor legacy of helping others is carried on by Brooke Astor. Ms. Astor has directed the distribution of over $130 million to worthy causes.

These admirable men and women have left the world a legacy that goes far beyond anything left by billions of people who have passed through life with no other thought than to survive from birth to death. They were all willing to sacrifice, to work hard, and to change the world and the shape of history itself.

Let me give you just one more—although I could write an entire book about such people.

A story is told about Percy Ross, the Minneapolis tycoon. It is said that he invited over one thousand disadvantaged kids in Minneapolis to an all-you-can-eat Christmas Eve dinner at the Minneapolis Auditorium. I would give anything to see the expression on those children's faces when he pulled his grand surprise. Each child was filled with a meal unlike any other they had had all year, and just as they were preparing to leave, the curtain went up in the auditorium, revealing a gleaming, brand-new bicycle for each of them.

Can you remember back far enough to have any idea what joy he must have brought to a thousand young lives? Why did he do it?

He did it because there is no joy comparable to helping others. We would all love to experience the same joy, but most of us can't afford it. Yet.

People like these leave more than just a tombstone. Because of them a child can smile, an illness can be cured, people can live in peace. I think that these people will rest in peace also.

Change Your World

Well, here it is. We're almost at the end of the book, and the beginning of a new life for you, if you choose. In this chapter, I am going far beyond the reaches of any investment book I have ever read. I want to convince you to join the ranks of those listed above. Human beings have so much potential. Most of them, however, operate on two cylinders in an eight-cylinder world.

Why not set a greater goal than mere money and toys? Why not set the ultimate goal, the wealth that comes with knowing that when you face the last day of mortality, the world will be a better place for your having been there.

I plan to change the world. I want to teach an entire generation of negative-thinking, failure-programmed people that success is possible. I want to see all people who have the desire and ambition succeed in whatever goals they set. I want to teach Success 101, and I want graduates from sea to shining sea.

Why should you be any different? If you can take off the golden handcuffs and provide for your own retirement, instead of relying on the government, you will be able to build a strong castle that you can call your own. And then you can make the changes in the world that you want to make, but always starting first in your own life and your family.

Do you want to alleviate the hunger that claims hundreds of thousands of lives every year? Do you want to spend your days changing and influencing the way our country is governed? Of course, you don't have to change the world; you don't have to share my vision. Perhaps you want to spend your days in quiet worship, or with your children, nurturing them and spending the time with them that your own parents could never afford. That's every bit as important as what we may want to do.

The important point is that you are doing something that is valuable and important to you. Financial freedom is not just a dream. It is real and can be achieved through real estate investing. Success requires no real financial genius, but it does require a solid knowledge of basic principles. This specific knowledge, together with your motivation, your personal plan, and action, will help you to realize your financial dreams.

It doesn't matter "how much," it just matters that you do something. For a reference, read Mark 12:41–44 and Luke 21:1–4.

Whatever you do, you will have changed the world, and with it you have made your investment plan and program something of great worth. We wish you and yours happiness on your journey. We pray that your worthy dreams become reality.

Thoughts are but dreams 'til their effects be tried.

—*William Shakespeare*

Chapter 30

A Checklist for Success

TO GET YOU MOVING ON THE PATH OF SUCCESS immediately, we would like to ask you some very serious questions and then give you a handy, step-by-step "quick-start checklist." Ready? First, before getting to the checklist, please answer the following questions:

- Would you like to spend a week with us in one of our target markets on a BuyingTour?
- Would you like to have us as your mentor?
- Would you like to be introduced to several members of our InnerCircle of self-made millionaires who live in your area?
- Would you love to know the top five markets that we are working in right now?

For all of the above, along with any other questions, send us an e-mail with all your telephone/e-mail/fax/snail-mail contact information. If you do send us an e-mail, please start by telling us a little about yourself. Please write a paragraph about where you are right now in life. Next, tell us about what you have done to date in real estate investing, and what it is you want to do in real estate investing. Finally, don't forget to tell us what you are going to spend the money on that you will make on real estate investing.

Send that e-mail to Marc Stephan Garrison at marcstephan garrison@narei.com.

Checklist for Successful Real Estate Investing

We want to leave you with a step-by-step checklist of what we would do today if we were you—just starting fresh in real estate investing, or getting more serious about your current or past real estate investments.

1. Determine the economic cycle stage that your back yard investing market is in. Remember that you can go to *www. ecodevdirectory.com* on the Internet to find your local department of economic development.
2. Do some soul-searching, either all by yourself or, preferably, with a spouse or partner, about what you would risk your life for right now.
3. Define your personal goals based on your values. In terms of today's economy and troubled times, we would ask that your first big goal be to pay off all consumer debt. We would ask that your second goal be to own your own home free and clear and to hire an attorney to put it in the right legal entity so that no one can ever take it away from you for any reason. Next would be working on getting ten homes with as little or no money down as possible. Work to pay for these homes free and clear by your target retirement date. The reality is that there will be zero Social Security left for your retirement. These ten houses, once paid off, will give you an income tomorrow at a level that $10,000 per month would provide today. Can you live off of that? Yes. Then start working from

this rock-solid foundation on making your personal dreams a reality.

4. Keep in touch with us, and let us get to know you over time.

5. Purchase and study the National Association of Real Estate Investors brand-new video course. Get to know us better, and let us introduce some of our InnerCircle.

6. After completing your video course, use the phone number. You will have to set up a time when we can personally talk one-on-one on the phone.

7. Let us help you build your action plan toward financial freedom.

8. At that time, let us refer you to one or two of our InnerCircle of self-made real estate millionaires whom we have taught and trained from your area. You might want to get together with them for lunch, breakfast, or dinner. Just remember to pay the bill, just like I did with my first two mentors.

9. Slowly start working your own back yard.

10. Practice real estate investing. Look at the ads. Make phone calls. Get a list of all real estate in your area that has sold during the past thirty days. Go drive to each of the properties and form a true definition of value for your area based on actual sales prices.

11. Learn how to work with buyer's brokers.

12. Learn how to inspect a property.

13. Learn how to run the numbers on a property.

14. Learn how to write a contract with the right clauses.

15. Find out from us what our top five markets are that we are working in.

16. Start doing your own research at *www.realtor.com* to see what properties are selling for in our target markets.

17. Talk with several of our InnerCircle members. Ask to hear their stories, then ask them to allow you to tell your story. And then ask them the golden question: "If you were me, what would you do right now?"

18. Then jump into the water. Remember that with us, a free mentor is just a phone call away.

19. When you are ready, see if you qualify to be with us on a BuyingTour.
20. Whenever a real estate professional gives you a property to consider, always answer them back and tell them why or why not you are interested in that property.
21. Remember that real estate investing is a people game. You have to earn respect in real estate investing. You can never demand it.
22. Keep in touch. E-mail us pictures of your deals. We'll send you back some of ours.

Marc Stephan Garrison
marcstephangarrison@narei.com

Paula Tripp-Garrison
paulatripp-garrison@narei.com

The National Association of Real Estate Investors (*www.narei.com*)
4331 East Baseline Road, Suite B-105
Gilbert, Arizona 85234-2961

Appendix 1

Our Products and Trainings

Dear Potential and Active Real Estate Investor,

This last year was a record-breaking real estate investing year for our 64,000 members in the United States and Canada. Is it any wonder that so many real estate investment markets are so good? Major companies continue to flee large cities, where the costs of operations have become horrific and the local governments have become extremely anti-business. These regions of obsolescence give great opportunities to investors who know how to invest in the twenty-first century and who have paid the price to learn the new paradigms and economics of real estate investing that we teach.

This fifth migration (the flight of businesses from regions of obsolescence to regions of opportunity) also gives the informed and trained real estate investor the opportunity to create wealth beyond their wildest dreams by investing in the areas where these businesses are relocating. These absorption/recovery markets are the single greatest opportunity for creating wealth that there has been.

Interest rates are low. High-tech stocks are down, along with the rest of the market. Bank interest rates for savings accounts and CDs are abysmal. Enron has made investors doubtful about the caliber and integrity of corporate management.

Real estate investing allows one to use one's own judgment and values.

Our entire program for both the beginning and active real estate investor has been improved to help you build more wealth than ever. Each of our courses, trainings, BuyingTours, and mentoring programs have been focused to give you the advantage both during economically uncertain times and during the upswing that will certainly follow.

Good times or bad, the courses, trainings, BuyingTours, and mentoring programs offered by us and/or through one of our strategic alliance partners will help you prosper. If you have always wanted to make big money in real estate investing, now is your chance.

We are sure that you will agree that these new and improved products and programs are the most exciting and dynamic wealth systems ever offered by a company in the real estate investment industry. Our programs are time-tested, practical, and easy-to-learn techniques. Our current curriculum continues our long-standing tradition of being the very best source of wealth-building training in the personal finance and investment arena.

Our very best to both you and yours.

Onward,

Marc Stephan Garrison and Paula Tripp-Garrison
The National Association of Real Estate Investors (NAREI)

P.S. What we have are simply the very best courses, trainings, BuyingTours, and mentoring programs in the universe. There simply is nothing better. We have a seventeen-year track record and well over 64,000 satisfied members to prove it.

P.P.S. You can make money or you can make excuses, but you can't make both. Go for it!!!

The Twenty-Nine Secrets of Self-Made Millionaires

Since 1984, Marc Stephan Garrison has spoken to hundreds of thousands of people at countless real estate seminars, conventions, workshops, BuyingTours, trainings, and via radio, television, and newsprint. He has personally trained hundreds of self-made millionaires. He shares the twenty-nine secrets that he has found in many, if not all, self-made real estate millionaires whom he has become friends with and gotten to know. This course is worth its weight in gold. This program is on a standard CD.

Since 1985, the National Association of Real Estate Investors (NAREI) has grown to be the largest association of real estate investors in the world. A one-year membership in NAREI is a must for every single new or experienced real estate investor in the United States of America or Canada.

"The Challenge" Twenty-One–Video Course

In 1986, after Marc Garrison started bringing fifteen real estate investors per month on his BuyingTours, he realized the need to bring all of his students (both beginning real estate investors and experienced real estate investors) up to speed before attending a BuyingTour. Over the years he started the "Challenge" program, which consisted of a seven-day hands-on training taught in Phoenix, Arizona. One-half of this training was taught in the classroom, and the other half of the program was taught in a bus, using actual properties that either he or his students had bought and sold. In June of 2002, that seven-day training was professionally filmed and edited into a complete A–Z basic and graduate school for successful real estate investors and potential self-made millionaires. This seven-day video course is not only taught by the Garrisons but also by some of their very best students and other self-made millionaires in the real estate investing arena. For more information or to purchase this course, call (480) 813-6043. Please understand that no student (whether new or seasoned) can attend a BuyingTour without completing this twenty-one–volume course.

Our BuyingTours

Started in 1986, our BuyingTours have become the "Granddaddy" of all real estate training programs—but at the same time, miles above the rest. Marc had become tired of speaking from 1983 to 1985 at real estate seminars, workshops, and conferences where most of the attendees never did anything with the knowledge that he or the other speakers gave them. Marc decided to take a chance and put his money where his mouth was by inviting a group of NAREI members into one of his hottest target absorption markets.

He worked for months to get this program ready. He planned to teach all aspects of residential single-family and multifamily real estate investing in domestic absorption markets to this group. They also were going to be able to view dozens and dozens and dozens of available screened income properties available for pennies on the dollar. He knew that it would work. From that initial group of fifteen, over $18 million of income-producing real estate was purchased during their BuyingTour. Every member of that group bought. And every member of that group made an incredible amount of money. This group followed Marc Stephan's timing signals and sold each of their properties within the first three years of ownership at prices ranging from 300 to 500 percent of their initial purchase price. They proved that Marc's new paradigms of real estate investing work. This is a hands-on experience for serious investors in residential income single- and multifamily housing. We offer one BuyingTour each month. You will meet us in one of the top five absorption/recovery markets in the United States and Canada. Participation is by application only.

Intensified Real Estate Investing Training

This intensified training is offered by one of our strategic alliance partners. This is truly a hands-on and dynamic training program. It will put you on the fast track to success in real estate investing. This extraordinary training is designed to teach the real-world ins and outs of identifying, negotiating, buying, and managing massive cash-flow real estate.

At this Intensified Real Estate Investing Training, you will learn:

- How to find investment properties
- How to talk to sellers
- How to finance purchases
- How to find the right professional:
  - Mortgage brokers
  - Real estate brokers
  - Bankers
  - Grant officers

You will even venture into the field on an exciting field trip to tour, analyze, price out, and possibly make offers on properties. All of these techniques are designed to help you take the next step toward your successful real estate investing career.

Since its doors first opened in 1991, hundreds of this program's graduates have learned the insider essentials of creating their own fortunes. As a result, many graduates have gone on to achieve their own success in both real estate and/or in their chosen business. The key, they said, was actually spending three days with millionaire mentors who are doing it themselves and showing you the ropes, step by step. Now, it's your turn to discover what our other students know. What better way to start building your own wealth than to have a proven millionaire show you how?

Wholesale Buying Training

Learn how to locate, evaluate, and negotiate for wholesale properties in one of the nation's most dynamic real estate markets. Then learn how to apply your knowledge of wholesale buying right in your own community! During this exciting and action-packed training camp, each student will even learn how to buy one or more properties in the Fort Worth area for his or her own portfolio. These properties can then be held as positive cash-flow rentals or, in some cases, quick-flipped for an immediate profit.

Our instructors will teach you how to do these things:

- How to identify wholesale properties
- How to locate owners and negotiate with them
- How to purchase and finance wholesale transactions
- Techniques to "quick-flip" for instant cash
- Closing strategies that can make you money
- How to develop an investor database
- How to work with out-of-state properties
- When to hold, when to sell
- Managing properties from miles away
- How to develop your own five-year investment plan

This training has been designed to show you how to create immediate cash and then structure that into wealth. Reality-based training, coupled with top-notch instruction, provides both an eye-opening and energizing experience. If real estate entrepreneurship is what you seek, then the Wholesale Buying Training is a must.

Foreclosure Training

You can make more money in foreclosures than in any other comparable portion of real estate investing—if you know how. Think about what factors make the best prospects for an investor: a distressed property with a distressed owner! With foreclosures, you also learn to work with lenders who are anxious to get bad loans off the books. Banks want out of the property management business—it's something they're not too good at in the first place—and you can help. Foreclosure Training is a proverbial win-win for anyone who wants to master this phase of investing.

A highlight of this training is a special field trip where you will learn how to knock on doors and approach owners actually in foreclosure. You will be taught an effective way to meet and negotiate with them, get to feel their plight, and understand their circumstance. Learn how to turn a dire financial situation into a workable solution where all the participants win—especially you!

During this training camp, you will also learn the following:

- The foreclosure process
- How foreclosure happens
- The various steps taken by the banks
- How to fix it so everyone wins
- The laws affecting foreclosures in each state
- Where foreclosure records are kept in the county courthouse
- How to research title and property tax information
- How to read real estate legal notices to unlock their meanings
- How to refinance and get tax-free cash at closing
- How to inspect, estimate, and rehab houses at 50 to 75 percent less than the going rate

Many homeowners facing foreclosures do not realize their options—and we will teach you how to exercise every one of them

357

to your advantage! By being creative, you can rescue their credit and give them a way out of the problem with their lender, while you build equity and cash flow in the process.

Purchase Option Training

Want an easy, low-risk way to attain financial freedom? Want to quit your job and live the life of your dreams on your own massive cash flows? Then you must attend the Purchase Option Training camp. Discover solid, proven strategies for attaining financial independence through real estate. Learn how to enjoy all the benefits of owning property without the risks and hassles. The key to this training is how to buy or control property by putting very little to absolutely no money down. Learn how to get cash back in your pocket when you buy a property. Discover how to acquire properties in any areas of your town with nothing down by using the purchase option method. See how you can cash in your purchase option properties to unlock thousands of dollars for yourself as soon as you get home from this training.

During this dynamic training, you will learn the following:

- How to create a "lease-option money machine" that pays you quick cash and steady monthly income
- How to create contracts that allow you to purchase property for little or no money down
- How to structure your offer and your financing so you can consistently get cash back in your pocket when you buy properties
- Solid, proven strategies to create huge monthly cash flow to allow you financial freedom

At the end of the training, you will be given a personalized outline of a game plan for the next ninety days, ensuring that when you return home you will hit the ground running. Following this proven plan can eliminate all doubt and uncertainty. Your experienced trainer brings you proven strategies, not textbook information and theories. A special session will even teach you how to negotiate and then arrive at your best contractual advantages with sellers, prospective tenants, buyers, and lessees.

When you attend the Purchase Option Training, you will learn a proven, step-by-step system that is so powerful that you can put it to work to build your financial freedom as soon as you step out the door. Through purchase option training, you can learn how to create a faster path to monthly income than by following any other comparable real estate investment strategy.

Property Management Cash-Flow Training

Learn to maximize cash flow and your net worth during this enjoyable three-day training camp devoted to a hidden element in real estate investment—property management. You will even learn numerous insider techniques in property management that could be the foundation of a successful and profitable new career.

This information-packed training camp will include the following, plus much, much more:

- How to build a solid positive cash flow to allow you to quit your job
- The secrets of earning $15,000 to $30,000 on each transaction
- Proven techniques to build a substantial net worth
- Step-by-step procedures for managing your own portfolio
- How to earn another income by managing other properties
- Marketing techniques to keep your investments producing profits
- How to find and keep good tenants—and deal with problem tenants
- How to deal with governmental regulations

- Cost-effective, quality approaches to maintaining your properties
- Ways to manage risk to keep costs and exposure low
- Discover profits in student housing and rooming houses
- Learn all of the positive tax implications of real estate
- Obtain an array of forms that will get you off to a good start

This dynamic training camp also features a field trip and tour of properties. You will be encouraged to apply what you've learned in the classroom to the real world, to properties that are ready to rent or sell. You will learn everything you need to know to begin a successful career in real estate investing.

Commercial Real Estate Investing Training

Taking on the challenge of the Commercial Real Estate Investing Training means rethinking a good many of your assumptions about what a good investment is all about. Learning to prospect for investment opportunities in the commercial sector of your own market is just part of the excitement of this three-day total immersion into a world to which most people have no access. Participate in a highly exciting workshop in which you will discover all the fundamentals of buying, managing, and disposing of properties in the four major categories favored by commercial real estate investors.

You will get hands-on experience in the following:

- Buy low/sell high secrets
- Finding good buys when no one else can
- Buy or control property with none of your own cash
- Marketing for good tenants
- Dealing with government regulations
- Strategies for enhancing your portfolio
- Turning junk properties into cash-flow jewels

On a four-hour field trip on the second day, you will view several potential investments and do a complete analysis of one of them. Each training camp student will also have a chance to broaden his or her outlook, make strategic alliances, and develop strategies to make more money in their own back yard, without heavy start-up capital and without years of apprenticeship. Walk out of the camp on Sunday evening with a head full of ideas, the confidence to put them into action—and a written plan for doing so!

Asset Protection and Tax Relief

Lawsuits, taxes, and death are inevitable. You can't ignore them. You pay thousands in unnecessary taxes. You can lose everything in a lawsuit. The government gets most of what's left when you die. However, you do have an alternative. You can take action and take control of your life and your business. You can design a step-by-step personal wealth plan that will make your personal and business assets "bomb-proof," dramatically reduce your income taxes, and eliminate estate taxes.

During the three-day Asset Protection and Tax Relief Training camp, you will learn the following:

- Asset protection techniques used by the wealthy
- Different forms of ownership and how they can help you:
  - Joint ownership
  - Corporation
  - Land trust
  - LLC
  - International trust
- How to work with the IRS—and save thousands
- How to cut taxes
- How to shield your assets from problems, and turn those problems into solutions
- Foolproof techniques to ensure your family's financial future

We'll cover corporations, partnerships, trusts, and international entities and help you understand what is right for you. After participating in this interactive event, you'll have designed your personal wealth plan, understood each part, reviewed it with your instructor, and you'll know each step to take in order to gain control of your life now and in the future.

Discount Notes and Mortgages

This dynamic training can go hand in hand with your ongoing real estate investing because it fits into your business plan as a natural moneymaker. Discover from industry experts how you can broker mortgages and notes at a discount. Learn how to find existing notes and then create new notes through simultaneous closings. These strategies can work in virtually every real estate transaction—single- and multifamily residences, commercial property, and vacant land. Learn how to cultivate sources right in your community who will depend on you to bring them opportunities to buy discount notes and mortgages—and then pay you for your services. You will also learn how to build wealth through brokering invoices and other debt instruments.

Here is an overview of what you will learn at this training:

- How note-buying can make you money
- How to find deals each day, every day
- Where to get the money to do the deals
- How to buy real estate for yourself by discounting notes
- How to discount invoices to create monthly income
- How to discount other debt instruments such as:
  - Business leases
  - Business notes
  - Conservation reserve program contracts
  - Inheritances
  - Lotteries

- Senior life insurance policies
- Structured settlements
- And much more . . .

The discount mortgage industry is enormous. Brokering the purchase of all kinds of notes and mortgages will put you right in the middle of the action. Our experts will teach you how to pinpoint funding sources who will say to you, "Find the deal, bring it to me, and I will fund it." And the best part is, you make money! Learn how to take the skills and talents that you already have and apply them to an industry that is willing to pay you well for your time and effort.

Keys to Creative Real Estate Financing

Every successful real estate investor knows that finding the right property is only half the battle. They know that financing the deal is when they win—or lose. Learning the keys to creative real estate financing gives you the knowledge and the power to go after any property worth buying. You'll never again say "If I only had the money," because you'll learn to master virtually every single real estate financing strategy there is, giving you the strength and confidence to close any deal. And now, for the first time, your training will leave you feeling like you've earned a Ph.D. in the subject.

Our nationally acclaimed experts will show you state-of-the-art ways to do the following:

- Create a mortgage, and then flip it for financing
- Exchange properties without tax consequences
- Structure financing with bad credit or no credit
- Prepare and present a powerful financial statement
- Make your home equity worth ten times its value
- Develop a no-fear approach to real estate negotiations
- Convert real estate notes into purchase money

- Discover money partnerships in your own hometown
- Win favorable terms from equity-only, "hard" lenders

Knowledge that you acquire from this training will instantly prove to be a powerful, wealth-building tool. Our faculty of national experts and practitioners will guide you through all of the latest methods, helping you to make real estate financing a strategic asset in your investment arsenal. It will level the playing field between you and your lenders!

The Personal Mentoring Program

The Personal Mentoring Program is the most exciting real estate investment training to come along in years. Our hand-picked mentors—each and every one a successful real estate investor and a self-made millionaire—specialize in teaching highly motivated students the latest techniques on how to amass wealth through cash-flow real estate. For four dynamic days, your mentor takes you step-by-step through our system of evaluating and then buying cash-flow properties right in your own hometown. Your mentor will also personally instruct you on the most effective use of our materials and techniques.

Mentoring is an especially valuable wealth-building program for students who have attended or viewed our Challenge program, BuyingTours, trainings, or boot camps. Mentoring is for students who are serious as a heart attack about their investing success and ready to put all of their training to work.

Here's a sampling of what your mentor will share with you, one-on-one:

- A telephone conference will put a mentor into your investment career
- Professional assessment of your finances, goals, and experience

- Complete income and marketing analysis of your properties
- Thorough evaluation of the real estate market in your community
- Identify, evaluate, and then locate cash-flow properties for acquisition
- Find financing options through bankers and lenders in your area
- Build a powerful investment plan—and then put it into action

Our one-on-one Mentor Program can provide unlimited opportunity for students who are serious about their real estate investment careers. Mentoring is the fastest track to financial independence for students who are selected to participate in this dynamic program.

E-mail Marc Stephan Garrison directly at marcstephan garrison@narei.com or Paula Tripp-Garrison at paulatripp-garrison@narei.com to find out more about our personal mentoring program.

Appendix 2

The Language of Real Estate Investing Today: A Glossary

A

additional principal payment: A payment by a borrower of more than the scheduled principal amount due in order to reduce the remaining loan balance.

adjustable rate mortgage (ARM): A mortgage loan whose interest rate fluctuates over the term of the loan based on the movements of an assigned index or a designated market indicator. ARMs generally limit how often and by how much the interest rate can vary.

agent: A person authorized to act for and under the direction of another person (called the principal) in dealings with third parties. An agent can enter into binding agreements on the principal's behalf and may even create liability for the principal if the agent causes harm in carrying out his or her duties.

amortization: The operation of paying off indebtedness, such as a mortgage, by installments. Common amortization periods are fifteen or thirty years.

appraisal: A determination of value, whereby a professional appraiser makes an estimate by examining the property and comparing the initial purchase price with recent sales of similar property.

appreciation: An increase in value or worth of property; the opposite of depreciation.

asking (list) price: The price placed on property for sale.

assessor: A government official who determines the value of the property for taxation purposes.

assumable mortgage: An existing mortgage that a buyer may be allowed to take over on the same terms given to the original borrower.

attachment: A method through which a debtor's property is placed in the custody of the law and held as security pending the outcome of a creditor's suit.

B

balloon mortgage: A mortgage where the final payment is considerably larger than the preceding payments.

brokerage: For a commission or fee, bringing together parties interested in buying, selling, exchanging, or leasing real property.

buyer's broker: A licensee who has declared to represent only the buyer in a transaction, regardless of whether compensation is paid by the buyer or the listing broker through a commission split. Some brokers conduct their business by representing buyers only.

C

cap: The maximum allowable increase, for either payment or interest rate, for a specified amount of time on an adjustable rate mortgage.

capital gains: The profit on the sale of a capital asset, such as stock or real estate.

capitalization: The estimation of the value of income producing property; it is determined by dividing the annual net income by the capitalization rate.

capitalization rate: The rate of expected return on investment property; it is a ratio of income to value.

cleaning fee: A nonrefundable fee that a landlord may charge when a tenant moves in that covers the cost of cleaning the rented premises after the tenant moves out, even if the place is left spotless. These fees are illegal in some states and allowed in others, though most state laws are silent on the issue. Landlords in every state are allowed to use the security deposit to clean a unit that is truly dirty.

clear title: A land title that doesn't have any liens (including a mortgage) against it.

closing: The conclusion of the sales transaction when the seller transfers title to the buyer.

closing costs: The costs that the buyer pays at the time of the closing in addition to the down payment. These may include points, title charges, credit report fee, document preparation fee, mortgage insurance premium, inspections and appraisals, prepayments for property taxes, deed recording fee, and homeowners insurance.

cloud on title: A claim or encumbrance that may affect title to land.

commission: The compensation paid to a licensed real estate broker or by the broker to the salesman for services rendered; it is usually a percentage of the selling price of the property.

comparables: Other properties that are similar to a particular property and are used to compare and establish a value for it.

contingency: A provision in a contract that states that some or all of the terms of the contract will be altered or voided by a specific event. In one common example, a buyer enters into the purchase of another home before his current home is sold and asks the seller to make the sale contingent upon the sale of the buyer's current home.

contract of sale: An agreement between the buyer and seller on the purchase price, terms, and conditions necessary to convey the title to the buyer.

conventional loan: A real estate loan that is not insured by the FHA or guaranteed by the VA.

conveyance: A written instrument, such as a deed or lease, that provides evidence of the transfer of some ownership interest in real property from one person to another.

cost approach to value: An estimate of value based on current construction costs, less depreciation, plus land value. This is in contrast to the income approach to value and the market approach to value.

counteroffer: The act of rejecting an offer to buy or sell while simultaneously making a different offer that changes the terms in some way.

covenant: A restriction on the use of real estate that governs its use, such as a requirement that the property will be used only for residential purposes.

D

deduction: In tax law, an amount that you can subtract from the total amount on which you owe tax. Examples of federal income tax deductions include mortgage interest, charitable contributions and certain state taxes.

deed: A written instrument by which title to land is conveyed.

depreciation: A loss in value.

disclosure: A revelation of a previously unknown fact. In many states you must disclose major physical defects in a house you are selling, such as a leaky roof or a potential flooding situation.

discount points (or points): An amount paid either to maintain or lower the interest rate charged. Each point is equal to 1 percent of the loan amount.

down payment: An amount of money the buyer pays that is the difference between the purchase price and the mortgage amount.

E

earnest money: A deposit that the buyer makes as evidence of good faith in offering to purchase real estate. Earnest money is typically held by a title company, in an escrow account, during the time between acceptance of the contract and the closing.

encumbrance: A cloud against clear, free title to the property that does not necessarily prevent conveyance, such as unpaid taxes, easements, deed restrictions, mortgage loans, etc.

equity: The difference between a house's present value and the mortgage amount owed.

escrow account: This may be a third-party account that holds money while a sale is in progress; it may also be an account used by lenders to save for the eventual payment of property taxes, hazard insurance, etc.

exclusive agency (EA): A listing agreement that gives a listing agent the right to sell the property for a specified time. The owner reserves the right to sell the property himself without paying a commission.

exclusive right to sell (ERS): A listing agreement that gives a listing agent the right to sell the property for a specified time, with the right to collect a commission if the property is sold by anyone, including the owner, during this period.

F

Fair Housing Act & Fair Housing Amendments Act: The federal laws that prohibit housing discrimination on the basis of race or color, national origin, religion, sex, familial status, or disability. These laws apply to all aspects of the landlord/tenant relationship, from refusing to rent to members of certain groups to providing different services during tenancy.

Fannie Mae: Created by Congress in 1938, Fannie Mae was originally part of the Federal Housing Administration (FHA). In 1968, Fannie Mae became a private company, and its role was expanded to buy mortgages beyond traditional government loan limits. Today, Fannie Mae works to increase the availability and affordability of homeownership for low-, moderate-, and middle-income Americans. Fannie Mae establishes strict guidelines for mortgage loans it is willing to purchase, and these guidelines have become the industry standard for the majority of home loans.

Federal Housing Administration (FHA): Founded in 1934, the FHA was consolidated into the newly established Department of Housing and Urban Development (HUD) in 1965. FHA loans require a special appraisal/inspection that determines whether a property meets the agency's minimum property standards. Though somewhat more expensive than a conventional loan in terms of interest rates and insurance fees, FHA loans offer slightly more liberal qualifying criteria.

finder's fee: A fee charged by real estate brokers and apartment-finding services in exchange for locating a rental property. Some landlords charge finder's fees merely for renting a property; this type of charge is not legitimate and, in some areas, is illegal.

first mortgage: A mortgage that is in first lien position, meaning it takes priority over all other liens (which are financial encumbrances).

fixed rate mortgage: A mortgage with an interest rate and monthly payment that don't vary for the term of the loan.

For Sale by Owner (FSBO): The process where an individual home-owner attempts to sell his property without a real estate broker. The acronym, FSBO, is pronounced "fizzbo."

foreclosure: A legal process instituted by a mortgagee or lien creditor after the debtor's default.

Freddie Mac: Chartered by Congress in 1970, Freddie Mac is a publicly held corporation that purchases mortgages in the secondary mortgage market.

G

Ginny Mae: The common nickname for the Government National Mortgage Association. Created in 1968 as a wholly owned corporation within the Department of Housing and Urban Development (HUD), Ginnie Mae does not loan money for mortgages. Instead, it operates in the secondary mortgage market, buying loans and selling mortgage-backed securities to investors, which in turn increases the availability of mortgage credit.

good faith estimate: A written estimate of closing costs that a lender must provide you within three days of submitting an application.

H

home equity loan: A fixed or adjustable rate loan secured by the equity in a home. The interest paid on such a loan is usually tax-deductible.

homeowners' insurance: An insurance policy designed to protect homeowners from financial losses related to the ownership of real property. In addition to covering losses due to vandalism, fire, hail, etc., most policies also provide theft and liability coverage. Flood-related damage requires a separate flood insurance policy or rider.

house closing: The final transfer of the ownership of a house from the seller to the buyer; it occurs after both have met all the terms of their contract and the deed has been recorded. Also known as "closing."

Housing and Urban Development, Department of (HUD): The U.S. Department of Housing and Urban Development; this agency is responsible for enforcing the federal Fair Housing Act.

I

income approach to value: An estimate of value based on the monetary returns that a property can be expected to generate; this can be contrasted with the cost approach to value and the market approach to value.

inspection clause: A stipulation in an offer to purchase that makes the sale contingent on the findings of a home inspector.

interest: Either an amount paid in return for the use of money, or the type and extent of ownership in property.

J

joint tenancy: A way for two or more people to share ownership of real estate or other property. When two or more people own property as joint tenants and one owner dies, the other owners automatically own the deceased owner's share.

L

landlord: The owner of any real estate, such as a house, apartment building or land, that is leased or rented to another person, called the tenant.

latent defect: Structural defects and flaws that are hidden.

lease: An oral or written agreement (a contract) between two people concerning the use of one person's property by the other.

leverage: The use of borrowed funds in order to finance an investment.

lien: A monetary claim against a property. Any liens should be settled before a sale is made final.

listing agreement: The legal agreement between the listing agent/ broker and the vendor; it sets out the services to be rendered, describes the property for sale, and states the payment terms.

M

market approach to value: An estimate of value based on the actual sales prices of comparable properties; this can be contrasted with the cost approach to value and the income approach to value.

market value: Also known as fair market value, it is the price that a willing buyer and a willing seller, both with full information, and neither under pressure to act, would agree upon.

mechanic's lien: A legal claim placed on real estate by someone who is owed money for labor, services, or supplies used to improve the property.

mortgage: A contract that provides security for the repayment of a loan; it is registered against property, with stated rights and remedies in the event of default. Lenders consider both the property and the financial worth of the borrower when deciding on a mortgage loan.

Multiple Listing Service (MLS): A system by which a number of real estate firms share information about homes for sale.

N

negative amortization: An amortization situation in which the payment made is insufficient to fund complete repayment of the loan at its termination.

net listing: A price, which must be expressly agreed upon, below which the owner will not sell the property and at which the broker will not receive a commission; the broker receives the excess over and above the net listing price as commission. In this situation, the broker's interests are potentially at odds with the interests of the seller.

O

offer: A proposal to enter into an agreement with another person. A legally valid acceptance of the offer will create a binding contract.

open listing: A listing under which the owner reserves the right to list his property with other brokers.

option: The right to purchase property within a definite time at a specified price. The holder of an option is under no obligation to purchase, but the seller is obligated to sell if the option holder exercises the right to purchase.

origination fee: A fee charged by lenders, in addition to interest, for services in connection with granting of a loan; this fee is usually a percentage of the loan amount.

P

points: Fees that are paid to induce lenders to make mortgage loans at a particular interest rate (sometimes called "discount points"). Each point is equal to 1 percent of the loan principal.

prepayment: The paying off of all or part of the mortgage before the scheduled date.

prepayment penalty: A fee that is paid to the lending institution for paying a loan prior to the scheduled maturity date.

principal: The amount of money owed to the lender, not including future interest.

property taxes: Taxes that are paid yearly on real property; these taxes are based on the assessed value of the real property.

purchase offer: A document that indicates the price, terms, and conditions under which a buyer is willing to purchase a property.

Q

qualify: To meet a mortgage lender's approval requirements for taking out a loan.

R

real estate agent: A person who is licensed to negotiate and transact the sale of real estate on behalf of a property owner.

Real Estate Appraiser, licensed: A person licensed to legally appraise real estate property for a fee.

Realtor: A real estate broker or an associate who holds active membership in a local real estate board that is affiliated with the National Association of Realtors.

realty: Land and buildings and other improvements from a physical standpoint. In common usage, real estate and real property are used interchangeably with realty.

refinancing: Applying for a new mortgage in order to gain better terms, such as a lower interest rate or a different principal amount.

REO: A Real Estate Owned property is one that goes back to the mortgage company after an unsuccessful foreclosure auction. The bank owns this property, and the mortgage loan no longer exists.

RESPA: The Real Estate Settlement Procedures Act (RESPA) is a federal law that concerns the procedures to be followed in a real estate closing; it is intended to make borrowers more knowledgeable about possible costs and charges.

restrictions: The limitations on the use or occupancy of real estate that are contained in a deed or in local ordinances pertaining to land use.

S

sales contract: A written agreement that states the terms of the sale agreed to by both buyer and seller.

Section 8: A government program that provides very low-income families with housing choice vouchers, which allow them to purchase or lease safe, affordable, privately-owned rental housing.

security deposit: A payment required by a landlord to ensure that a tenant pays rent on time and keeps the rental unit in good condition. If the tenant damages the property or leaves owing rent, the landlord can use the security deposit to cover what the tenant owes.

short sale (of house): A sale of a house in which the proceeds fall short of what the owner still owes on the mortgage. Many lenders will agree to accept the proceeds of a short sale and forgive the rest of what is owed on the mortgage when the owner cannot make the mortgage payments. By accepting a short sale, the lender can avoid a lengthy and costly foreclosure, and the owner is able to pay off the loan for less than what he owes.

T

tenancy by the entirety: A kind of property ownership that is only possible for married couples. When one spouse dies, the surviving spouse gets title to the property. Similar to joint tenancy, this type of ownership is available in only about half the states.

tenancy in common: A type of ownership in which two or more people have an undivided interest in property, without the right of survivorship.

Upon the death of one of the owners, his or her interest passes to his or her heirs or devisees (those to whom real estate is given by will).

term: The actual life of a mortgage. At the end of the term, the mortgage becomes due and payable unless the lender renews the mortgage.

time is of the essence: A clause, which when included in a contract, makes failure to perform by a specified date a material breach or violation of the contract.

title: The right of ownership of a property.

title company: A company that provides title insurance policies.

title insurance: A type of insurance that provides protection for lenders or homeowners against any financial loss that results from legal defects in the title.

title search: The procedure of checking all the records relating to the property to determine whether the seller has the right to sell the property, and can do so free of liens.

V

VA: The Veterans Administration (VA) is a federal agency that guarantees loans made to qualified veterans on approved property.

variable rate: An interest rate that changes periodically in relation to a specified index. The payments due on a loan may increase or decrease accordingly.

W

walk through: Either a buyer's on-site inspection of the property being purchased immediately prior to closing, or a detailed inspection of a new construction home, in which a punch list (a list of outstanding construction items to be completed by the contractor) and cosmetic items are addressed, prior to final acceptance.

Index